LEGENDARY LOCALS

OF

CARLSBAD

NEW MEXICO

DONNA BLAKE BIRCHELL AND THE
SOUTHEASTERN NEW MEXICO
HISTORICAL SOCIETY

LEGENDARY LOCALS

ISBN 978-1-4671-0226-1

Legendary Locals is an imprint of Arcadia Publishing
Charleston, South Carolina

Printed in the United States of America

Library of Congress Control Number: 2015938520

For all general information, please contact Arcadia Publishing:
Telephone 843-853-2070
Fax 843-853-0044
E-mail sales@arcadiapublishing.com
For customer service and orders:
Toll-Free 1-888-313-2665

Visit us on the Internet at www.arcadiapublishing.com

Dedication

To Jared "Jed" Howard, whose dedication to the preservation of Carlsbad's history is nothing less than completely awe-inspiring. You are indeed the epitome of a legendary local!

On the Front Cover: Clockwise from top left:
Roderick Mead, artist (Courtesy SENMHS; see page 24), Dan Blocker, actor (Courtesy SENMHS; see page 43), Cody Ross, professional baseball player (Author's collection; see page 86), Pete Panagopoulos, humanitarian (Courtesy SENMHS; see page 57), Maggie Oso, black bear artist (Author's collection; see page 29), Frank Pompa, early settler (Courtesy SENMHS; see page 18), F. Drew Gaffney, astronaut (Author's collection; see page 71), Josephine Anderson, nurse (Courtesy SENMHS; see page 19), Chief Clyde Sunny Skies Hunt, jewelry maker, with Frank Kindel, daredevil (Courtesy SENMHS; see pages 38 and 68, respectively).

On the Back Cover: From left to right:
The Carlsbad Springs, where the town of Carlsbad garnered its name due to the mineral waters that continue to host a favorite relaxing spot for residents today as in 1899 (Courtesy of SENMHS), The Carlsbad Caverns National Park, where a group of local residents and cavers made one of the first descents into the world-famous cave in 1923. (Courtesy of SENMHS).

CONTENTS

Acknowledgments 6

Introduction 7

CHAPTER ONE Historical Figures 9

CHAPTER TWO Artistic Flair 23

CHAPTER THREE That's Entertainment 41

CHAPTER FOUR Business Sense 55

CHAPTER FIVE Personalities Galore 67

CHAPTER SIX A Salute to Our Military Heroes 75

CHAPTER SEVEN Sports Legends 83

CHAPTER EIGHT Public Servants 95

Index 126

ACKNOWLEDGMENTS

The Southeastern New Mexico Historical Society has played a huge role in the preservation of Carlsbad's history, mainly through the efforts of historian Jed Howard and his photography archives. The historical society has shared a wealth of vintage images with the world through the implementation of www.nearlovingsbend.net, a website initialized by Jed.

For all of those legendary locals who more than deserve to be included in these pages, but are not, my sincerest apologies. I would have loved to have space for everyone. There were some excruciating decisions to be made, and I hope I did not offend anyone.

Samantha Villa, technical services librarian and awesome friend, you paved my way for this journey and opened a whole new and fascinating world to me with the simple act of forwarding a phone call. Thank you, once again, is not enough!

I am so grateful to all of those who were willing to be included in this book and the enthusiasm you showed for the project, not to mention putting up with my often crazy requests. Many thanks to Jeanne Thompson of city hall for going above and beyond to help me in my quest.

I also wish to thank my editor at Arcadia Publishing, Erin Vosgien, for her gentle guidance, patience, and expertise. Erin and her colleagues are awesome!

As always, a heartfelt thank-you and much love goes to my family—Jerry, Michael, and Justin Birchell—who eagerly gave me the encouragement and strength to forge ahead with all of my projects. I could not have done any of this without your support. Thank you for still loving me after all the drama.

Unless otherwise noted, all images appear courtesy of the Southeastern New Mexico Historical Society (SENMHS).

INTRODUCTION

For the first settlers of Eddy (Carlsbad), the flat, treeless landscape was not too impressive, but visionary Charles B. Eddy had an unusual insight into the future. Established in 1888, the town, which carried his name, would grow quickly thanks to the massive promotional plans, nearly unheard of for the time. People from all around the world, especially Italy, Switzerland, and England, would come to southeastern New Mexico to carve out their own piece of what was touted as an agricultural paradise. Eddy would soon be known as the "Pearl of the Pecos" and would be first incorporated on January 16, 1893.

Part of Lincoln County, which was the largest county in the United States at that time, Eddy soon expanded rapidly with the vision of the men and women mentioned in this book.

Water played a huge role in the development of the desert into farmland. Irrigation was a new concept in the area, but through the capital of the investors and hard work of the laborers, a premier irrigation system, complete with flume and canals, fed the arid desert and allowed it to flourish.

With the addition of water, settlers began to move into the region, creating a great need for business, industry, and entertainment. A natural mineral spring that bursts forth from the banks of the Pecos River was said to have healing qualities, much like a famous spa in the country of Czechoslovakia, Karlsbad. This similarity inspired Mary Tansill to suggest changing the name of Eddy to Carlsbad.

Founding father Charles Eddy had moved on to start new enterprises elsewhere in Cloudcroft and Alamogordo, New Mexico, so a vote was held on May 23, 1899, and the name of Carlsbad was adopted. The burgeoning town has seen many changes throughout the years, particularly in population size and industrial focus, but remains a great family-oriented community.

Ranching was the first big draw to the area, followed by farming. The arid climate helped tubercular patients as well, and tourism entered the picture with the promotion of the Carlsbad Caverns. Potash mining along with oil, gas, and nuclear waste repository opportunities in the region have sustained residents for generations with long-lasting, high-paying jobs.

Although the community has had its share of bad times and good times, Carlsbad is resilient, bouncing back even stronger after such events. Its citizens band together in times of trouble by giving an often overwhelming amount of support for those affected.

Carlsbad is most famous as the home of the Carlsbad Caverns National Park, which did wonders to put the small community on the world map. This magnificent cave system, comprised of massive limestone formations, is an ever-changing underground environment with discoveries of new chambers occurring even in recent history. With over 300 recorded caves in the Guadalupe Mountains, the Carlsbad Caverns comprise 120 of those, not to mention the many more yet undiscovered.

Often given credit as the discoverer of the Carlsbad Caverns, Jim White may not actually have been the first to explore the cave. That honor was claimed by Abijah "Bije" Long, who filed a placer mining claim on the cave for the purpose of guano removal from 1903 to 1905, according to his book *The Big Cave*.

White may not be the cave's first explorer, but he certainly can lay claim to being its biggest promoter and fan. Seeking employment from the guano mining operations, White would use the opportunity to go into the cave as a time to deeper explore the bowels of the expanse. His bosses were not pleased by this fact, and White would shuffle from company to company as his true motives were discovered. Eventually, White was granted his greatest desire of getting paid while exploring the cave. He conducted tours and provided a meal afterwards all for the fee of a couple dollars.

Carlsbad is a beautiful town with tree-lined streets, although very few of the over 6,000 cottonwood trees originally planted by the founding fathers still exist today. Determined to have an aesthetically pleasing town, the early residents had to ship in the cottonwoods to Eddy at great costs, so protecting them was paramount. Burros roamed the area and created havoc on the tasty young saplings, so a guard was hired for the sole purpose of discouraging the beasts from eating the beauty. Over the years, many of the cottonwoods were replaced with hardy mulberries.

Known also for housing a large concentration of artists, Carlsbad certainly reaps the benefits of creative beauty. Sculptures, murals, and metalwork can be found all around town for the public to enjoy. Galleries, antique stores, and unique gift shops draw tourists and residents alike to the revived downtown. The farmers' market can be found on the courthouse lawn Saturday mornings starting in June. Thanks to the award-winning Carlsbad MainStreet Project, downtown and the local economy have been revitalized.

It is safe to say, if Charles Eddy were to see his town today, he would be quite pleased by the progress his tiny village has made since 1888. Community leaders have strived to maintain the integrity of the town and keep the standards that were initially intended by those who put so much of their hearts and souls into its success.

The current community of Carlsbad has a lot to offer both prospective and current residents. The mild climate, which has always been a huge draw, provides the opportunity for many outdoor activities, like hiking, boating, swimming, gardening, walking, golfing, and four-wheel driving. Whether you've lived in Carlsbad all your life or just a few years, it is the friendliness of the people that will make you want to call this booming community home.

LEGENDARY LOCALS

OF

CARLSBAD

NEW MEXICO

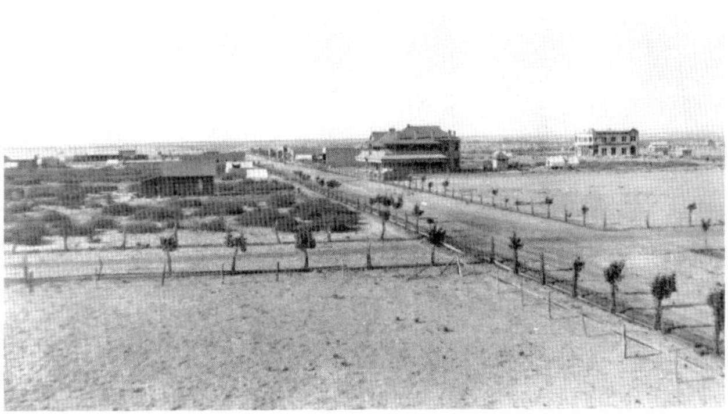

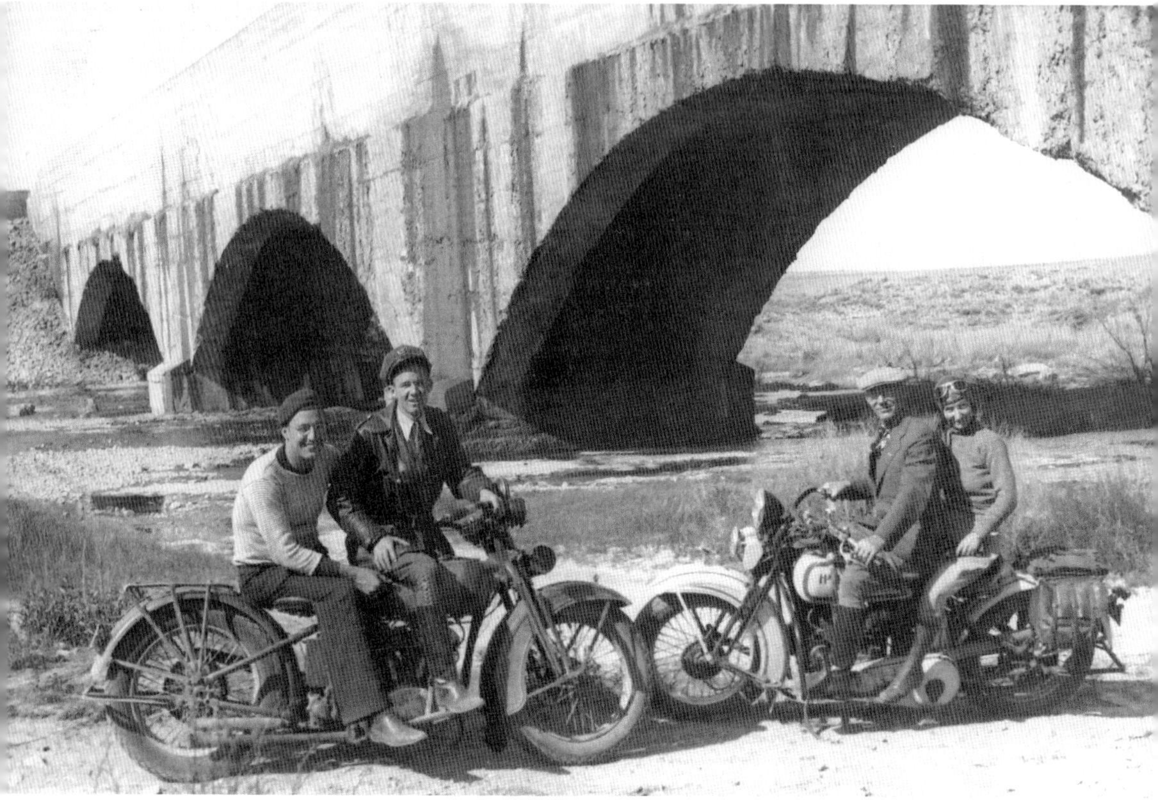

At the Flume

Resident and photographer Bob Nymeyer (shown on left), joins three visitors to Carlsbad in 1933 on their motorcycles at the Flume, which crosses the Pecos River. The concrete Flume was completed in 1903 and is a key component of the Carlsbad Irrigation Project. (Courtesy of the Southeastern New Mexico Historical Society.)

Page 1: Early Eddy

Quite progressive for its time, Eddy (now known as Carlsbad) was home to a modern hotel that featured a fireplace in each room as well as 6,000 freshly planted cottonwood trees to break the monotony of the stark landscape. These trees became snacks for a herd of burros that thought the saplings were quite a tasty treat. (Courtesy of the Southeastern New Mexico Historical Society.)

CHAPTER ONE

Historical Figures

In all communities, there are the movers and shakers who mold and shape with the promotions and opportunities afforded them. Carlsbad was fortunate to have such a high concentration of people who were all in the mindset of making the Pecos Valley prosper. It was also lucky to have the interest of many influential and prosperous men who invested heavily in the dream sold to them by Charles Bishop Eddy. Millions of dollars and hours were spent to develop the town we know today.

Although the key players did not always agree, they did concur on wanting the new town to succeed in a big way. Eddy assembled his dream team very strategically: a newspaperman for promotion (Charles Greene), a fellow dreamer who wanted an irrigated valley (Patrick Garrett), a railroad man and deep-pocketed investor (James J. Hagerman), and a Punch cigar maker (Robert Tansill) who was sold on the area not only as a great investment but as a miracle spot for the restoration of health.

Women also made great changes to the landscape of Carlsbad by building the first hospital and library through donations given to the Women's Club by local citizens. Raffles, banquets, and dances were all the rage and proved to be great fundraisers. Keeping with tradition, a dance would be held at every new home or business constructed, but so many were held that the townspeople quickly changed that custom. Carlsbad grew so quickly that they could not keep up.

Setbacks and tragedies would slow the progress of the town at times, almost to the point of extinction, but throughout Carlsbad's history the residents would bounce back more determined to succeed.

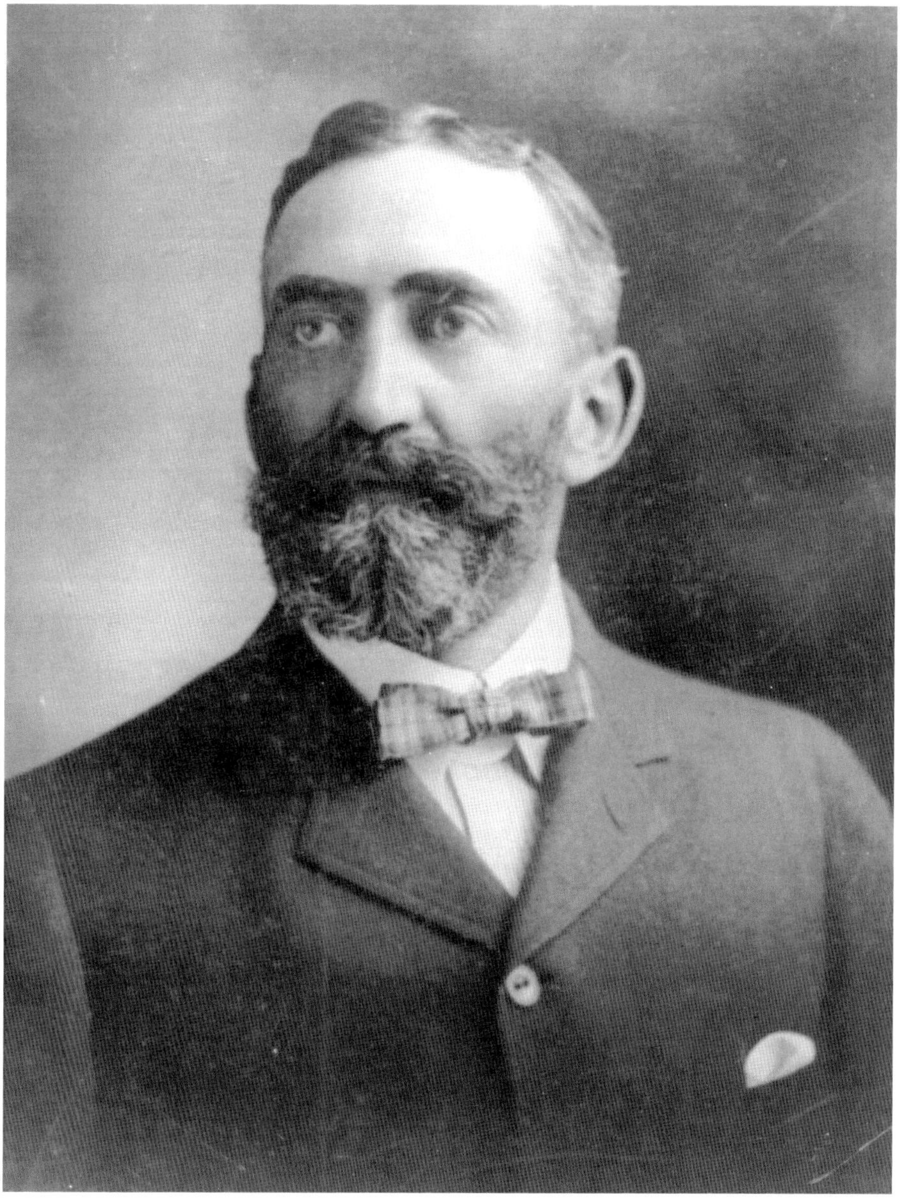

Charles B. Eddy

Founding father of Eddy (now Carlsbad), Charles B. Eddy, came from New York. Seeing the potential of the arid region, Eddy was involved in the Eddy-Bissell Cattle Company and developed the Pecos Valley Irrigation Company, setting into motion an unequaled promotional campaign for his time. He also established the communities of Alamogordo and Cloudcroft and developed a much-needed railroad system before returning home to New York in 1889. Eddy was characterized by friend Francis G. Tracy as "always on the go and drank quantities of strong, black coffee at every meal." Charismatic and a born salesman, Eddy gathered some of the most influential men in the country to invest in his dream. It was through their generosity that the town of Eddy was born. The Eddy Line Camp is still standing in Heritage Park next to the Flume, where it was moved one stone at a time through the herculean efforts of the Southeastern New Mexico Historical Society in 1981.

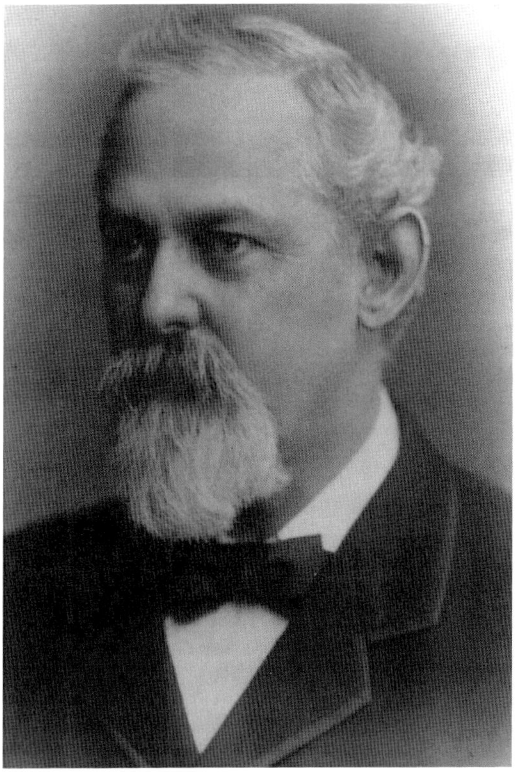

Charles Greene
Santa Fe newspaperman Charles Greene was vital to the promotion of Charles Eddy's dream. Through his connections, brochures that expounded upon the opportunities in southeastern New Mexico were distributed internationally. Greene's promotions would bring many large groups from Switzerland, Italy, and France. Greene and Eddy would get together at Eddy's ranch to "swap dreams, exchange air castles, and become mutually enamored with each other's capabilities." The result was the town of Eddy.

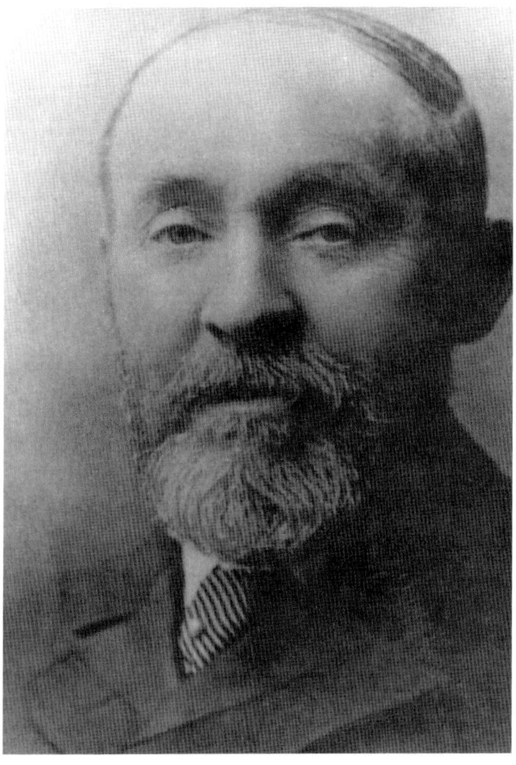

James John Hagerman
A multimillionaire, James John Hagerman was one of the most influential men in the Pecos Valley. Pumping nearly $3 million into Carlsbad, Hagerman brought irrigation and the much-needed railroad. He built a showcase home on Hagerman Heights, east of town, which still stands today. After becoming disenchanted with the Pecos Valley, Hagerman traveled to Milan, Italy, where he passed away on September 13, 1909.

Robert Tansill

Best known for his multimillion-dollar invention of the 5¢ Punch cigar in Chicago, Illinois, Robert Tansill was a world traveler but failing in health. When he contracted tuberculosis, his doctor suggested he move west for a drier climate. Colorado Springs would be Tansill's next home, where he met a charismatic man by the name of Charles Eddy, who sold him on the idea of an "Oasis in the Desert." Tansill was soon to be Charles Eddy's newest convert and largest investor. The newly formed town of Eddy had an important resident in Tansill, who was immensely proud of its progress. Tansill was one of Eddy's largest cheerleaders for the 14 years in town before his death in 1902.

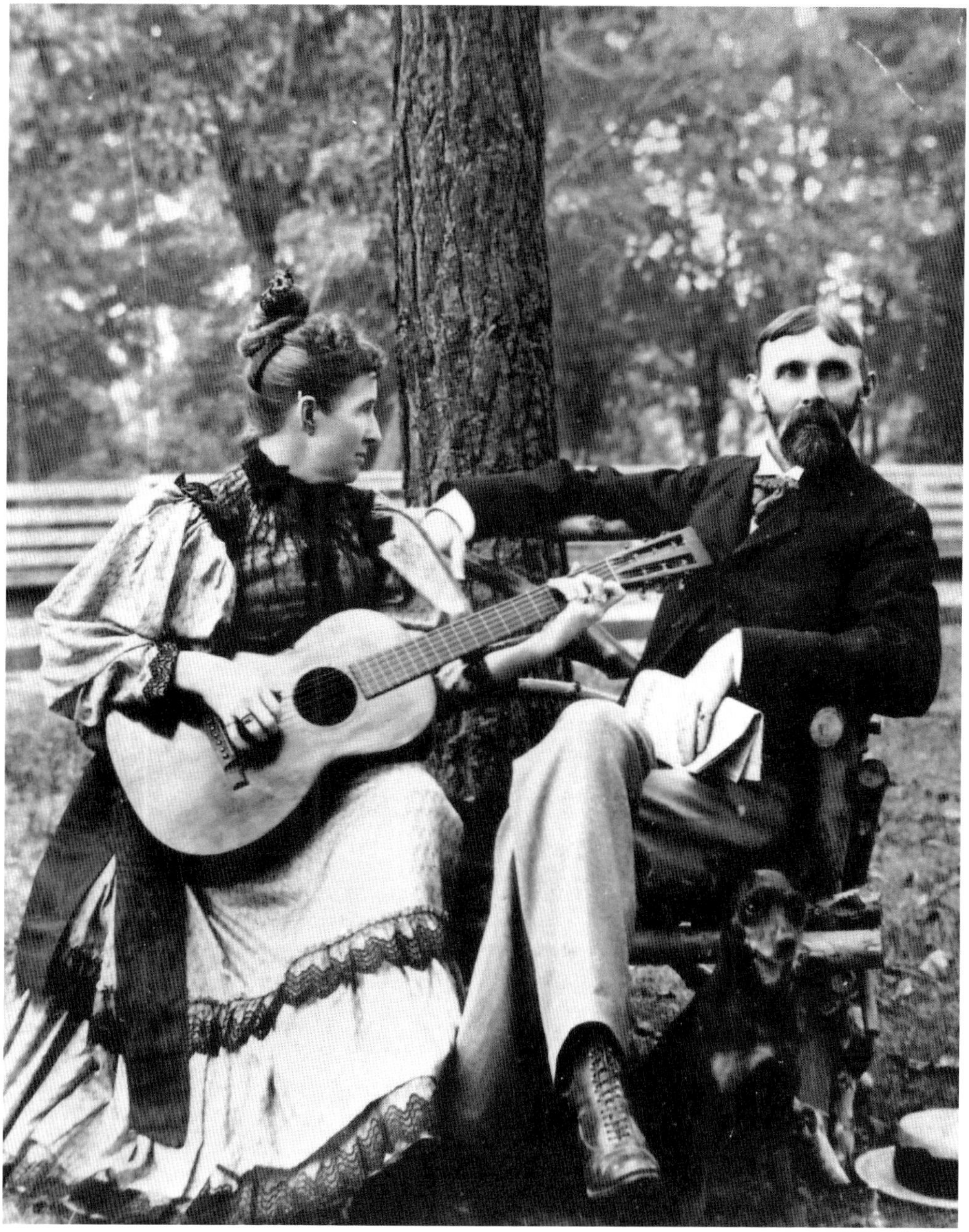

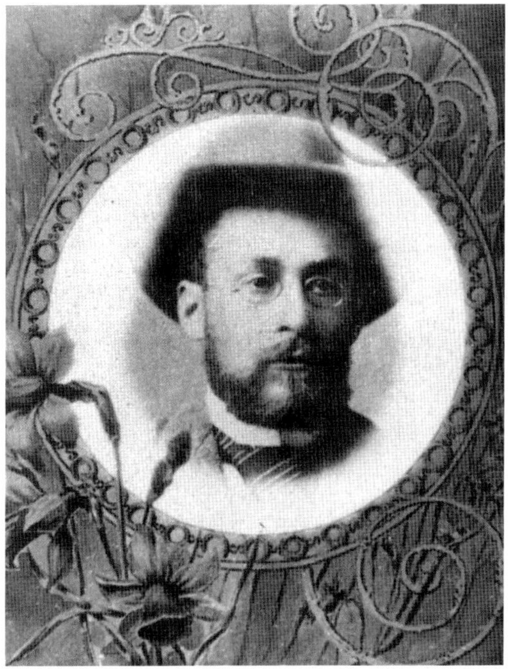

Francis G. Tracy

Businessman and gentleman farmer Francis G. Tracy introduced the Pecos Valley to Egyptian cotton and peaches. Peaches would especially become a huge crop for the region. His comprehensive writings detail the birth of Carlsbad and give a good feel of what life was like in the early days. Tracy's relatives still live in Carlsbad today.

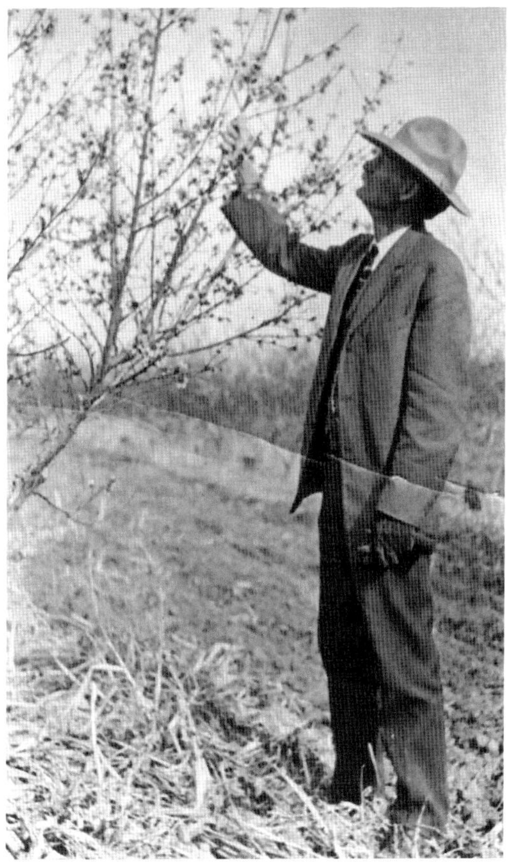

Charles H. McLenathen

Eddy's first real estate agent, Charles H. McLenathen, was instrumental in the development of the town structure. Eddy grew at such a rapid rate that it was difficult for McLenathen to keep up. McLenathen was also a business partner to Francis Tracy, and the two men produced the best crop of peaches in the area. A box of peaches from the "Teddy Roosevelt tree" in the Tracy-McLenathen orchard was sent to President Roosevelt in 1911.

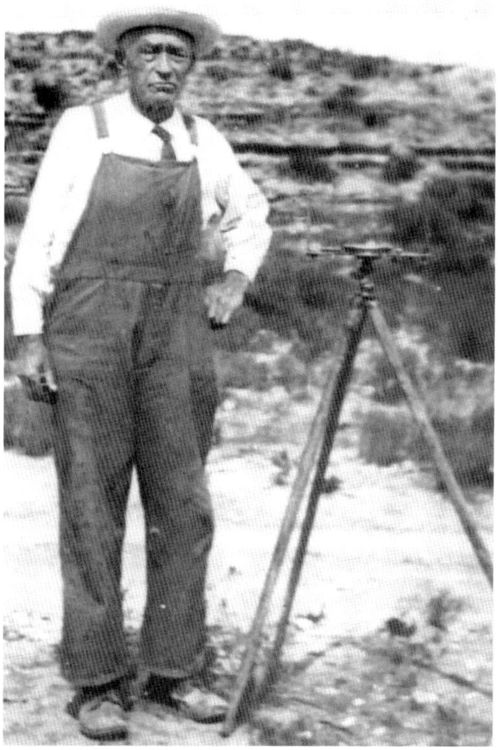

Bartholomew A. Nymeyer
The first surveyor of the Eddy townsite, Bartholomew Nymeyer, was also responsible for the proposed irrigation systems of Carlsbad. Town lots sold for $50 and came with a clause that stated no alcohol would be sold or manufactured on the land; if violated, the land reverted back to the town. Nymeyer and his family ran the Eddy House, the first hostelry in Eddy, until 1890.

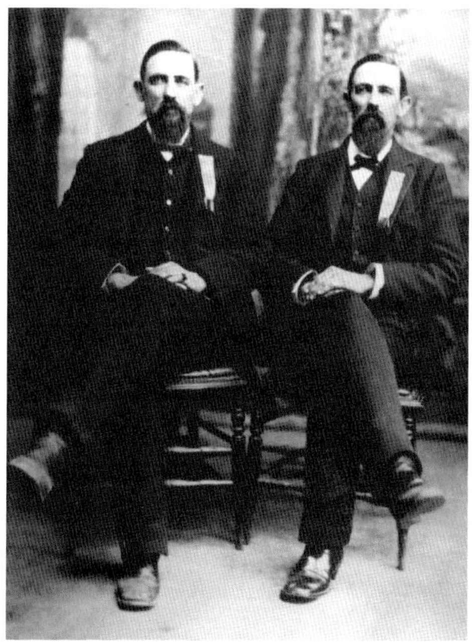

Claiborne Merchant
The Merchant family, early cattle ranchers, still own the San Simon Ranch in Lea County, New Mexico, acquired in 1897 by Claiborne Merchant and his business partner, James Parramore. The ranch encompasses 1.34 million acres (21 square miles) in New Mexico. The original purchase included a two-room adobe house, four watering holes, and grazing rights, but no land, since it was on public government property.

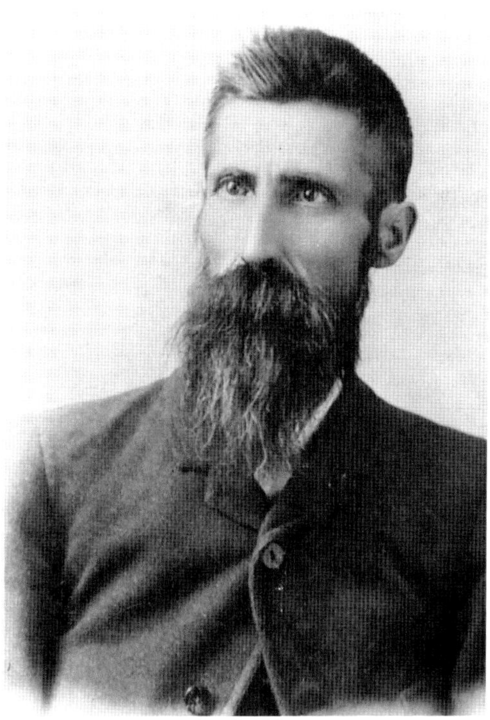

Alfred A. Freeman

Alfred A. Freeman served as the first judge of the Fifth Judicial District of the New Mexico Territory. His jurisdiction included both Eddy and Chaves Counties. Appointed by Pres. Benjamin Harrison, he settled in Socorro, New Mexico, which posed an inconvenience to the lawyers in southern New Mexico, a two-day ride away. Freeman owned land in La Huerta and set up private practice with his son-in-law.

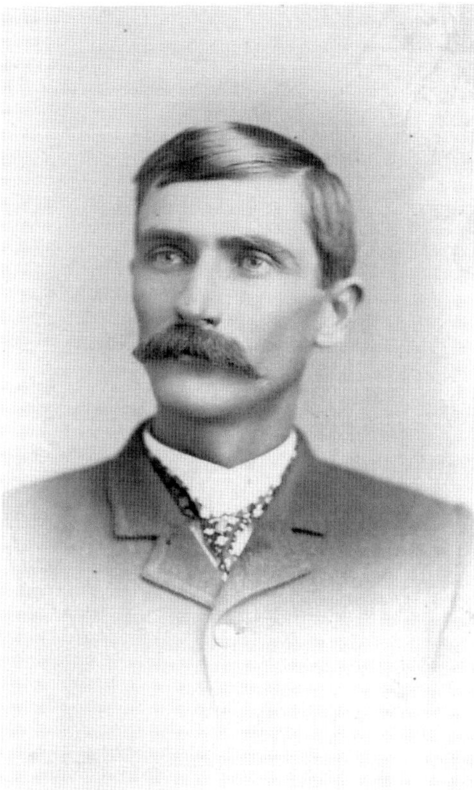

Patrick F. Garrett

Famous as the man who shot Billy the Kid, Patrick F. Garrett held many jobs. He was a cowboy, buffalo hunter, tax collector, rancher, and sheriff, and he also saw the value of irrigation in the desert. Garrett joined Eddy and invested in the region. He was asked to leave the Pecos Irrigation & Investment Company in Eddy, due to notoriety from the death of Billy the Kid.

Daniel "Dee" Harkey

The world was introduced to Eddy through author Dee Harkey's book *Mean As Hell.* Harkey played a large role in the early history of the region, first as a butcher for Dave Kemp, a saloon owner in Phenix, and finally a deputy sheriff. Harkey's book caused a stir in town; he carried a pistol on his hip when he went to gather his mail.

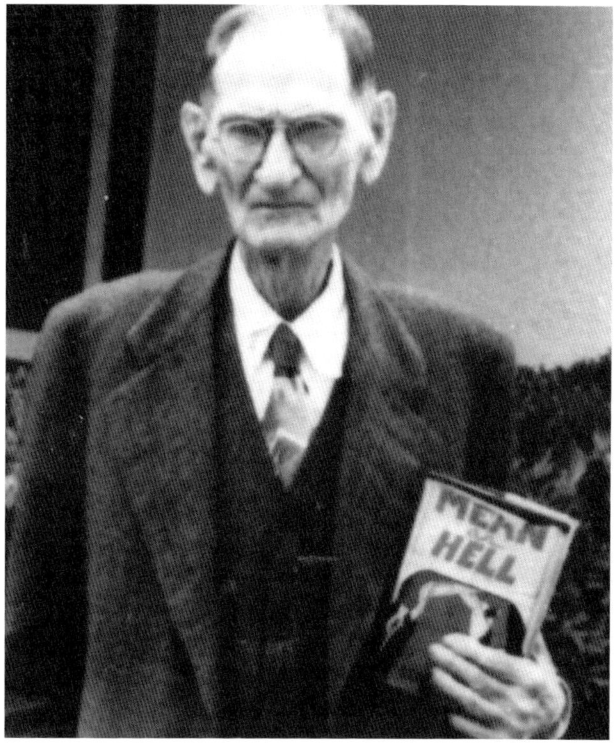

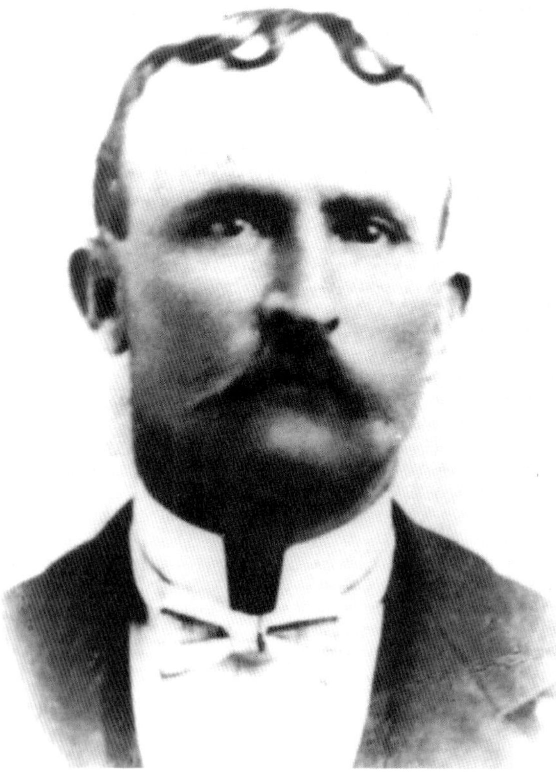

Dave Kemp

An early sheriff of Eddy, Dave Kemp had seen both sides of the law. Charged with murder as a teen, Kemp came to New Mexico after a Texas judge pardoned him for his age. Once in Eddy, Kemp became an owner of several local saloons and was accused of shooting his rival for the office of sheriff, Les Dow. He was acquitted, which caused controversy in the town.

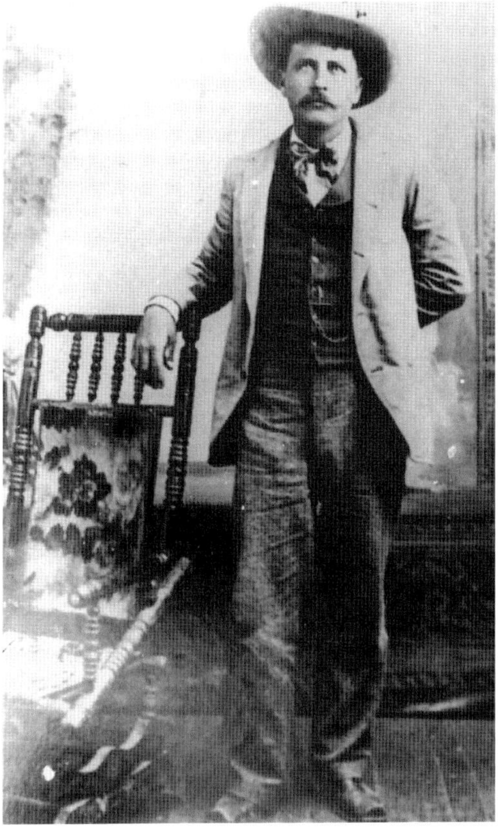

James "Les" Dow

Saloon owner and stock detective in Seven Rivers (a town north of Eddy), Les Dow shot outlaw Zack Light, who caused trouble in the town. Dow moved his family to Eddy where it was safer. Ironically, this decision would cost him his life. Dow created enemies by making accusations of cattle rustling and murder. He was described by the newspaper as "a man who feared nothing but assassination."

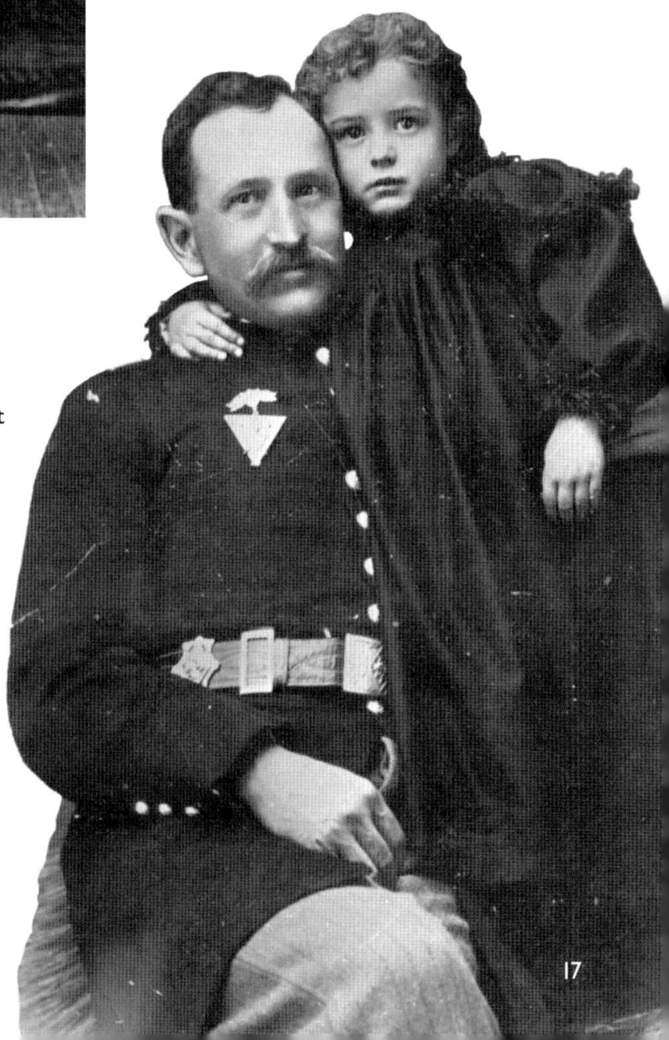

Dr. Anson Bearup

Arriving in Eddy from White Oaks, dentist Anson Bearup initially used Charles Eddy's line camp as his office. He quickly became one of the most beloved citizens of the town and was known to possess a good sense of humor. Bearup would play his phonograph as a patient was in his chair; he either liked loud music or it was to drown out the complaints of the patient.

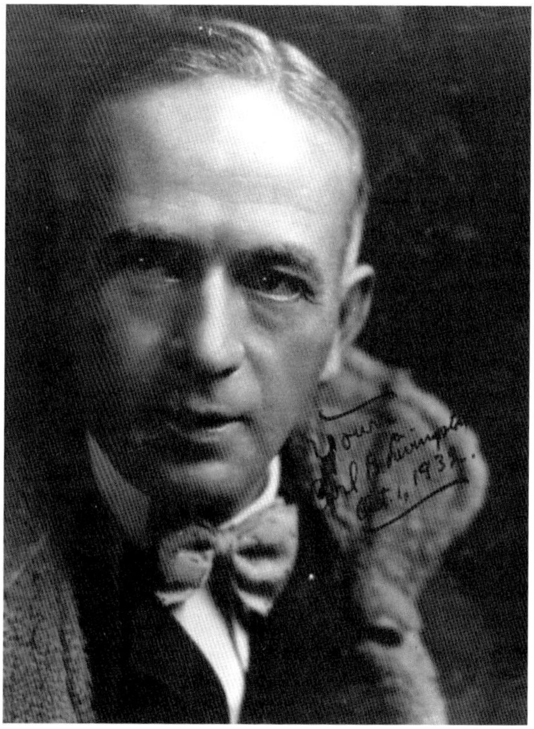

Carl Livingston

As an attorney, actor, writer, and archaeologist, Carl Livingston brought a spark to Carlsbad. Known as the discoverer of the ancient Basket Maker culture in the region, Livingston penned *Caves and Canyons of the Carlsbad Country* about the Guadalupe Mountains. As an orator, Livingston was described as a modest man who did not bore his audience with "I." He assisted with early exploration of the Caverns.

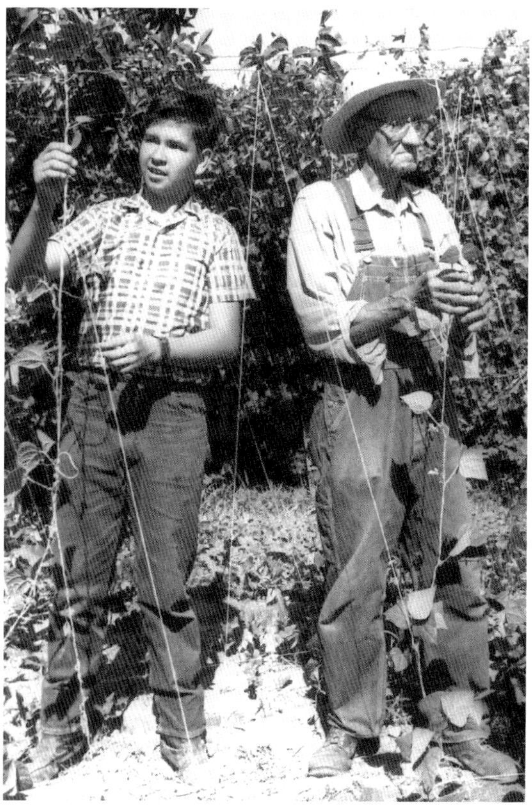

Frank Pompa

One of the first Hispanic families to arrive in Eddy, the Pompas came to the area to secure construction jobs with the irrigation project. They had no place to live, so they created a *chosa* (dugout) on the bank of the Pecos River. Later they moved into a cave in Wildcat Bluff (south of Eddy), an area known for the rattlesnakes. The Pompas still live in Carlsbad.

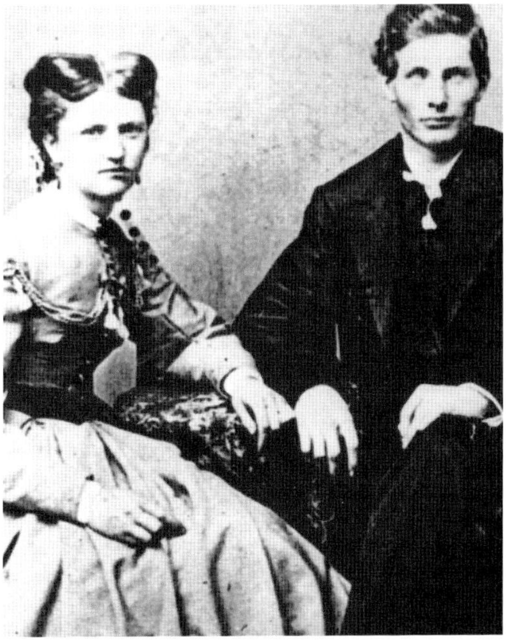

Josephine Cox Anderson

Called "Grandma" or "Angel of the Pecos," Josephine Anderson was the epitome of a pioneer woman. Josephine moved to California where she met her husband, Lucius. They started mining ventures before moving to Carlsbad, where Lucius was the first contractor and built most of the early structures. Tuberculosis drew new citizens to Carlsbad's climate, leading Josephine to open a sanatorium. During the 1918 flu epidemic, Carlsbad was not spared. Josephine gathered women to fight the spread by setting up tents along the Pecos River and making soups and cornbread; of the 60 patients they treated, all survived. Josephine also had a favorite pastime, creating oil paintings of the 104 varieties of flowers in the Pecos Valley. Several of her paintings were sent to the World's Fair. Josephine was honored by New Mexico with a historical roadway marker.

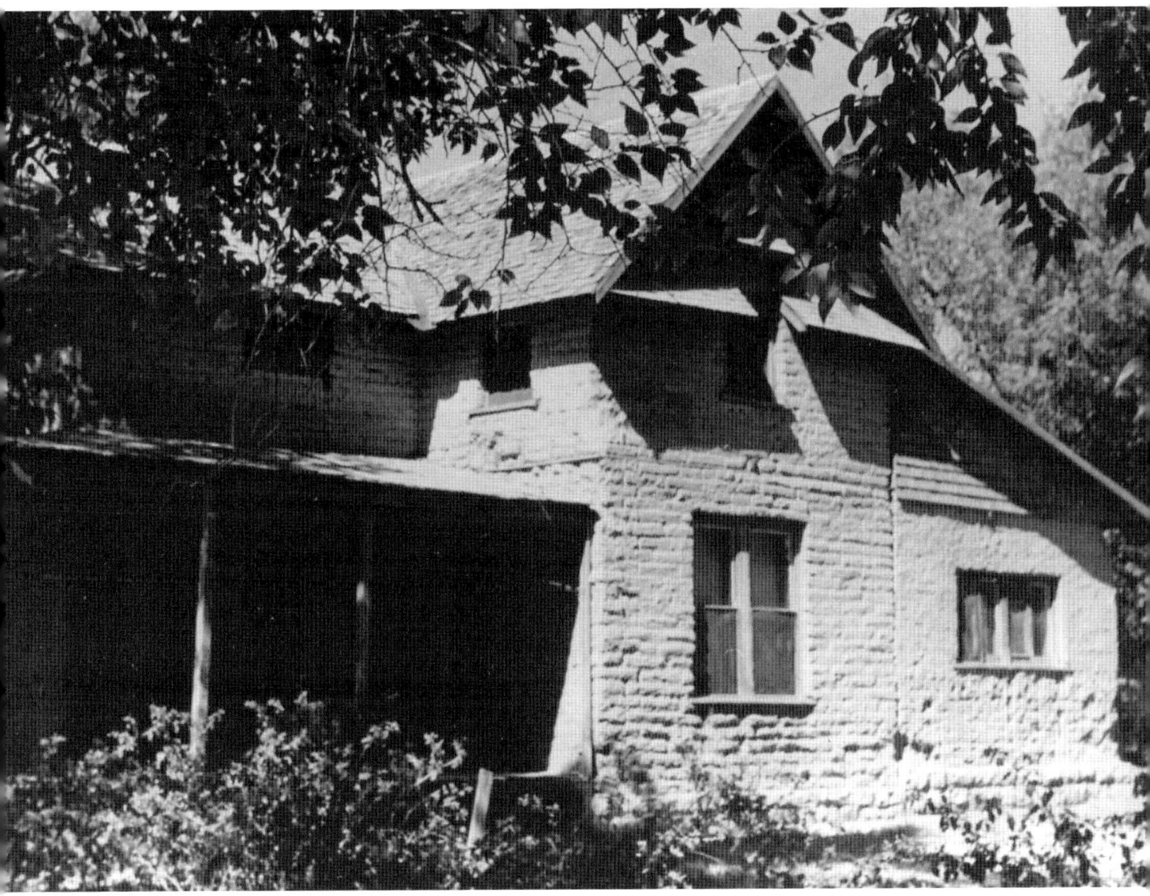

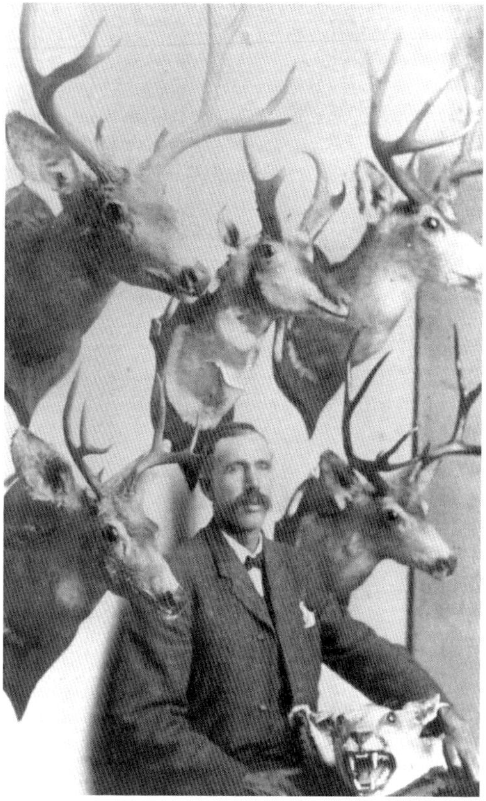

Matt Ohnemus

Carlsbad's first taxidermist, Matt Ohnemus, made a lasting impression in the community. A pair of cranes taken from a local lake and preserved by Ohnemus made the rounds of various businesses for years, showing up in many early photographs. Matt and his brother Rome would arrive in Carlsbad on the fifth train, brought to town from California to tend Charles Greene's vineyard.

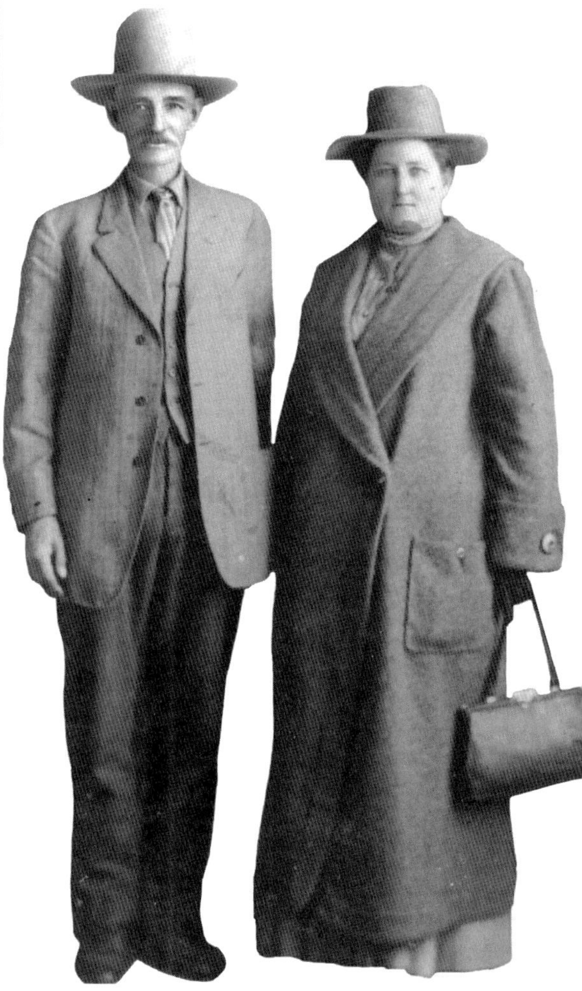

Walter Thayer

Rancher Walter Thayer knew the players of the "Old West" in the area. From Maryland, Thayer was sent to Texas in search of his brother, but neither would return. Thayer was employed by cattleman John Chisum and eventually owned the X Bar ranch in Queen, New Mexico. Thayer's second wife, Julia Shattuck, was a member of a founding family. Thayer died of an accidental gunshot wound in 1915.

Barbara Culp Jones

Affectionately known as "Ma'am Jones," Barbara Jones was a pioneer woman. The Jones family ran a trading post at Seven Rivers, where she sold her famous pies. The mother of nine children, Jones had her hands full, and her nursing skills were famous. Jones was befriended by outlaw Billy the Kid when she nursed him back to health after he had trouble with the Mescalero Apaches.

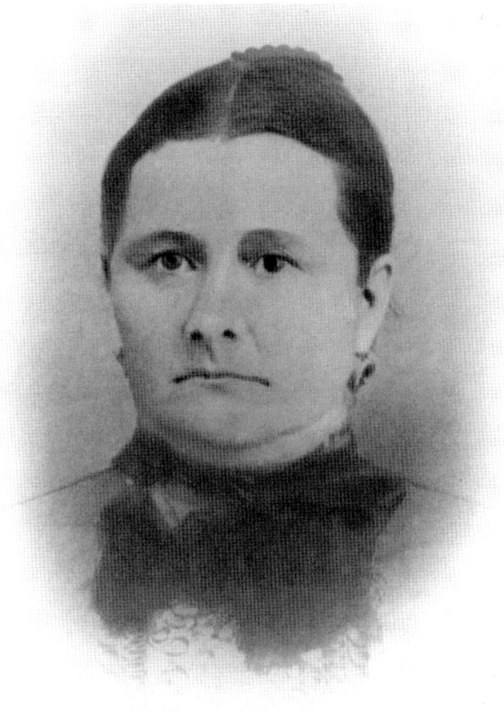

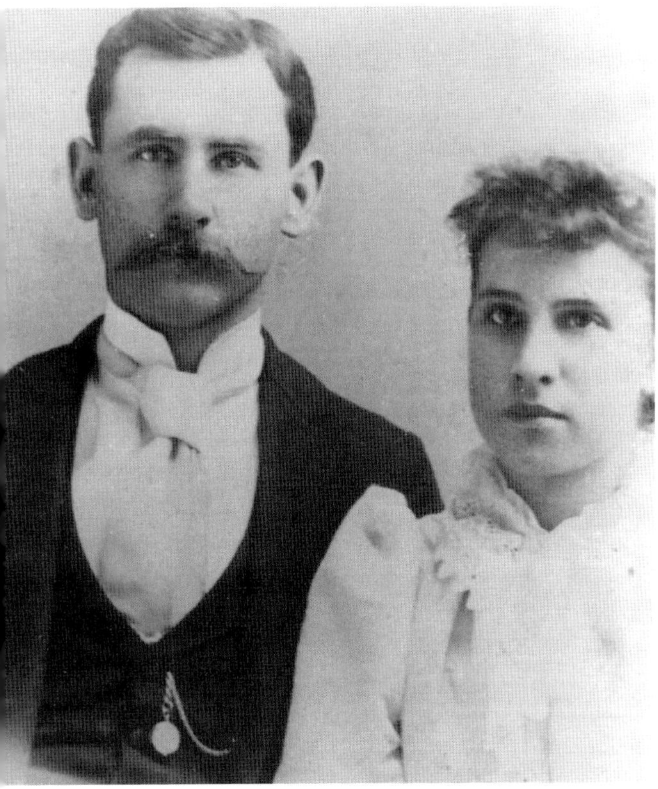

Flora Ryan

Beginning a career as a librarian in 1929, Flora Ryan was known to be a no-nonsense, matter-of-fact woman who did not pull any punches. Fiercely loyal to her library, Ryan would strike fear into anyone who threatened the institution. City officials would step lightly if in opposition to her policies. Possessing a quick wit and dry humor, Ryan ran a tight ship.

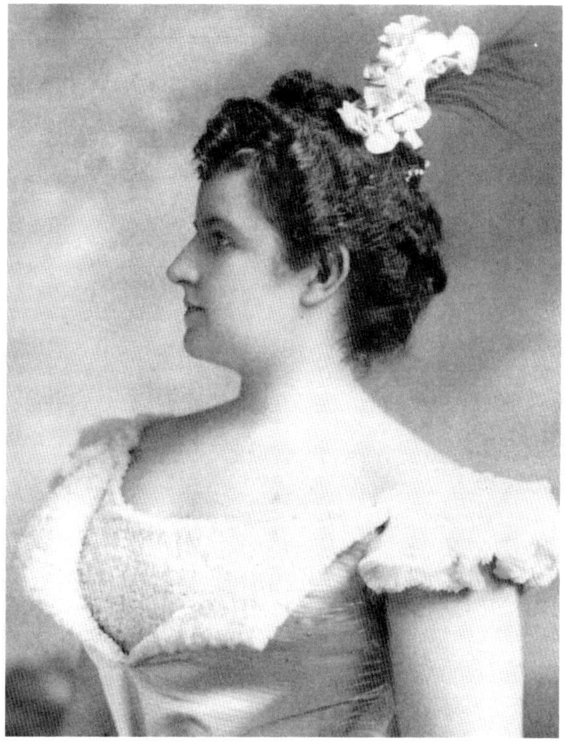

Cesarine Graves Lewis Kerr

Beautiful New York socialite Cesarine Graves Lewis Kerr came to Eddy in hopes that the dry climate would improve the health of her sister, Armadine Graves Bujac, who was suffering from tuberculosis. Cesarine would embrace her new community by donating the land she owned along the Pecos River (known as "The Beach") for the public to enjoy free forever. Cesarine was well known as a woman full of life with a generous heart.

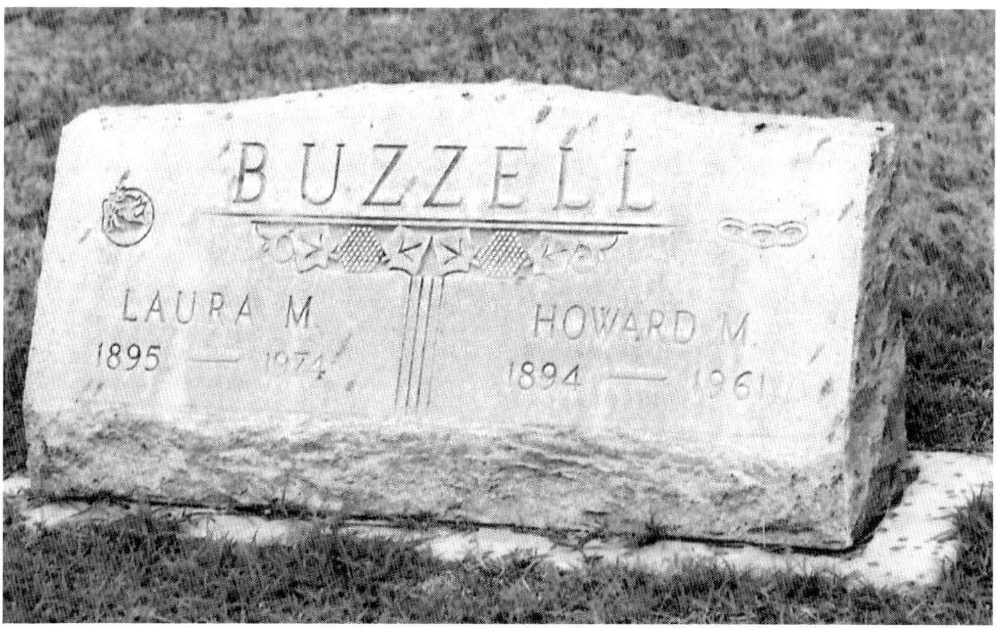

Laura Mae Cribb Buzzell

At 16, Laura Cribb was involved in the biggest story of the century—the sinking of the *Titanic*. Cribb and her father, John, were en route to New Jersey that fateful voyage. Cribb survived on Lifeboat No. 12, but her father would not. She married an American, Howard Buzzell, in England before returning to the United States, where her husband worked at the potash mines east of Carlsbad. (Author's collection)

CHAPTER TWO

Artistic Flair

Art plays a huge part in the everyday life in Carlsbad, from the lifelike metal sculptures in Halagueno Arts Park—which embraces the Carlsbad Public Library and Carlsbad Museum and Art Center—to murals that grace the sides of buildings, private galleries, and a museum collection that features the works of the "Taos Ten."

The expansive desert vistas around Carlsbad inspire those with an artistic heart to create beautiful works, no matter the medium. Carlsbad warmly embraces artists, enthusiastically celebrating their accomplishments with gala events, art walks, and art shows. The clean air must have something to do with the creative spirit felt while enjoying the outdoors. There is so much beauty around Carlsbad that it is hard not to want to record it by some means. The experience of one New Mexico sunset is invigorating and intoxicating.

This book touches on only a few of the individuals who should be recognized within these pages, but those not included are by no means less deserving.

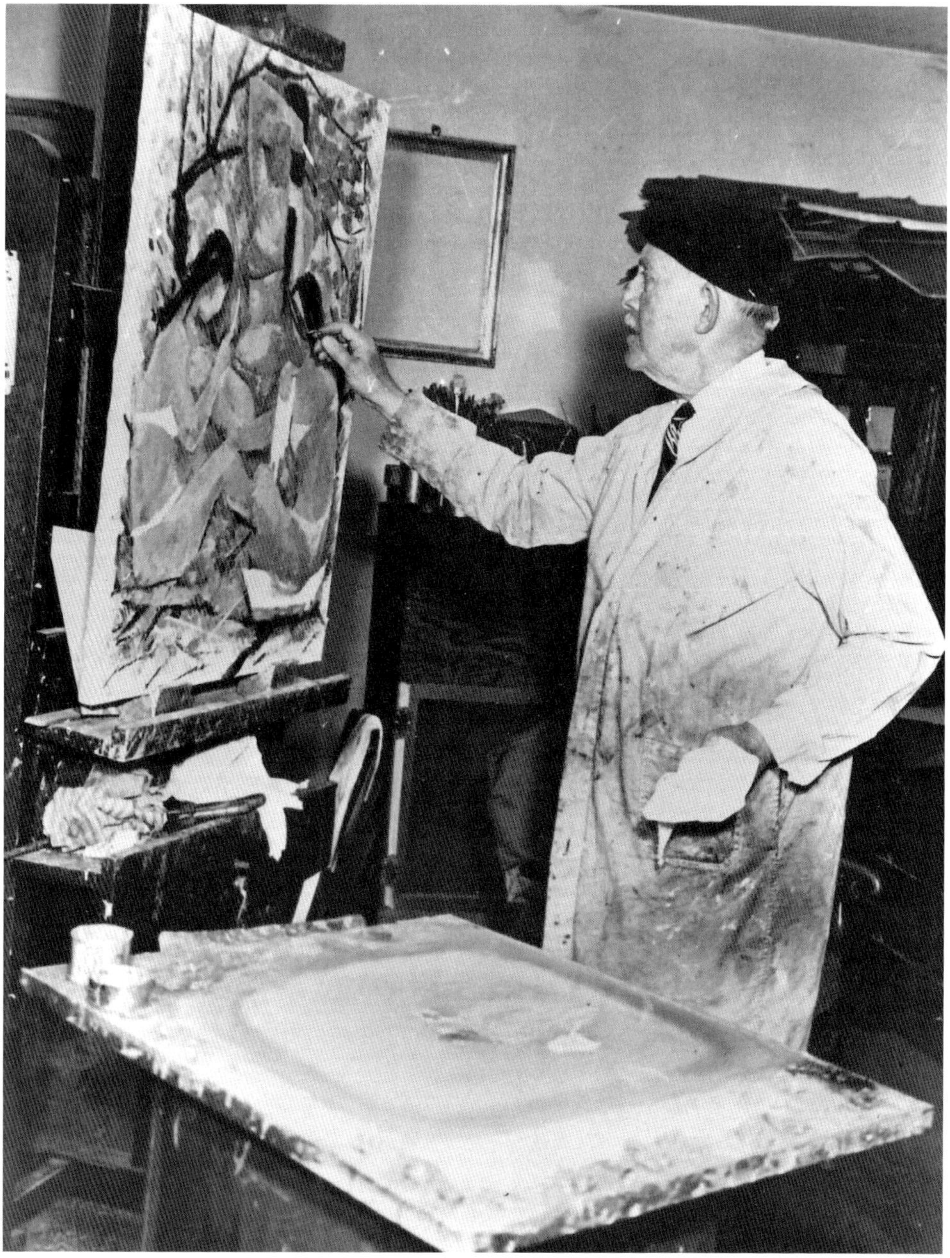

Roderick Fletcher Mead

The etchings, engravings, and paintings of artist Roderick Mead are in some of the finest collections and galleries in the United States, England, France, and Canada. Having owned one of the finest homes in Carlsbad, which offers magnificent views of the Pecos Valley, Mead was one of Carlsbad's most accomplished and well-known artists. He studied printmaking under Stanley William Hayter at the experimental Atelier 17 in Paris, France. He later gave art lessons to a few lucky pupils of Carlsbad. Mead's etchings and prints are highly prized and garner equally high prices from collectors. His studio was in his home, which James J. Hagerman built on the east hill outside Carlsbad, offering stunning views of the city. Mead's art collection is housed in a special gallery at the Carlsbad Museum and Art Center.

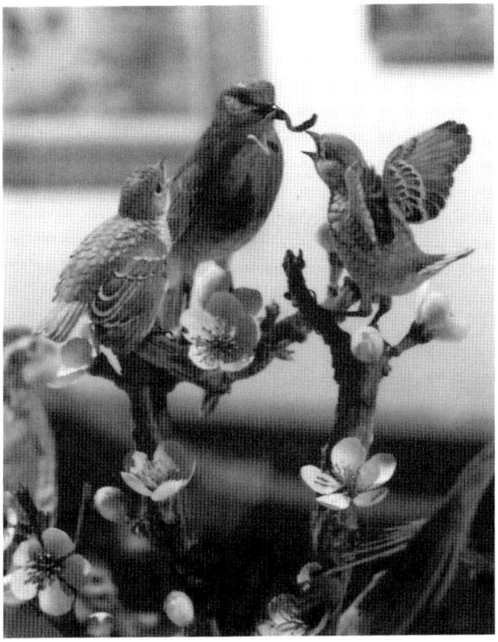

Jack Drake
Jack Drake created intricate wood carvings of local and exotic birds found in the White House and National Art Museum. A self-taught artist, Drake began by carving bars of soap. He once stated, "Facial expression is the most important thing. If you don't get that right to start with, you throw it away and start again." (Author's collection.)

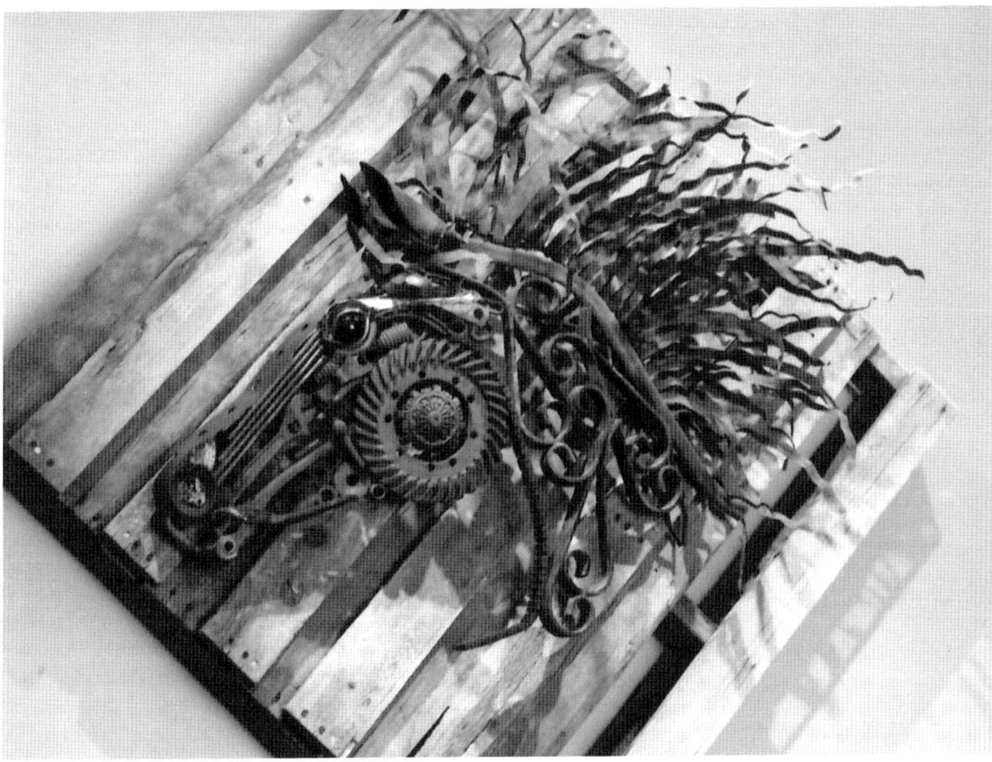

Peggi Johnson Bell
Peggi Bell, an artistic welder, turns recycled parts, tools, and metal scraps into gorgeous works of art. Bell's pieces features unusual items melded together to create fanciful horses. Each horse comes to life when Bell gives it a name, like *Wildfire* shown here. (Author's collection.)

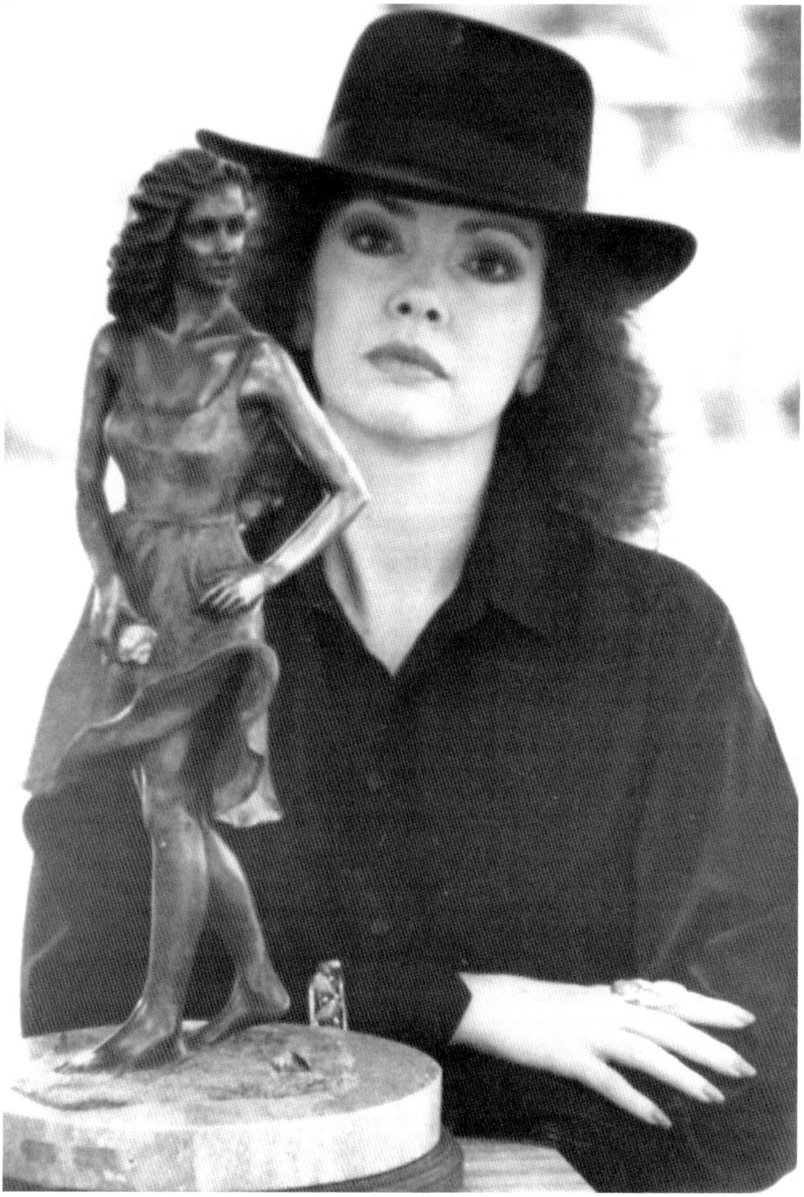

Wren Prather-Stroud

Through her love of dance and music, Wren Prather-Stroud won a scholarship as Miss New Mexico. During her travels abroad, she was exposed to many masterpieces of sculpture and fell in love with the art form. Examples of her own figurative bronze sculptures are in many private and public collections. Prather-Stroud's contribution to Halagueno Arts Park, *The Reader*, sits proudly by the entrance to the Carlsbad Public Library to commemorate its 100th anniversary in 1997. Most of her projects are portrait commissions, but Prather-Stroud is happy creating figural sculptures as well. Working in front of large mirrors in her studio, she is able to see her art, which she makes in oil-based clay, from all angles. Prather-Stroud likes to work in two-to-three-hour intervals to maintain focus and will step away occasionally to gain a fresh perspective. Once the work is completed to her satisfaction, she sends it to a Santa Fe foundry for the final steps.

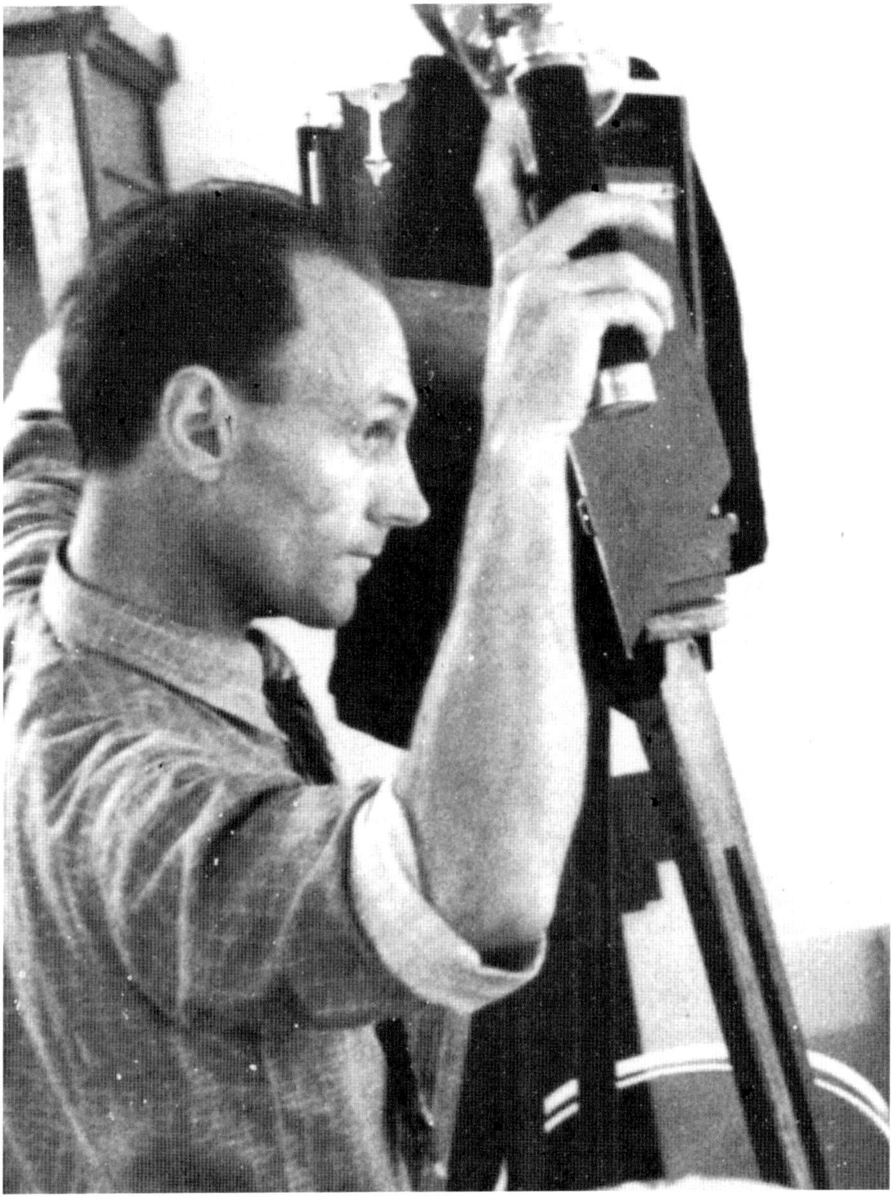

Ray V. Davis

Photographer Ray V. Davis had a different perspective on Carlsbad. Davis was responsible for bringing the beauty of the Carlsbad Caverns to the world via a photography spread in the 1923 *New York Times*. Davis owned a photography shop in Carlsbad, which he later sold to fellow photographer, Robert Nymeyer. Tragedy followed Davis throughout his life; he lost two sons during World War II. They were aboard a Japanese hospital ship nicknamed *Hell Ships* after they were rescued from the Bataan Death March, when the ship was sunk as a result of United States military strikes, unaware that US soldiers were aboard. Davis's life seemed to unravel after this heartbreaking event, and his already fragile health began to fail. In the yard of his home, Davis constructed brightly painted vignettes and grottos, which often held small replicas of human skeletons. Upon his death on April 17, 1980, the song "Rock of Ages" was played during his funeral, a tie to his connection with the Carlsbad Caverns.

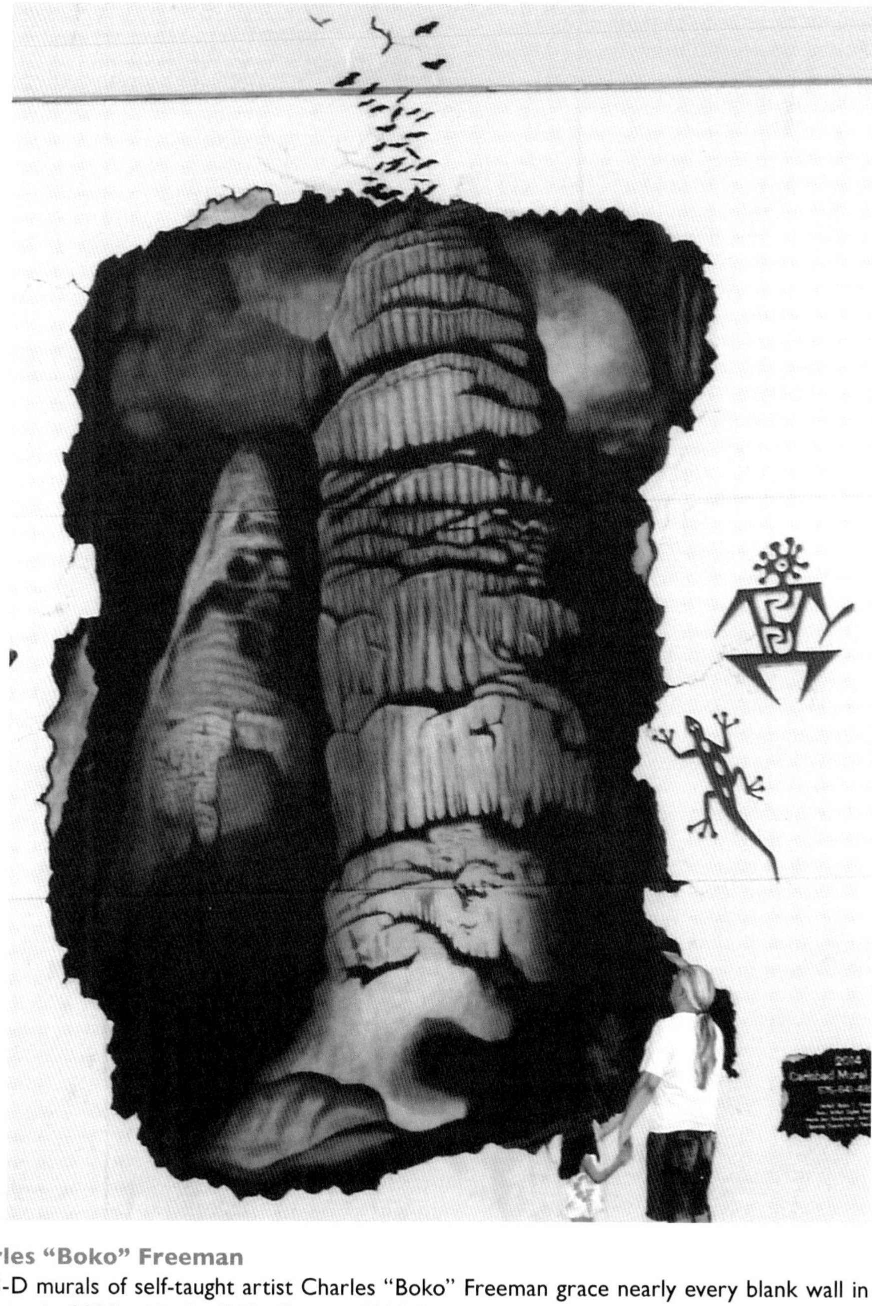

Charles "Boko" Freeman

The 3-D murals of self-taught artist Charles "Boko" Freeman grace nearly every blank wall in town, beginning in 2009 with the Eddy County DWI Program mural, which depicts the consequences of driving impaired. As part of the Carlsbad Mural Project, Freeman has immortalized the beautiful formations of the world famous Carlsbad Caverns National Park along with other local vacation spots in a commemorative postage stamp. He also worked closely with the budding artists of Carlsbad to complete lasting tributes. Freeman's works can be found in public buildings and private homes in Los Angeles, Atlanta, and Carlsbad. Freeman's most recent work is a traveling mural that commemorates the 40th anniversary of the Guadalupe Mountains National Park. Carlsbad is more beautiful due to the wonderful work of this humble artist. (Author's collection.)

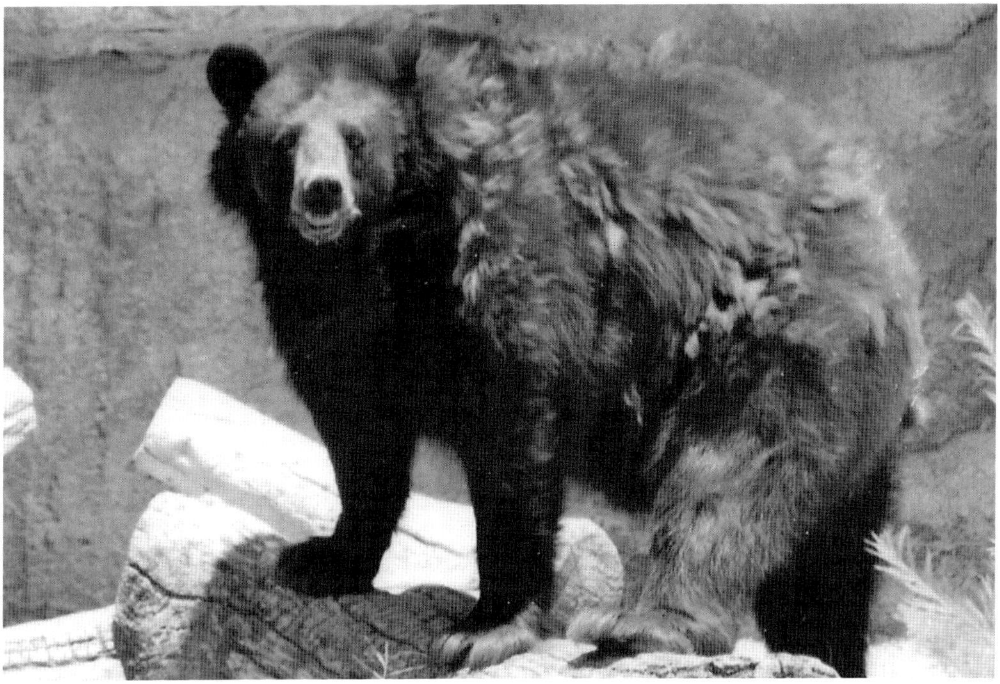

Maggie Oso

Maggie Oso, a black bear, is the star of the Living Desert Zoo and Gardens State Park. At six months old, Maggie found a place in the hearts of the staff and community. As part of an enrichment program, Maggie was given paper and nontoxic paint, from which she has created many award-winning paintings. The creations are sold by the Friends of the Living Desert to supplement the zoo's revenue. (Author's collection.)

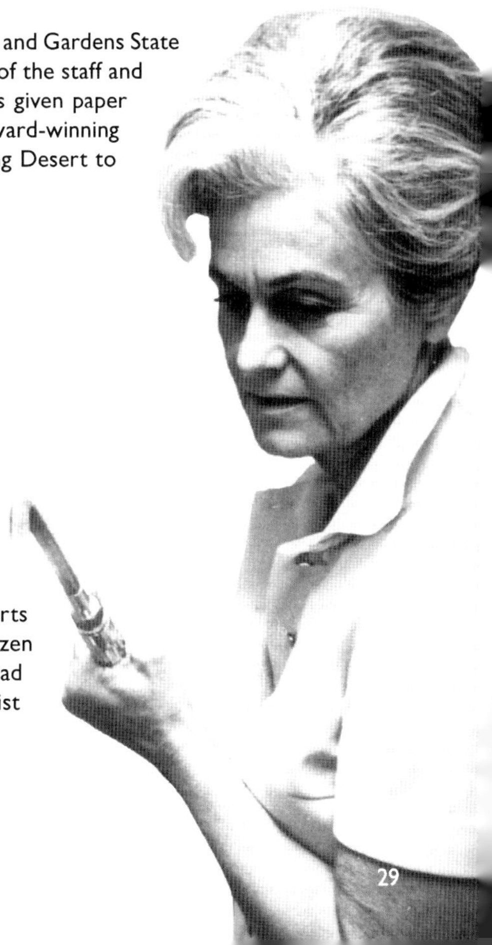

Dorothy Smith Lorentzen

Quoted as saying, "There's absolutely nothing that cannot be inspiration for creating art," fine jewelry designer Dorothy Lorentzen made a name for herself in the sports realm as a diving champion in her youth. A vignette of Lorentzen diving at Black River is featured on the facade of the Carlsbad Public Library Annex in a mural by Artesia, New Mexico, artist Noel Marquez.

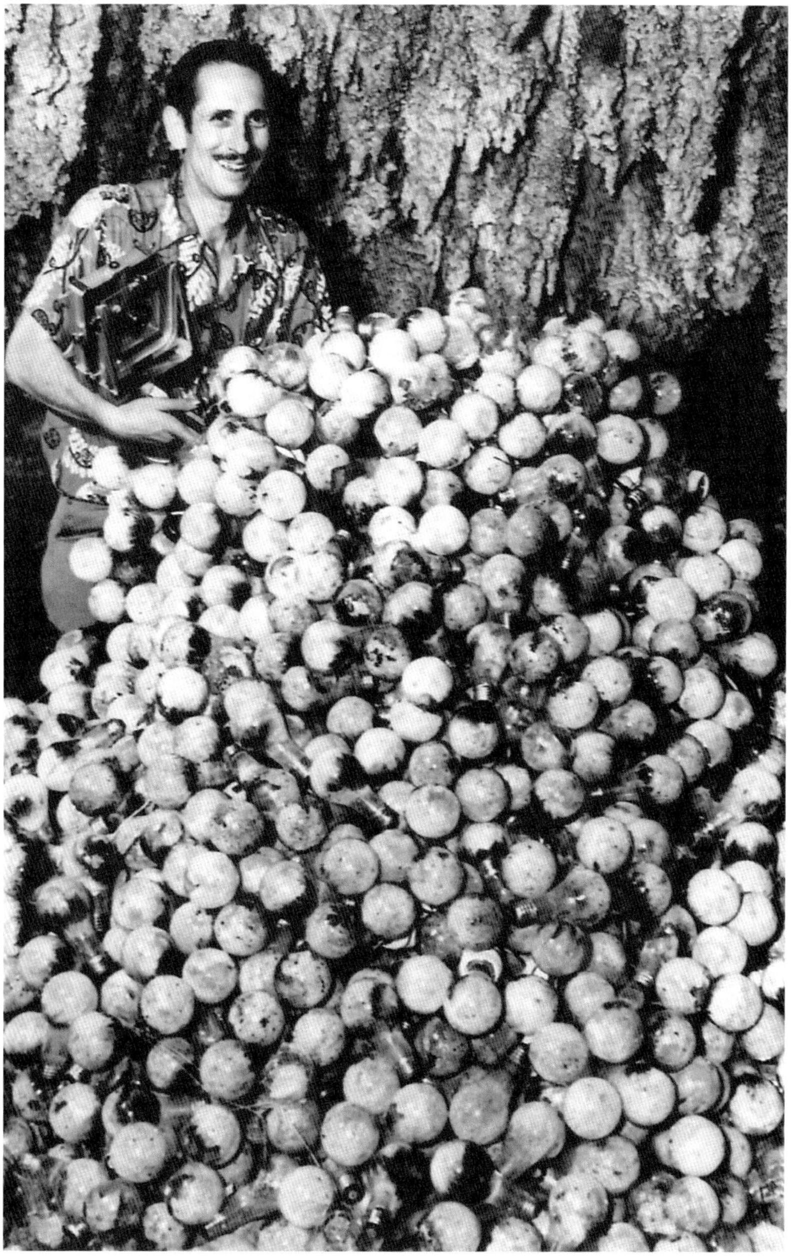

Ennis C. "Tex" Helm

The underground beauty of the Carlsbad Caverns was literally illuminated in color by the photography of Tex Helm and his world record *Big Shot*, which used over 2,400 Super No. 2 flashbulbs to light up 550,000 square feet in the Big Room. This photograph appeared in the October 1953 edition of *National Geographic* as the world's largest flashbulb color picture. The shot took Helm and his team 16 hours to set up and take down. As a newsman, Helm also chased Bonnie and Clyde across the nation, was the second newsman on scene at the Saint Valentine's Day Massacre in Chicago, and photographed early space flight tests for the government. One of Helm's best known accomplishments is his role as photographer in Admiral Byrd's third expedition into the Antarctic.

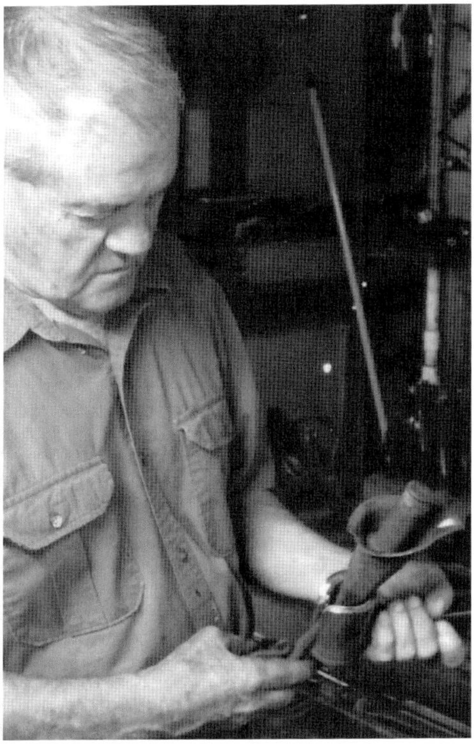

Frank Westfall
The transition from dentist to blacksmith artist was easy for Frank Westfall. In his small but efficient blacksmith shop, Westfall forges metal into beautiful creations that grace many homes and businesses in Carlsbad. From the smallest cluster of grapes to full-sized gates and stair railings, each piece shows the great love he puts into his dying art form. (Author's collection.)

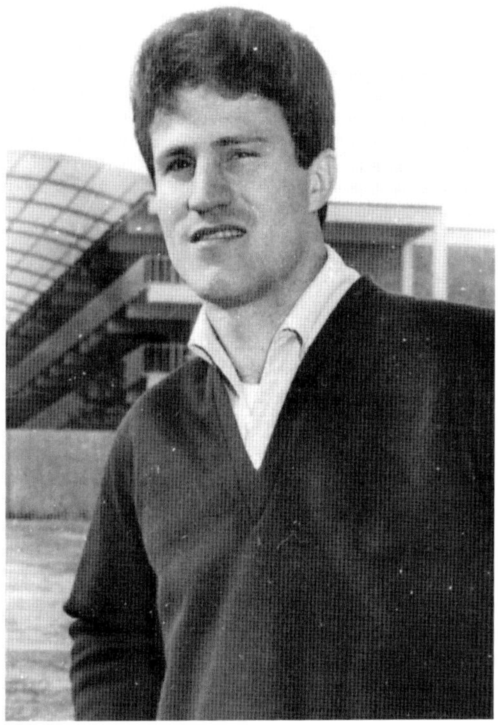

Gary Niblett
Western artist Gary Niblett rubs elbows with artists such as G. Harvey and Olaf Wieghorst. Earning his membership in the Cowboy Artists of America in 1975, Niblett's work received worldwide accolades, including a 1981 appearance on the *Merv Griffin Show.* Niblett also painted a portrait of Donna Douglas (Elly May Clampett of *The Beverly Hillbillies*) for the Trader Jim Mill Art Fair.

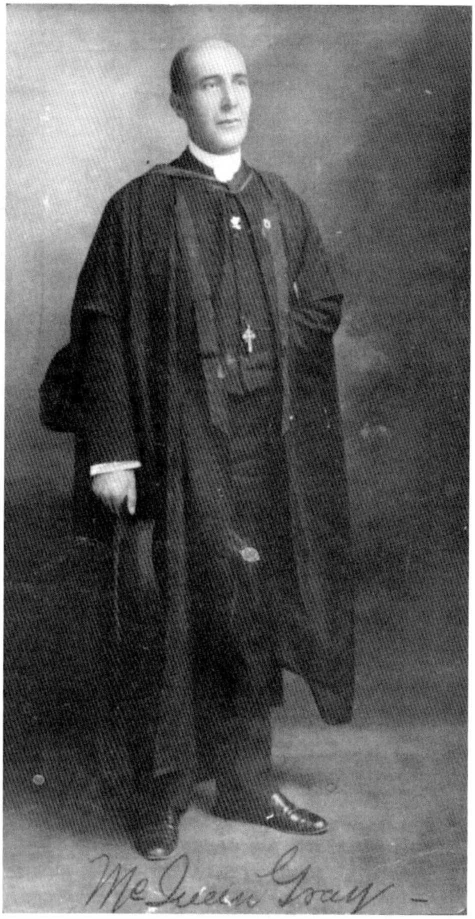

Edward McQueen Gray
Edward McQueen Gray, an Englishman who came to the desert, was an accomplished author, educator, and the fourth president of the University of New Mexico. Gray would delight Carlsbad residents by taking out his phonograph and give impromptu concerts on summer evenings from the balcony of the Schlitz Hotel. Gray lived in Loving for 14 years before he moved to Carlsbad, where his home was dubbed "Baronald."

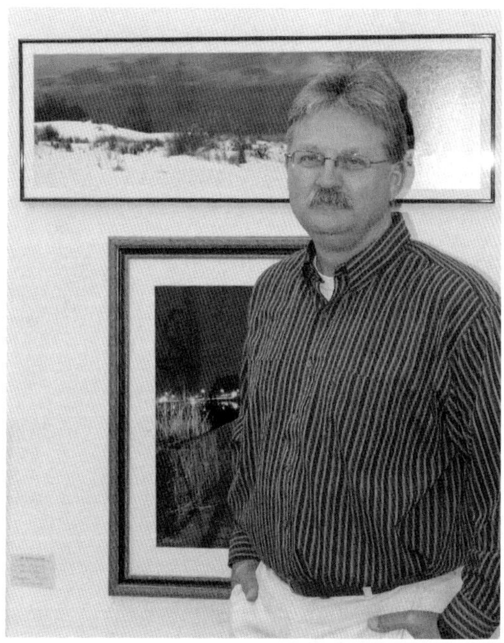

Brad Molgaard
Retired from the Carlsbad Police Department, Brad Molgaard captures the beauty around him through the lens of his camera. The award-winning photographer is a favorite at local art shows, which often grant his work a first place ribbon. Molgaard has a passion for photography and explores his craft through the use of different computer programs and enhancements, which results in stunning, unique works of art. (Author's collection.)

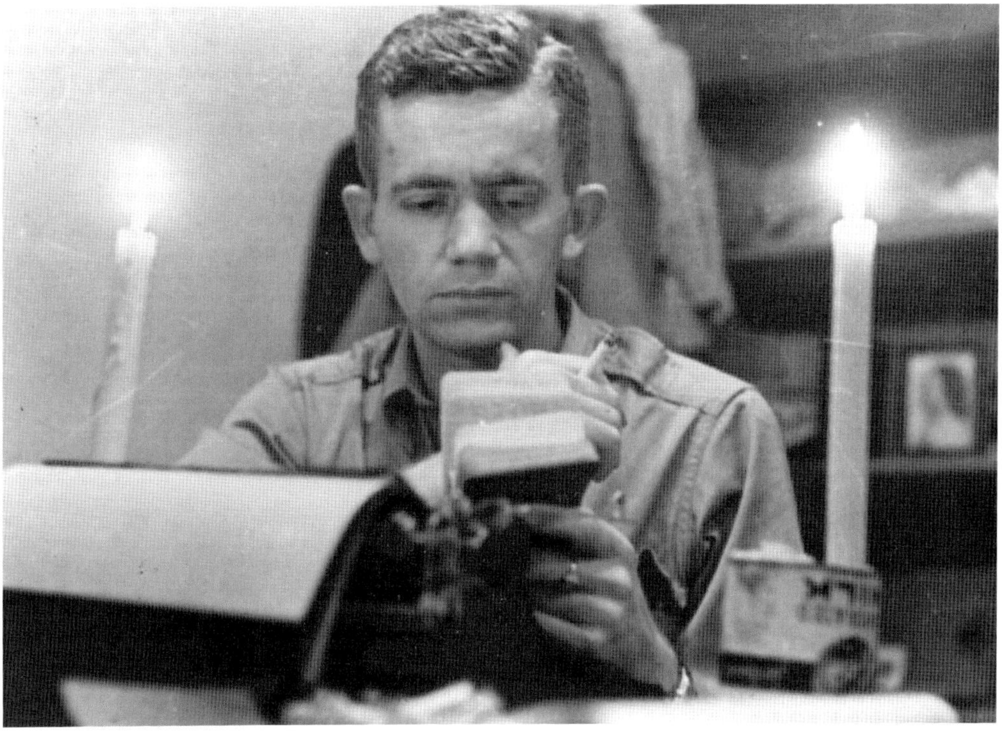

Kenneth L. Dixon

Born in Illinois, Kenneth L. Dixon was the editor of the *Carlsbad Current Argus* from 1936 to 1942. In 1942, Dixon joined the Associated Press as a foreign war correspondent, traveling to places such as Africa, Europe, and the Pacific Theater. Dixon covered the exploits of Maj. William Stewart Walker as he worked to rescue 380 American soldiers trapped during the Battle of the Bulge.

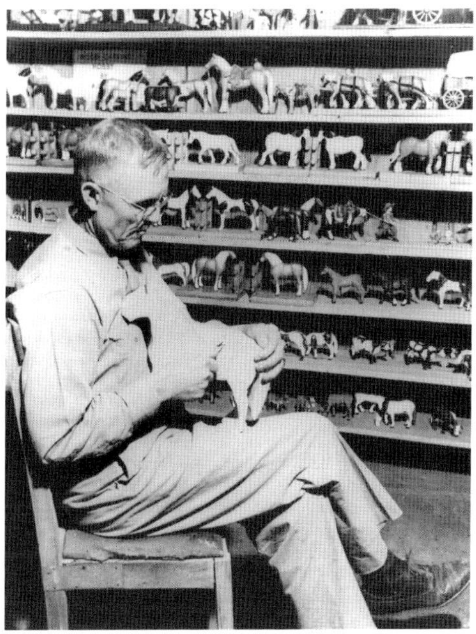

Lewis Means

Raised in the Guadalupe Mountains, Lewis Means attended Artesia College and Southern Methodist University to become the first preacher for the village of Weed, New Mexico. Means's love for horses was evident, as he filled many shelves of his home with his hand-carved creations. This collection is in many homes in the area and at the now debunked Million Dollar Museum in Whites City, New Mexico.

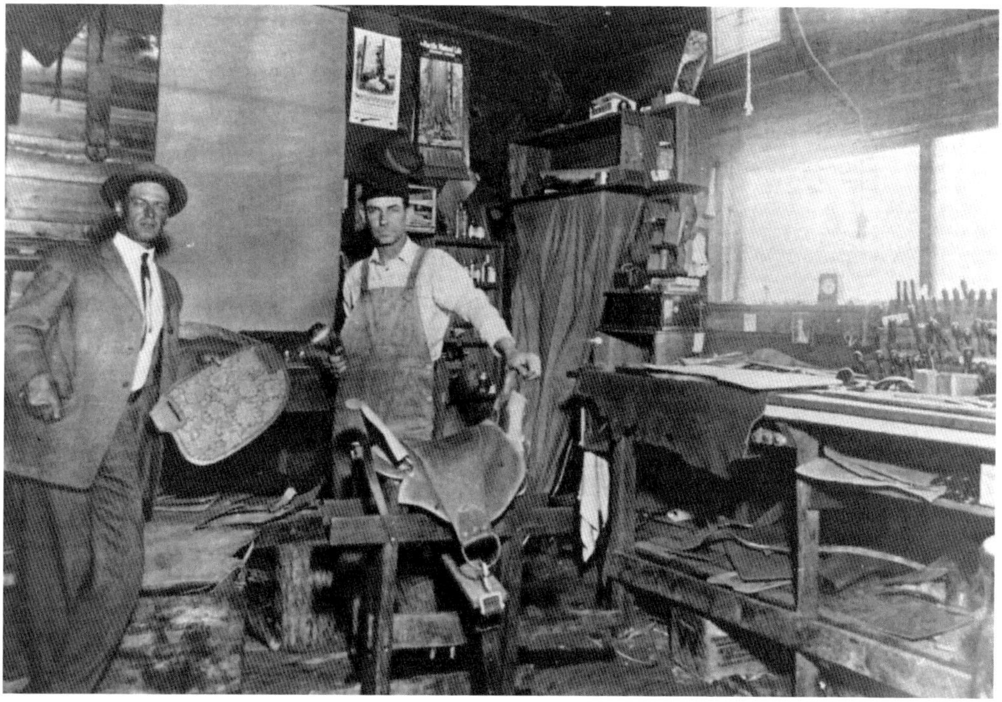

Ed "Kirk" Kirkpatrick

With a reputation as a respected saddle maker, Kirk Kirkpatrick supplied Carlsbad and the Pecos Valley with their tack needs. Kirkpatrick worked for Roberts-Dearborn, and his saddles were sought after by well-to-do cowboys and ranch owners all along the Pecos Valley. Fine leather carvings and details were his trademark. The Carlsbad Museum and Art Center has the saddle Kirkpatrick made for rancher Green Ussery on display.

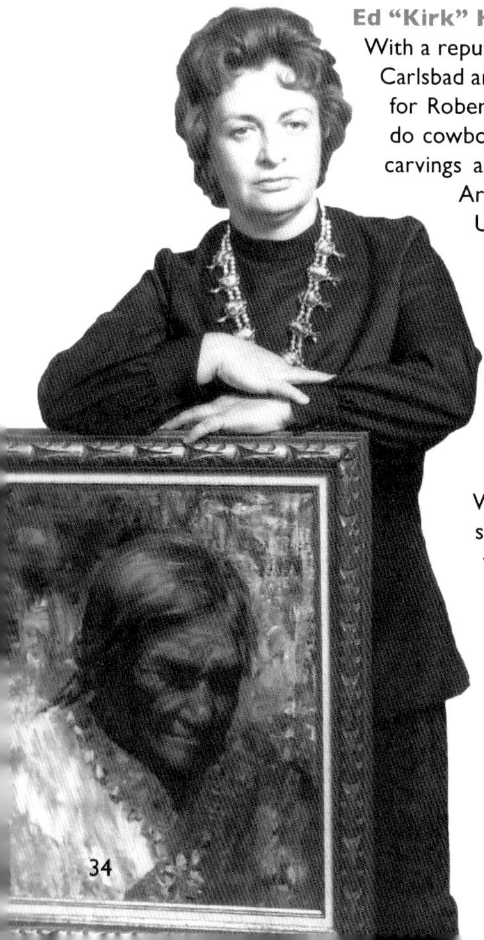

Grace Knox

Western artist Grace Knox has won many ribbons in the art shows given by the Carlsbad Area Art Association. Grace was kind in her skills and taught classes at the Senior Center, allowing others to know the thrill of creating a piece of art. Knox has judged many prestigious art shows, and her work has been featured in major magazines and selected by Leaning Tree for greeting cards.

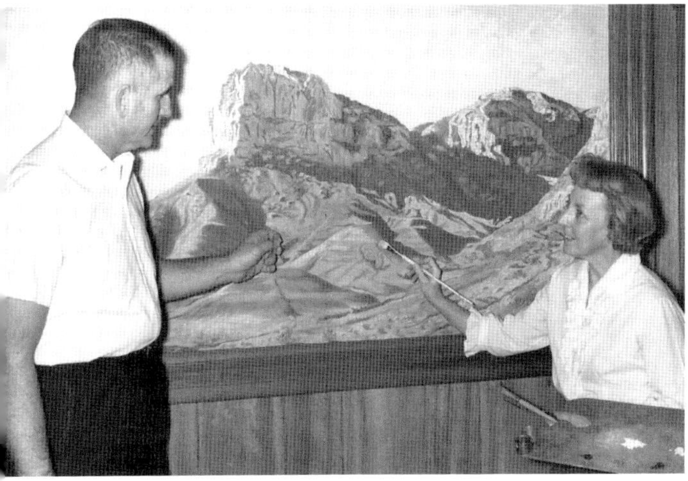

Lucille Martin
The Southwest was a favorite subject of oil painter Lucille Martin, whose works have won many prestigious awards in exhibits in Florida, Texas, and New Mexico. As a muralist, Martin created art to grace the walls of church and commercial buildings in Carlsbad as well as the Houston Medical Center and Western Tradition Gallery in Boulder, Colorado. In 1964, she was commissioned by Governor Campbell to create a roadrunner painting for aircraft carrier *Constellation.*

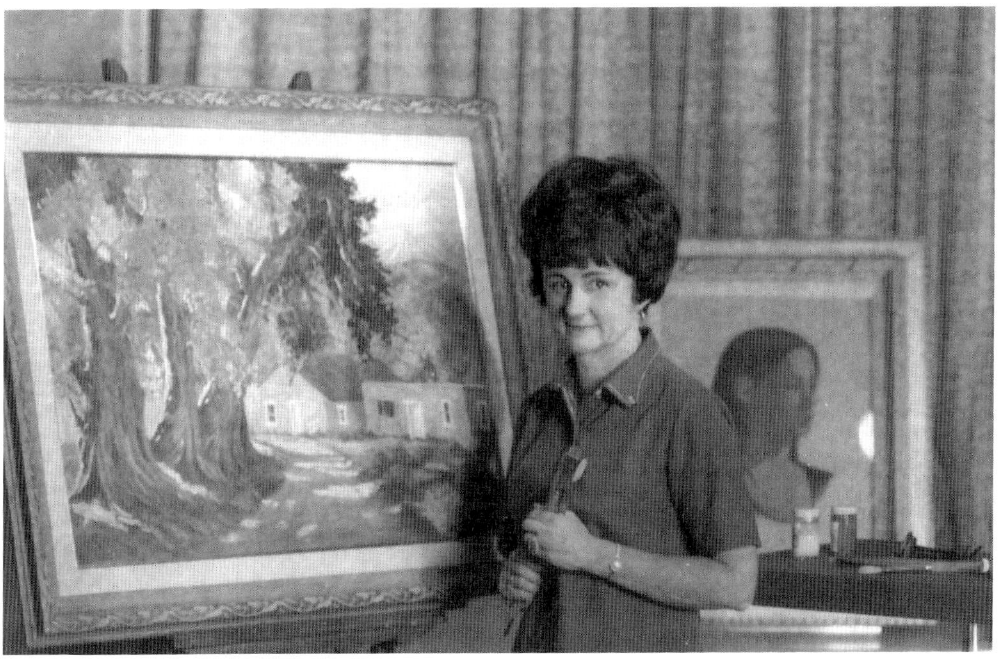

Nora Robertson
Passing away two days before her 93rd birthday in 2013, Nora Robertson was an award-winning oil painter and sculptor. Born in Rhyl, North Wales, she came to Carlsbad so her father could work as a mining engineer for the first potash mine in the basin, US Borax. Robertson taught at Carlsbad High School and New Mexico State University, and her landscapes captured the desert beauty that surrounded her.

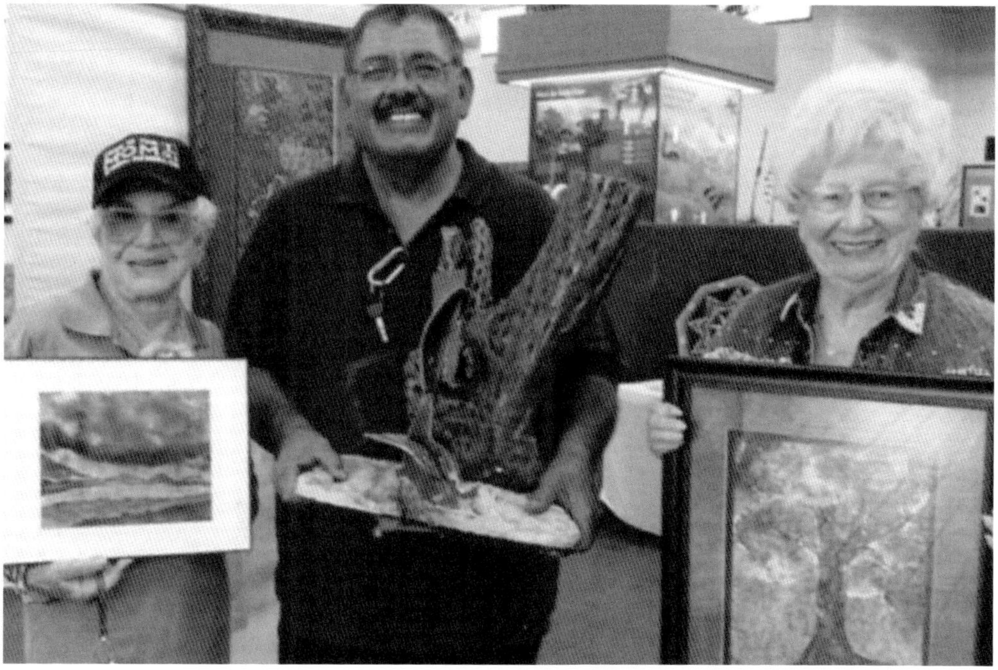

John Hernandez

World-renowned metal artist John Hernandez uses a CNC plasma cutter to render his art and has worked with other artists to create beautiful collaborations. Hernandez also works with the Carlsbad MainStreet Farmers' Market and encourages elementary children to walk to school through the "Walking School Bus," where he personally escorts children to school on foot. (Courtesy of John Hernandez.)

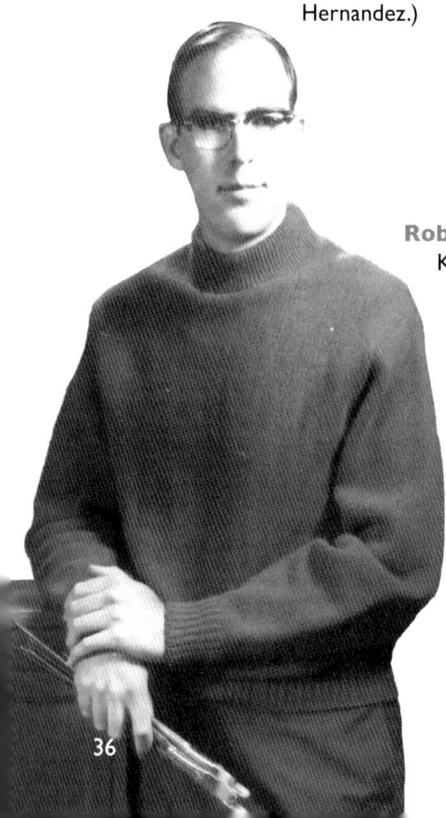

Robert Johanningmeier

Known for his ultrarealistic style, Robert Johanningmeier captures light through his paintings. Be it glass, candlelight, or a reflection, it is portrayed as nearly jumping off the canvas. As an author of a book on how to invest in art, Johanningmeier lets the world in on the secrets he has learned over the years.

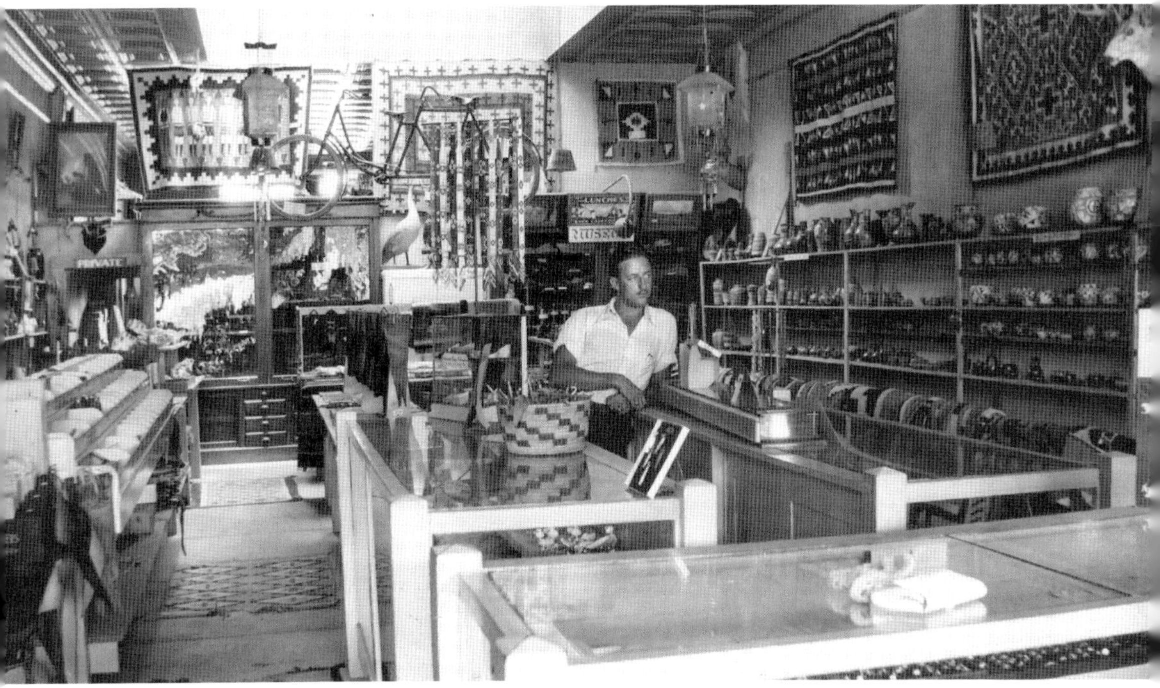

Robert "Bob" Nymeyer
Photographer, author, and store owner Robert "Bob" Nymeyer left a legacy of historical photographs. It is through his images that the world became familiar with the Carlsbad Caverns. As the author of *Carlsbad, Caves and a Camera*, Nymeyer explains his love of both caving and photography. Flashbulbs were too bulky and expensive, so Nymeyer would mix a little shotgun powder and magnesium to produce the desired effect.

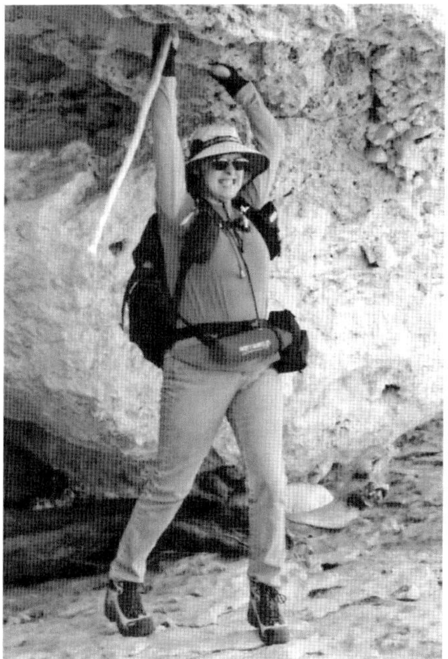

Valerie Cranston
Since being brought to Carlsbad as a child in 1960, New Yorker Valerie Cranston calls herself the "Swedish Yankee." Besides her family, Cranston's greatest loves are the mountains, writing, and animals. Cranston's Sunday feature for the *Carlsbad Current Argus* gives the citizens of Carlsbad a glimpse of their history as Cranston brings the stories of the past to life with her easy style. (Courtesy of Valerie Cranston.)

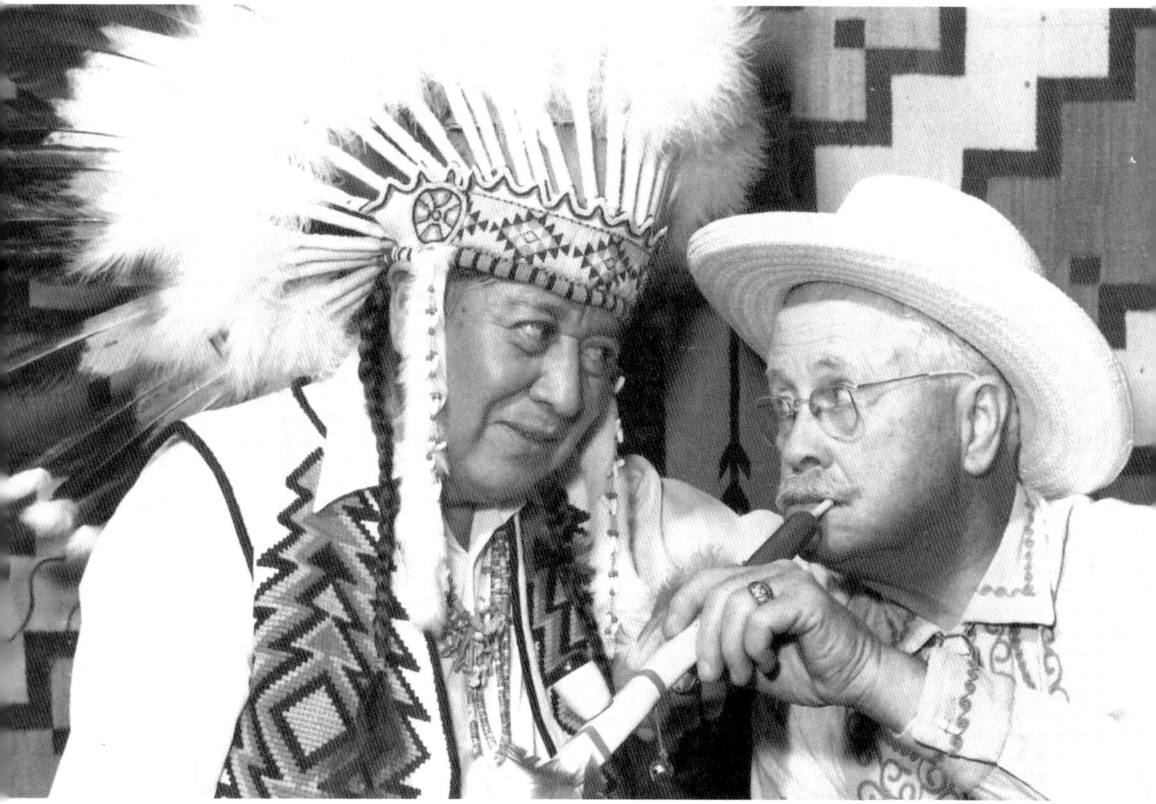

Clyde "Chief Sunny Skies" Hunt

Clyde Hunt, son of "Chief Big Snake," was a native of Acoma Pueblo. Big Snake's original name was Peter Nabokov, and he was the only Westphalian German Indian chief recorded in his time. Big Snake was an American Indian Scared Clown, an International Show Indian, and a medicine man. Though his son, Sunny Skies, was the last hereditary medicine man of Acoma, he moved to Carlsbad in 1937 at the request of his wife, Estelle. There, Sunny Skies opened a trading post, which he operated until his death in 1972; Estelle closed shop in 1977. Sunny Skies loved the tourists who would frequent his shop to see an "authentic Indian." Playing up to this, he put on full regalia and performed dance. He was extremely active in the community and never knew a stranger.

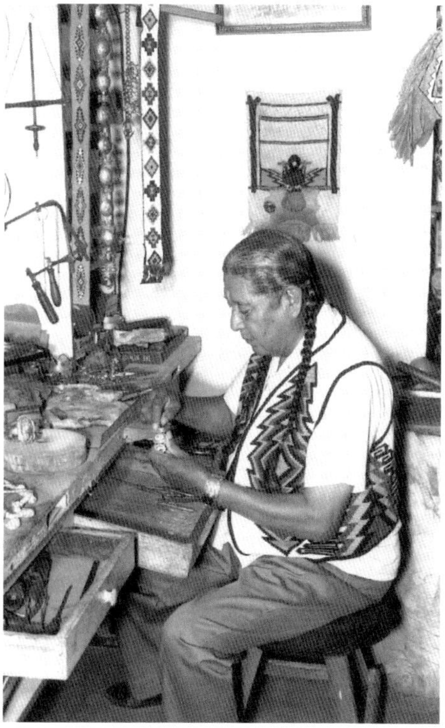

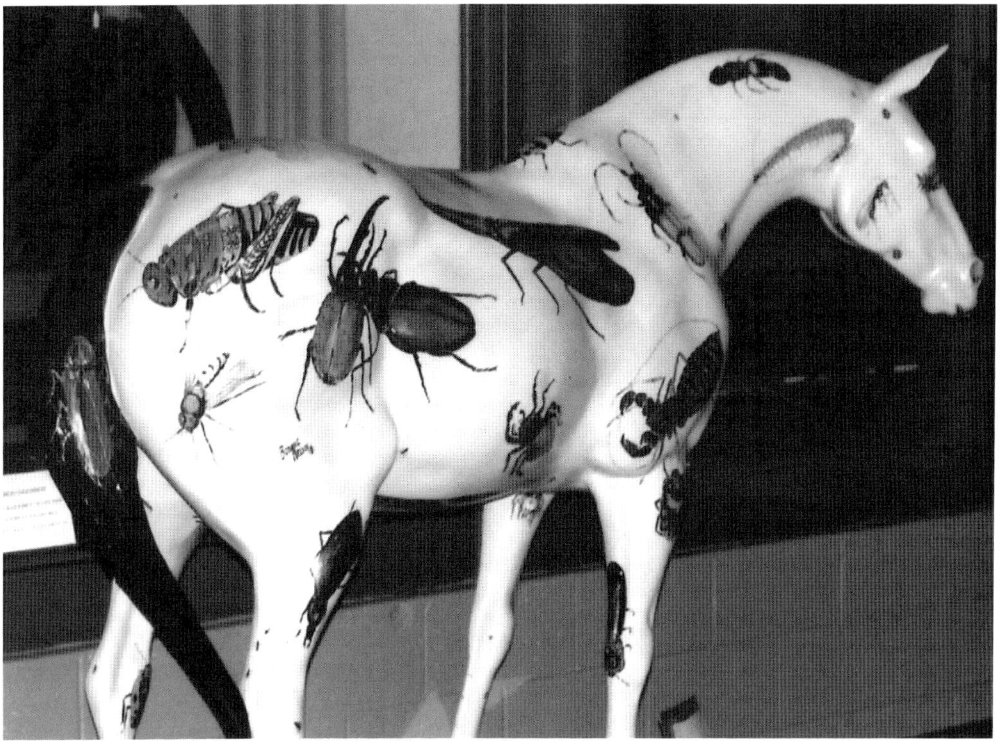

Trail of the Painted Ponies

Trail of the Painted Ponies is an art project that utilized local artists to design and paint life-sized acrylic horses to benefit charities. Carlsbad was one of the first to participate in the auctions in 2001. Local artists Gerri Mattson, Pat Beason, Carla Clark, Israel Palma, and Kay Brubaker created the ponies, many with humorous names like *Five Card Stud*, *Boot Scootin' Horsey*, and *Horse 'n Buggie*. (Author's collection.)

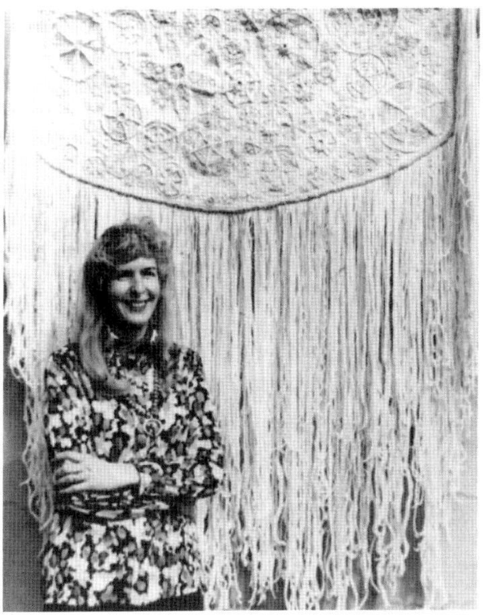

Helen Rumpel

Famous for her fiber art, Helen Rumpel has lived all over the world, including Carlsbad. Rumpel's fascinating work is exhibited in galleries from New York to Russia. Rumpel was presented the Governor's Award in 1990 as an Outstanding New Mexico Woman in Art among many other honors. Rumpel's works are in collections worldwide, and before her death in 2014, she published a book about her art.

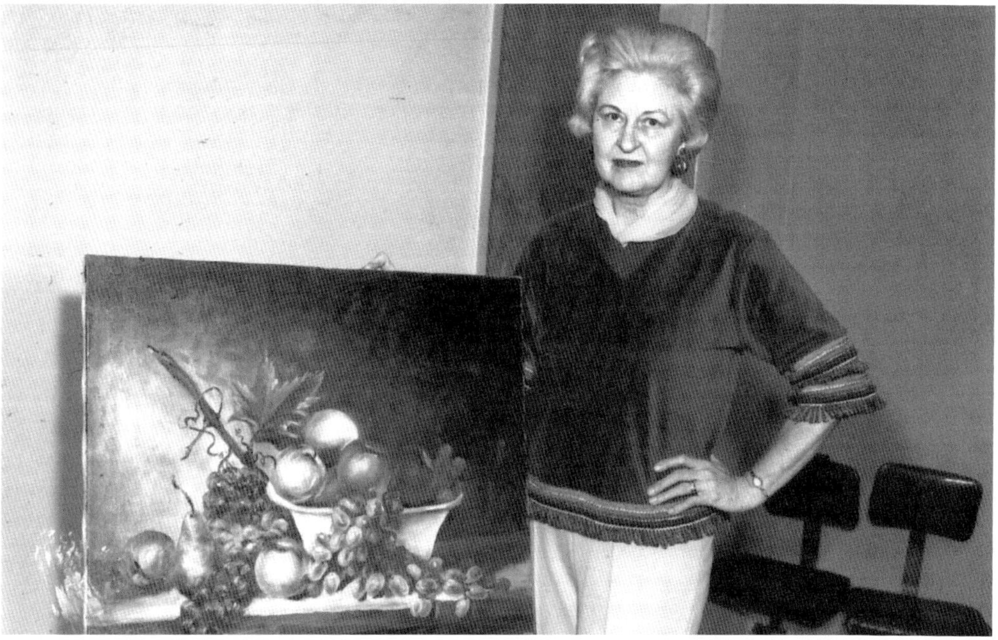

Velma "May" Howell

Trained nurse Velma May Howell became an artist later in life. In her studio on Wood Street, May used her favorite medium, oils, to create stunning still life paintings of fruits and flowers. Born in Hope, Arkansas, Howell moved to many places with her family before finally settling in Carlsbad.

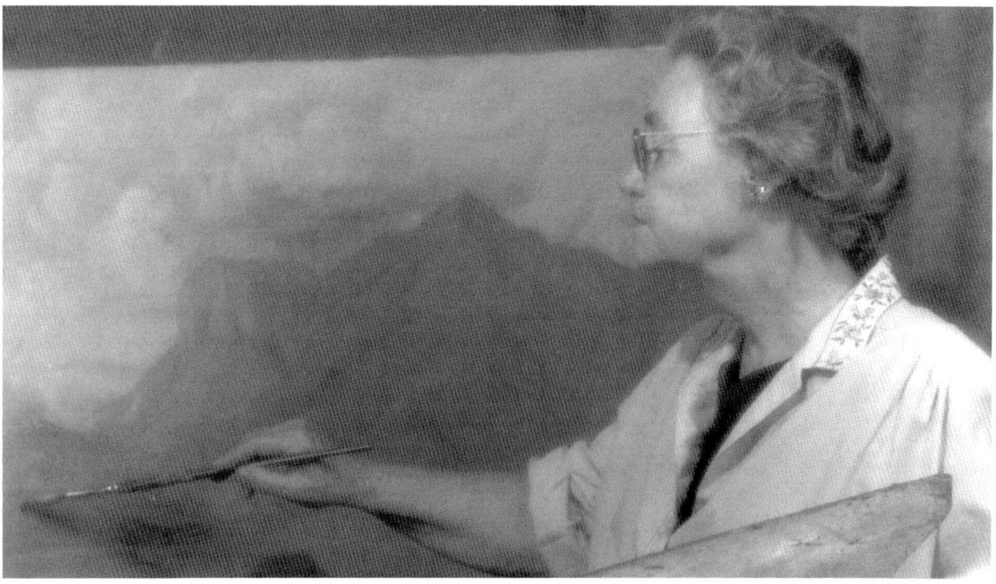

Camille Smith

Landscape artist Camille Smith is mother to jewelry maker Dorothy Smith Lorentzen. Hailing from pioneer stock, Smith put her knowledge of the area into every landscape painting she created. Smith's favorite subject was El Capitan in the Guadalupe Mountains, which she could see from the land at Black River that had been owned by the Smith family for generations.

CHAPTER THREE

That's Entertainment

Talent must be a key ingredient in the rich mineral water of Carlsbad. Residents have always been known to have a flair for the dramatic, and talent seems to come natural.

The Carlsbad Community Theatre puts on several productions during the year and employs local talent to fill roles. There are three dance studios in Carlsbad that cater to children. Although there is healthy competition between studios, they work together to put on joint productions to rave reviews.

The Carlsbad music scene has a wide genre range; country, mariachi, Tejaño, gospel, and rock bands all vie for attention. In the 1950s and 1960s, garage bands surfaced, producing some musicians who are still playing today. Carlsbad has played host to notable acts like Elvis Presley (at the start of his career in 1955), Waylon Jennings, Randy Travis, Spencer Campbell (who is from Carlsbad), Buddy Holley and The Fireballs, Tracy Lawrence, and Glen Campbell (who married Carlsbad beautician Billie Jean Nunley).

Several movies, such as *The Honkers*, *The Gargoyles*, and *Journey to the Center of the Earth,* used Carlsbad and the Caverns as locations. Talent learned in Carlsbad is well known to the world through the works of actors Bruce Cabot and Dan Blocker, who entertained us on the big and little screens with their memorable characters.

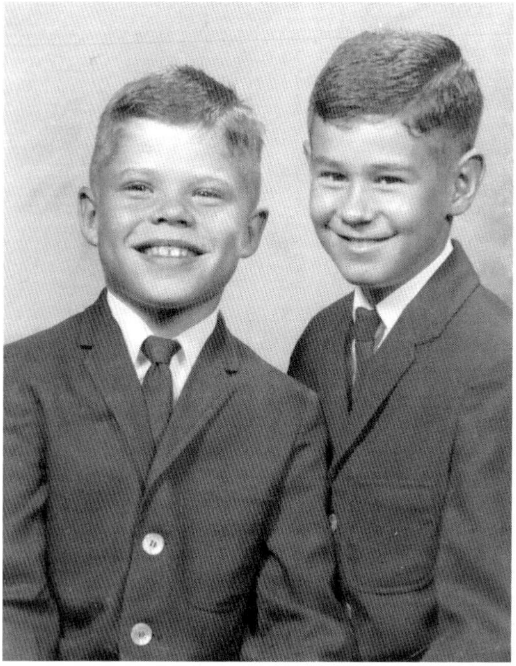

James Rees Lucas

As a product of pioneer stock, James Rees Lucas put his heart and soul into his music. As a native of Carlsbad, Lucas was known for his guitar playing and drumming abilities. Several bands over the years would be proud to have Lucas as a member, but his group The Proof was to be his last. Lucas passed away at age 52 from a heart attack after finishing a gig at a local Mexican restaurant. Tragically, one of the first EMTs on scene was his brother Barry. His shocking death left a huge void in the community; he is greatly missed by all who knew him. (Below, courtesy of Lanny Barnett.)

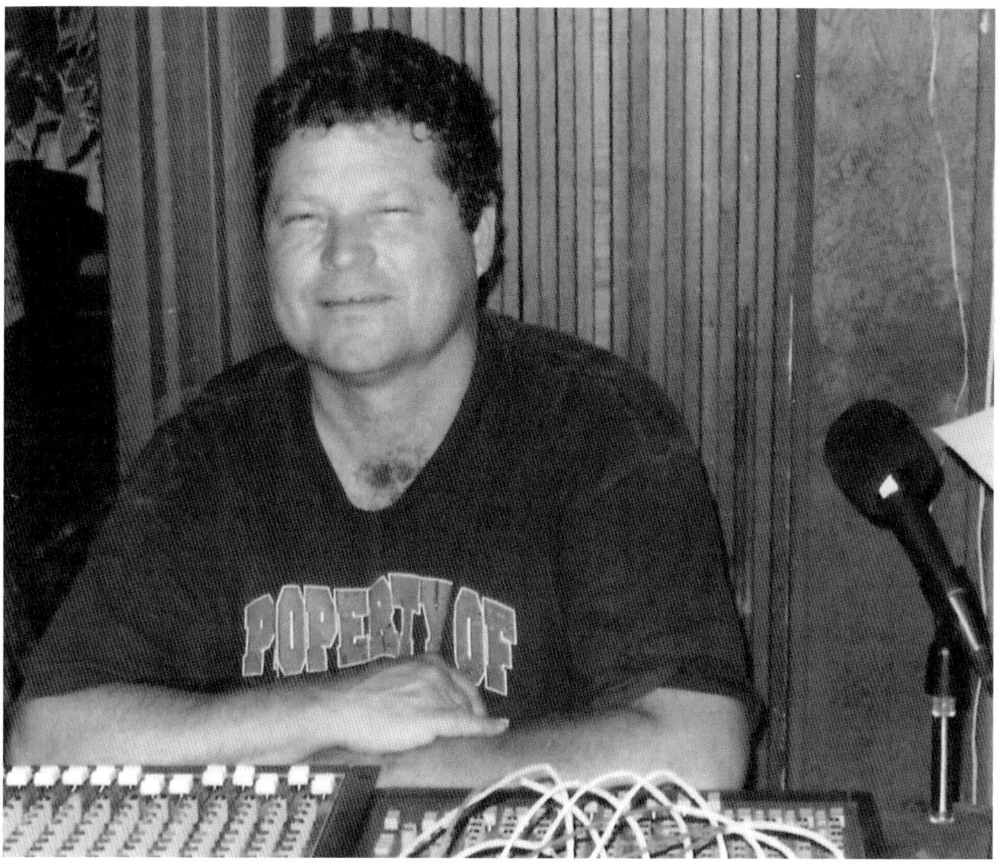

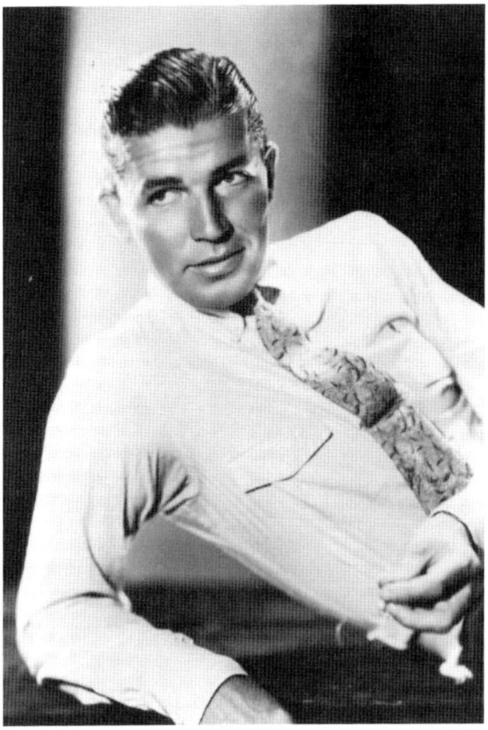

Bruce Cabot

Etienne Pelissier Jacques de Bujac Jr. grew up as the son of a lawyer, but he moved to Hollywood to act. He changed his name to Bruce Cabot before his first film in 1931. Cabot is best remembered as Jack Driscoll in the 1933 version of *King Kong*. He starred in over 100 films, many with his close friend, John Wayne. Cabot died at age 68 in 1972.

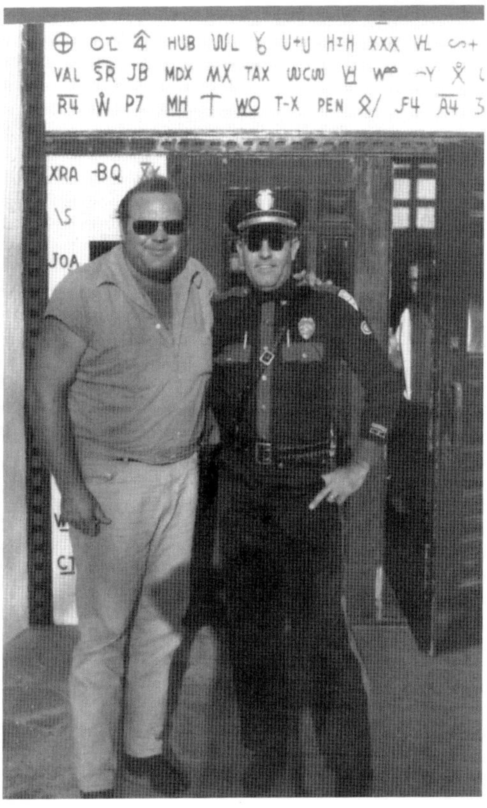

Dan Blocker

Dan Blocker will always be known to many as Eric "Hoss" Cartwright from the television series *Bonanza*, but to Carlsbad residents he was known as the sixth grade teacher and coach for Eddy Elementary School. Blocker (shown on left with Officer Jim Hickman) was a fan of performance cars; he owned a 1965 Chevrolet Chevelle SS396 "Z-16" and was a friend of dragster Dick Harrell.

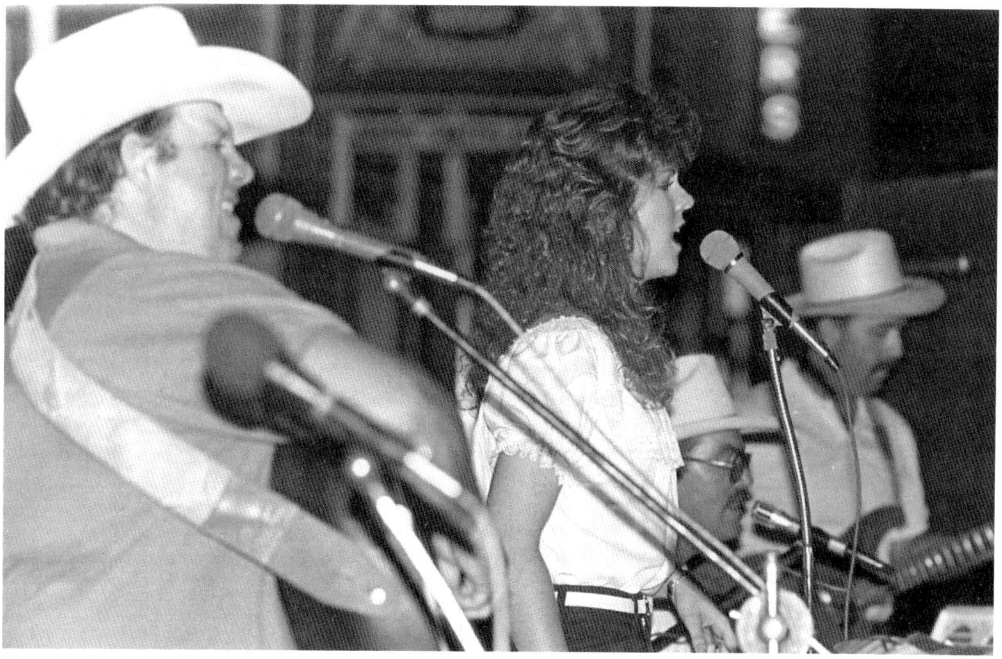

Billy Grandi

Friday and Saturday nights in Carlsbad during the 1970s and 1980s were sweeter due to the country-and-western sounds of the Billy Grandi Band. Playing to packed venues, the Billy Grandi Band was a fixture in the Carlsbad music scene, always providing fun and great sounds to normally quiet small town weekends. During Rodeo Week—usually in July—the Grandi Band played for the street dance.

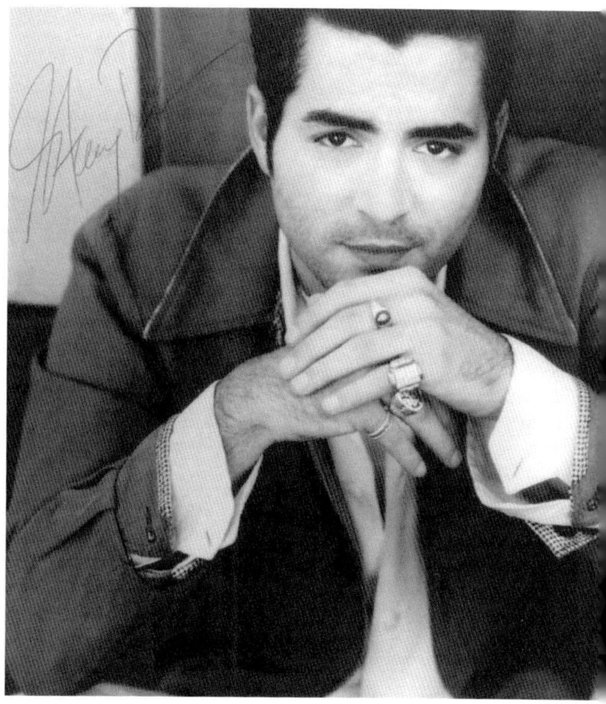

Stacy Dean Campbell

Singer/songwriter Stacy Campbell helped pen hits like "I'm Gonna Love You Anyway" for country artist Trace Adkins. Campbell also authored *Cottonwood*, which included a CD of songs inspired by the book and hosted a televised travel log called *Bronco Roads* that highlights life in the American West. He is best known for his 1990 critically acclaimed album, *Lonesome Wins Again*, produced by Columbia Records. (Author's collection)

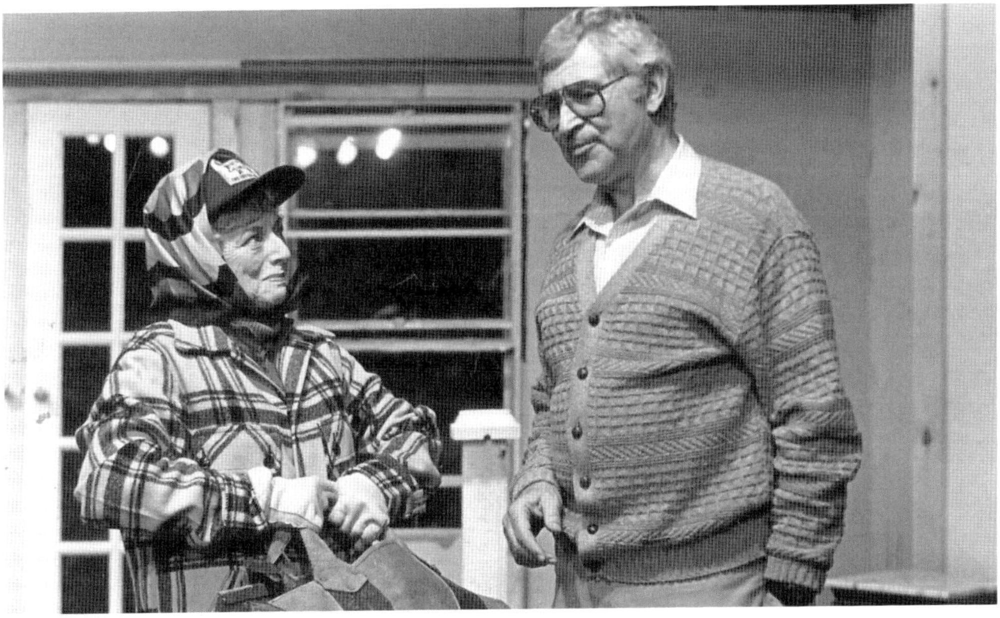

Lynne Pitcaithley

Tiny Lynne Pitcaithley wears many hats in the community of Carlsbad. Known for her work as a champion of animals through Noah's Ark Animal Rescue Center, Pitcaithley is also a well-loved actress, appearing in many productions in the Carlsbad Community Theatre. Pitcaithley's love of animals prompted her to start a spay and neuter program, in which animal owners get a certificate for a substantial discount on the procedures. In 1999, Pitcaithley retired as Carlsbad's oldest teacher at age 80. Lynne always tells people that her favorite perfume is a bit of chalk dust, some books, and a whole lot of children. She is also the author of *Acts I, II and III, a Memoir,* a story of her life that took 10 years to write and four years to get published.

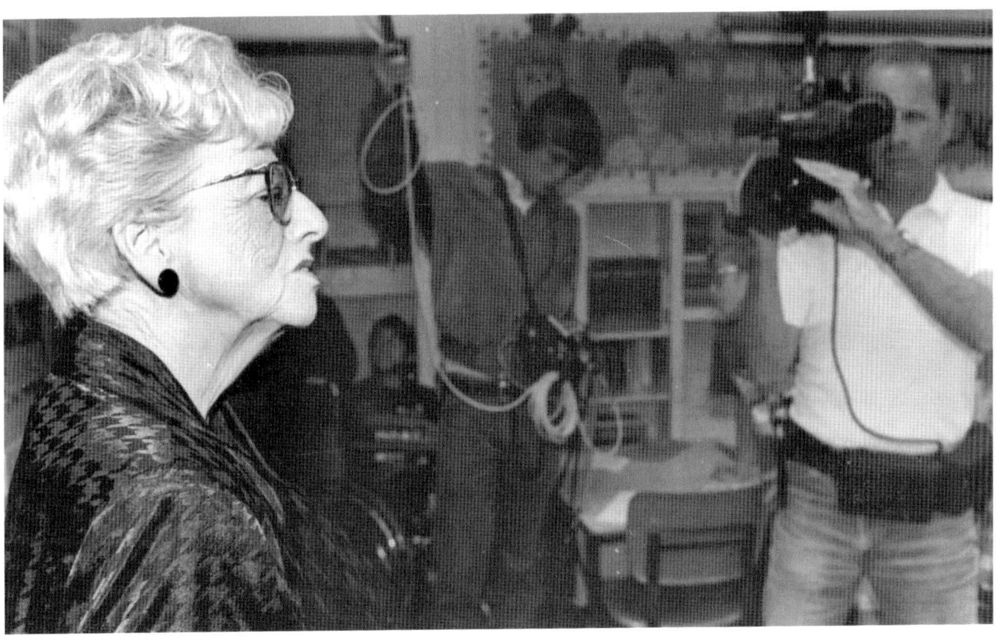

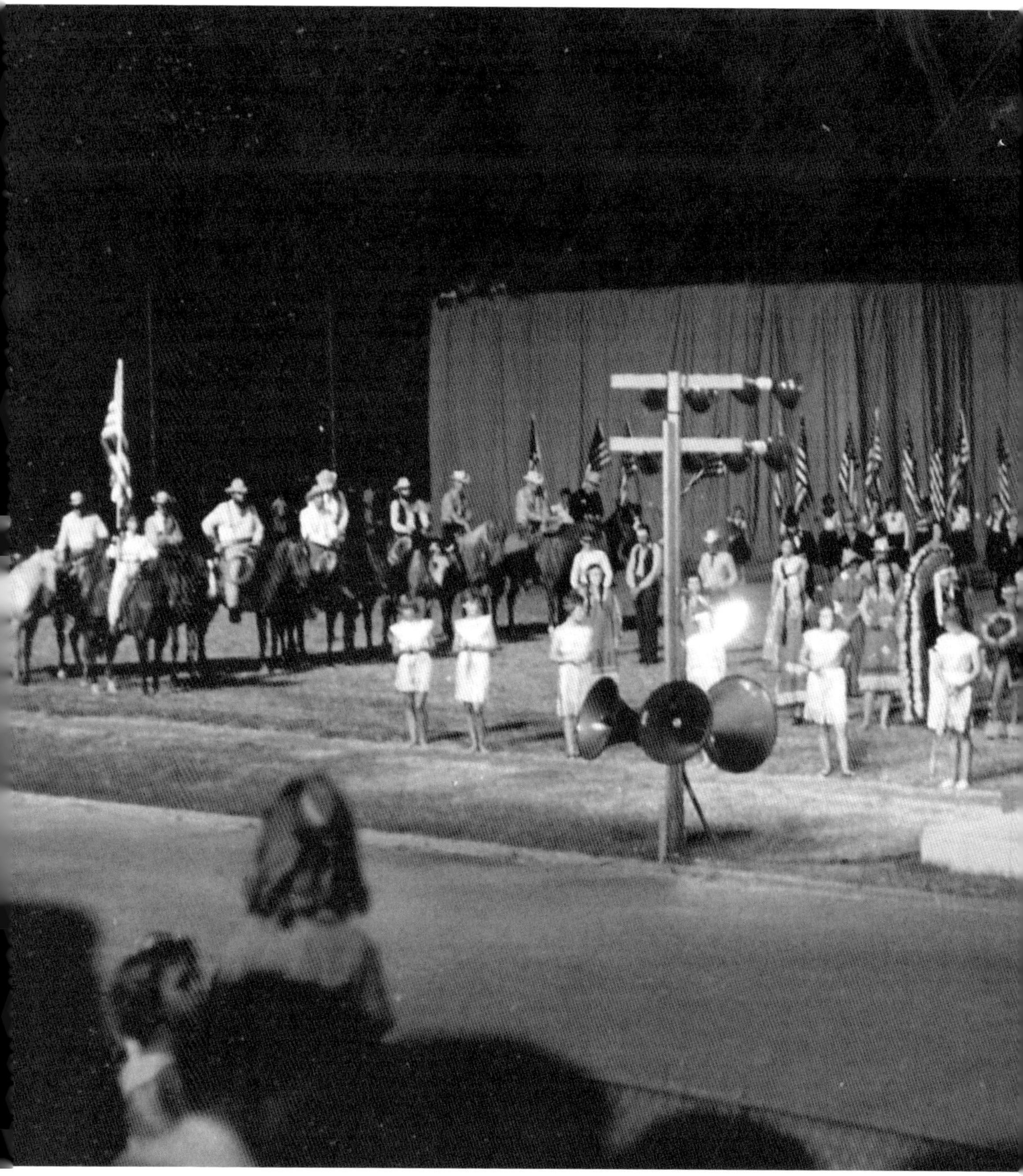

Pageant of Progress

For the 75th diamond jubilee of the founding of Carlsbad in August 1963, a large group of civic leaders gathered together and produced a substantial performance. An entire week was devoted to the telling of Carlsbad's rich history, highlighting all of the players, participants, and members of the community. A 68-page souvenir program of the event was published, which included the photographic images and brief history shorts of the area. The musical and oration extravaganza took place at the Carlsbad High

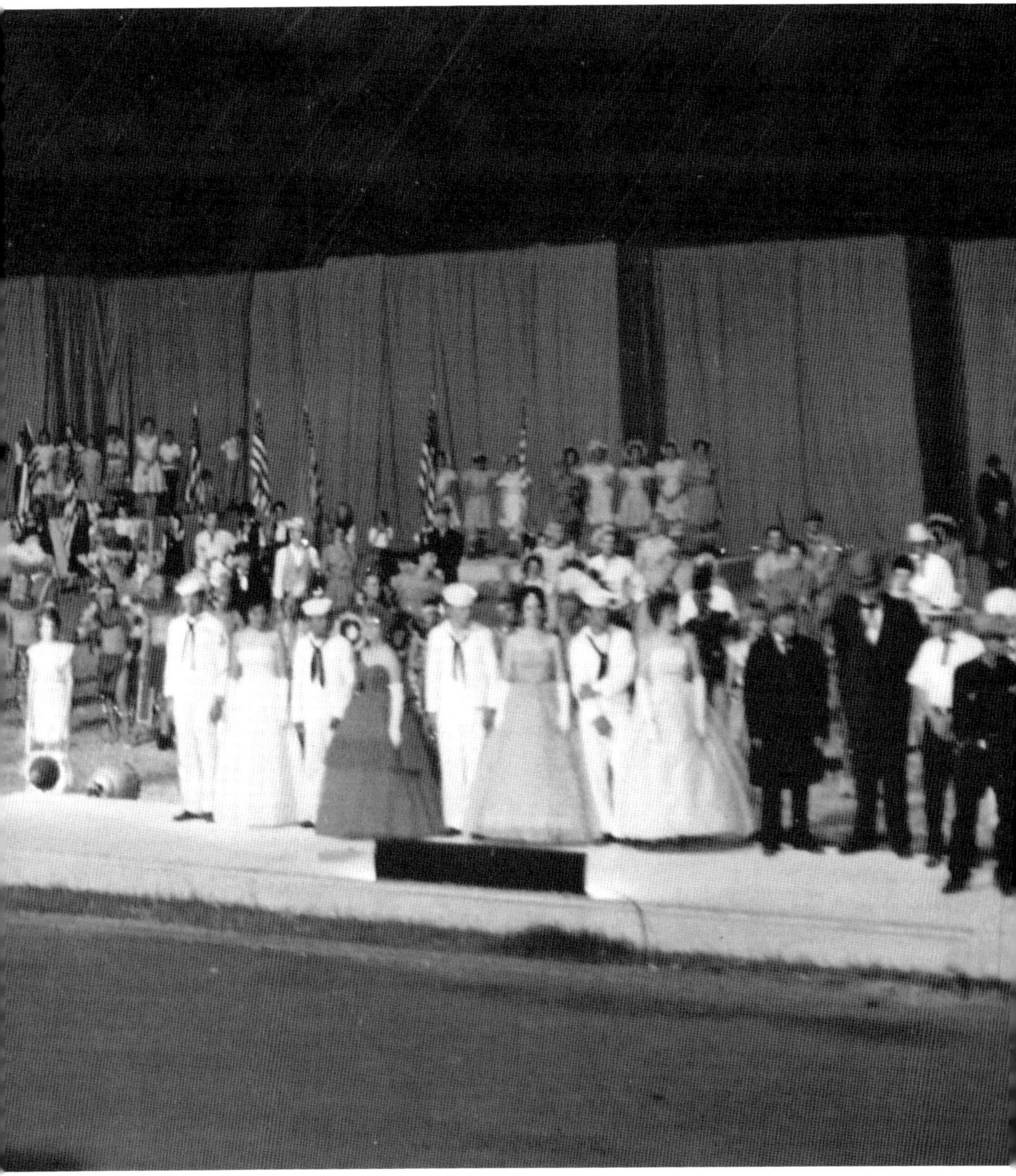

School, which is now P.R. Leyva Middle School. It was through this event that historian Jed Howard became interested in the old photographs of the town and began his work to preserve them. A cast of hundreds brought the rich history of Carlsbad to life, dressed in period clothing with antique props highlighted by beard-growing, most authentic dress, and jubilee queen contests. Jubilee queen Francine Sims (Hoffman) was given a six-day trip to Honolulu, Hawaii, as her prize.

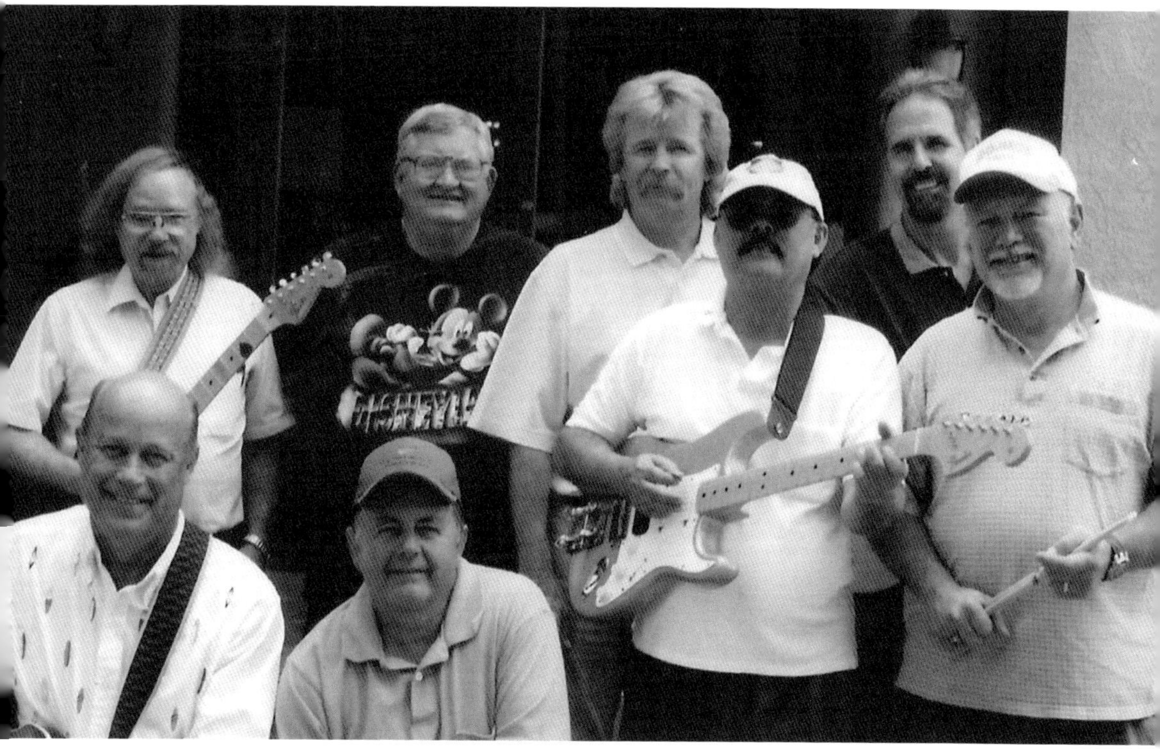

Stuck in the 60s Band
Born in 1963 from the dreams and abilities of four preteen boys from the tiny subdivision of Carlsbad known as Happy Valley, garage band The Hustlers would morph and endure over 50 years, surviving as Stuck in the 60s. Original members are David Huggins (lead guitar), Lanny Barnett (bass guitar), Bobby Joe Conger (drums), Glenn Getings (rhythm guitar), Mike Bartlett (saxophone and keyboard), Larry Gregory (lead and rhythm guitar), and Tom Riley (drums). They were later joined by new members, some from Carlsbad's other garage bands. There is Don Spruill (rhythm guitar and vocals), Mark Hutchins (bass guitar from The Imperials), Margie Gregory (wife of Larry), Jimmy Wiseman (drums from The Others), John Roberts (guitar from The Others), and Ronnie and Deedle Muncrief (vocals). Guest band members such as Rees Lucas joined the band when they played for high school reunions and dances. (Courtesy of Lanny Barnett.)

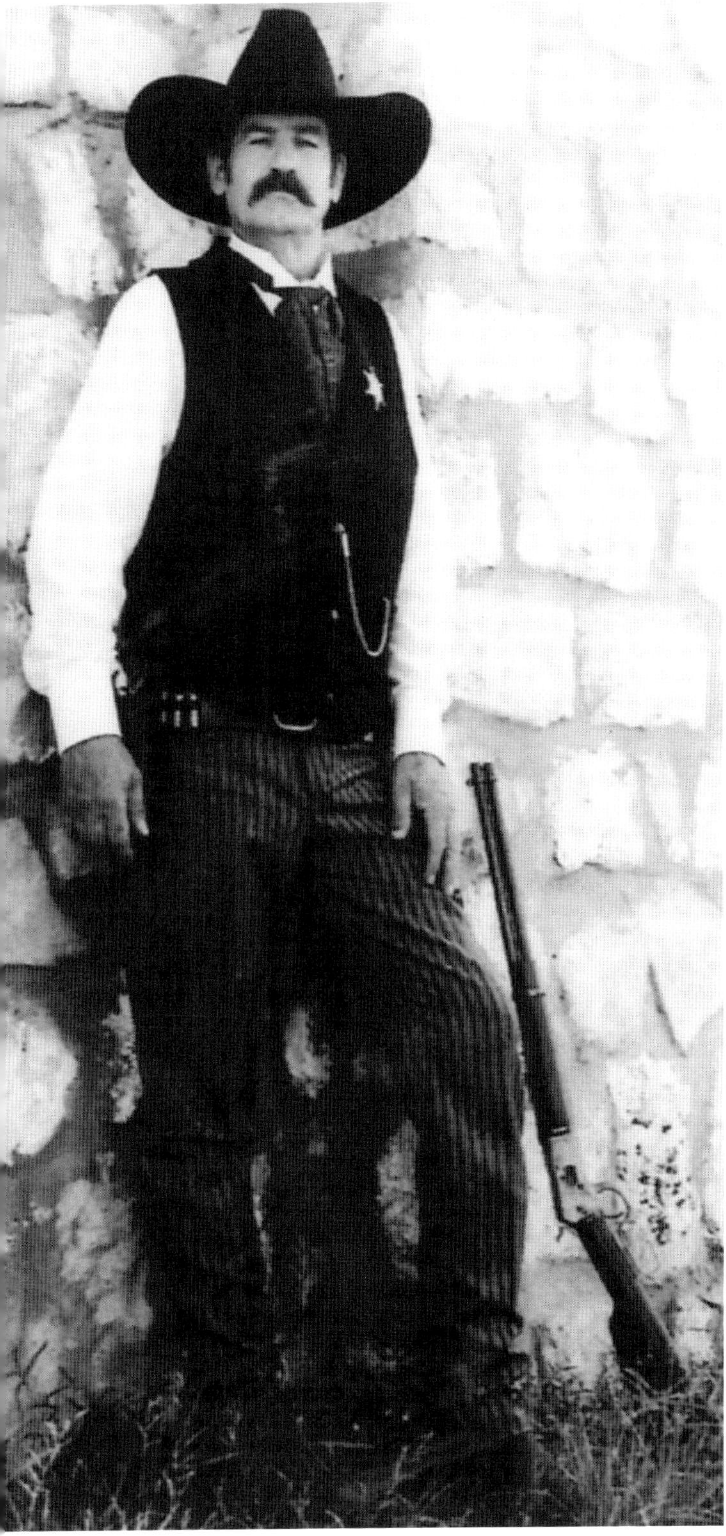

Ron Grimes
To say Ron Grimes has worn many hats would be a gross understatement. Grimes has been a journalism teacher, photographer, newspaper columnist, city editor, musician, historical writer, and Chautauqua presenter. He is well known throughout New Mexico for portraying the famed lawman Patrick Garrett, especially from his performance at *Old Lincoln Days* in Lincoln, New Mexico, and other historical presentations sponsored by the state. Grimes writes and publishes the popular *Pea Vine Express*, a historical newsletter that gives fascinating stories of the past garnered from old newspapers. Grimes is currently working on a book about his father, Wayne, who was a member of the 10th Horse Cavalry, which became the 200th Coast Artillery National Guard unit of Bataan fame. As part of the Flying X Chuck Wagon Band, Ron played the bass, sang, and cracked jokes for the audience. (Courtesy of Valerie Cranston.)

Jim O'Hearn

Jim O'Hearn could be heard as the voice of Carlsbad on radio station KBAD and television station KATK. He worked for US Potash until 1967; then, he lived out his dream as a news reporter. In 1974, O'Hearn joined the *Carlsbad Current Argus* to become an award-winning columnist and reporter. He was also a manager for a Shorthorn Little League team from 1953 to 1967.

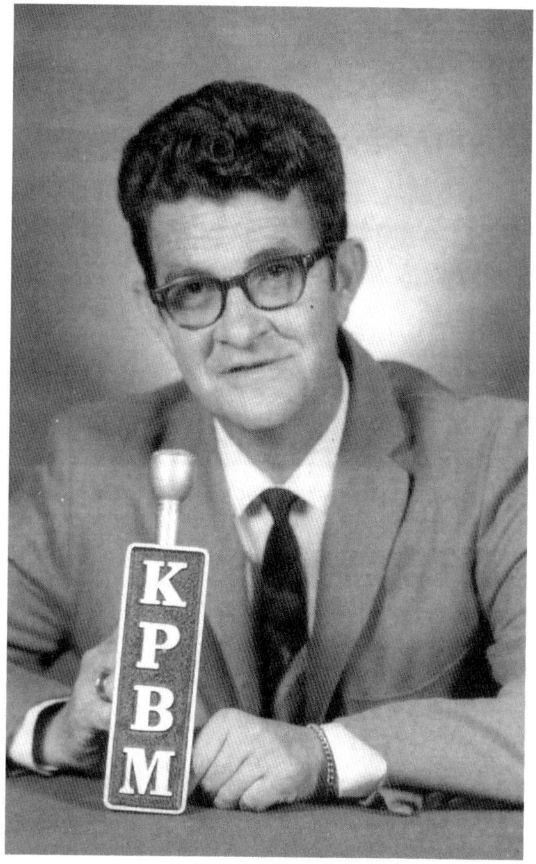

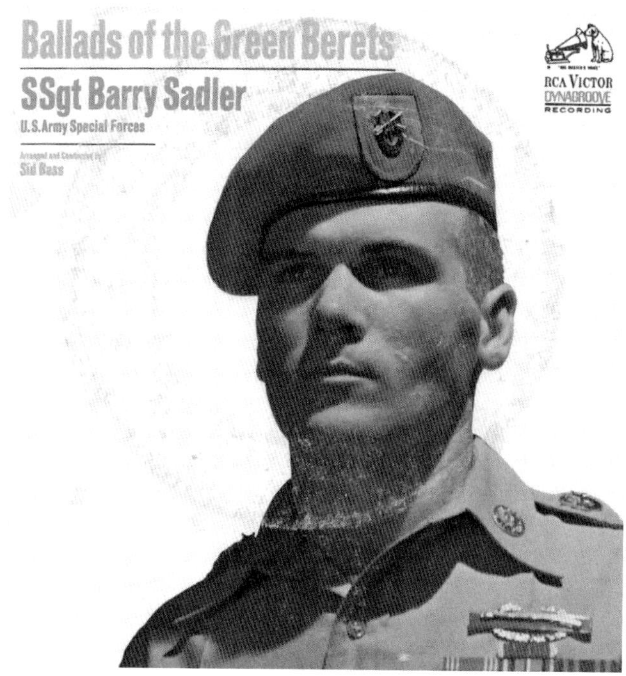

Barry Sadler

The Green Berets aired during the Vietnam War, in which Carlsbad native, S.Sgt. Barry Sadler released his song, "The Ballad of the Green Berets." Sadler wrote the ballad as a tribute to Green Beret James Gabriel Jr., the first Hawaiian native to be killed in Vietnam. Sadler, who sang the ballad on the *Ed Sullivan Show* in 1966, was also an adventure series author. (Author's collection.)

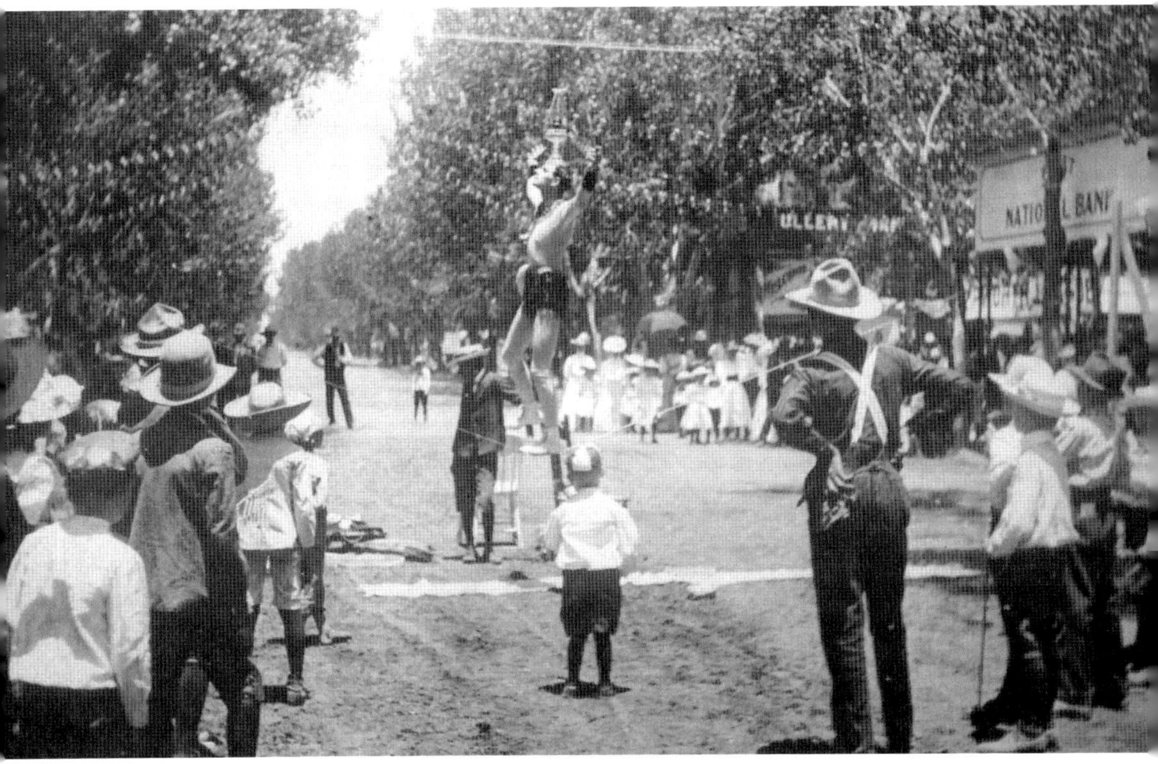

George Frederick
Dressed in head-to-toe leotards with an oil lamp on his forehead, trapeze artist George Frederick caused gasps throughout the crowd in 1907 as he performed his soft-wire act on a rope strung across Canyon Street.

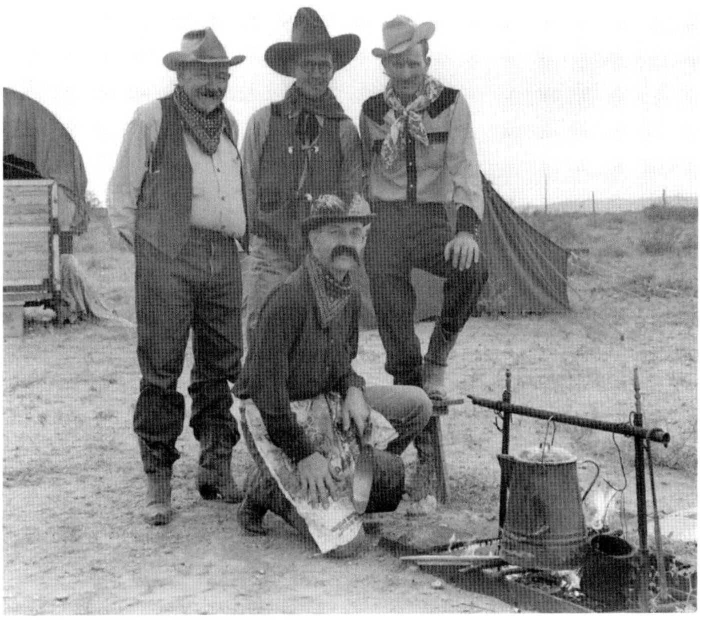

Cavern City Four
A barbershop quartet who performed at civic and community events was formed by local businessmen and notables in 1949. The original members are shown in costume around a campfire. From back left to right, they are Bill Burnett, Harold Thornberry, and Leon Small, with John E. Cutter in front. The quartet would see many member changes over the years but continued success around the region.

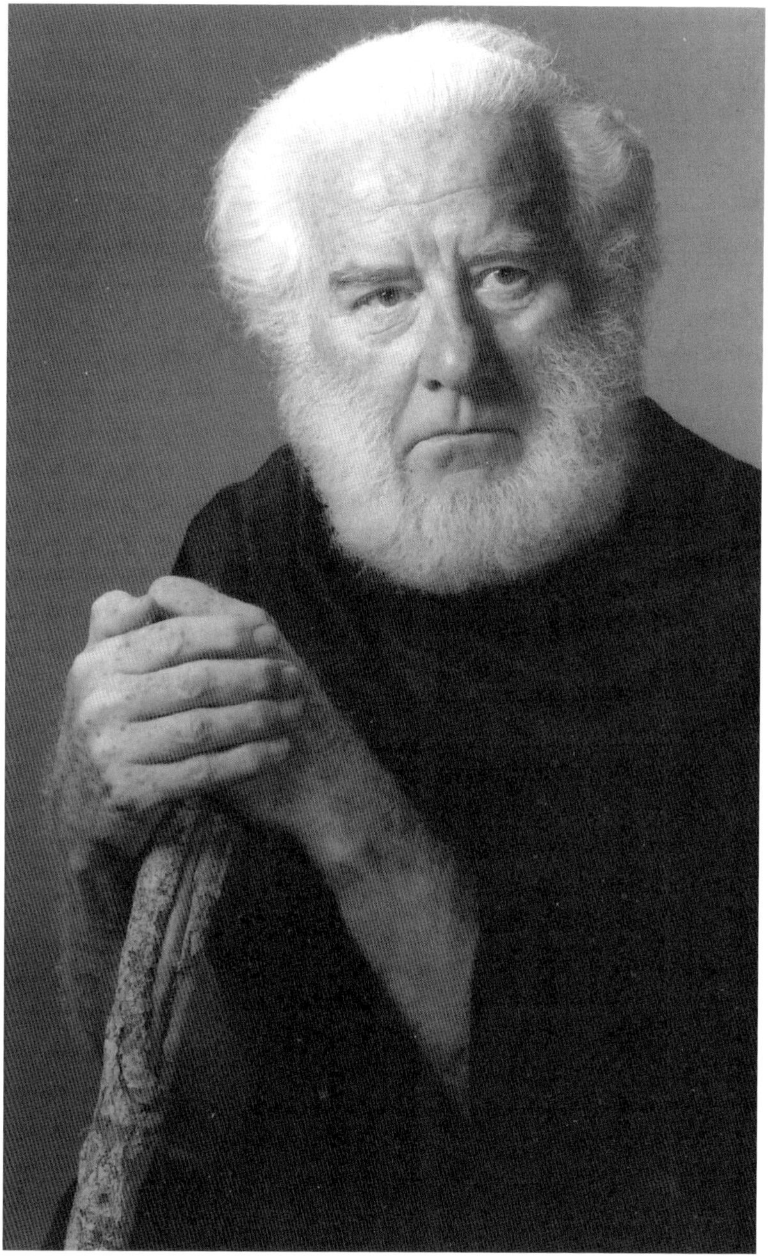

Al Pitcaithley

A man of many talents, Pvt. Al Pitcaithley was known as an avid model railroader, actor, and circus contortionist. He was the manager for the USO at the Carlsbad Army Airfield, the cashier for the theater, and program director at local television station KAVE, where he would produce and star in his *Man on the Street* program. His antics were immortalized in *Billboard* magazine several times. Pitcaithley's father, William, was connected with the Tripoli Music Hall, so his talent came naturally. Pitcaithley starred in many community theater productions with his wife, Lynne. The Pitcaithleys were known around Carlsbad as true characters and dispensers of great sage advice to aspiring actors and community leaders.

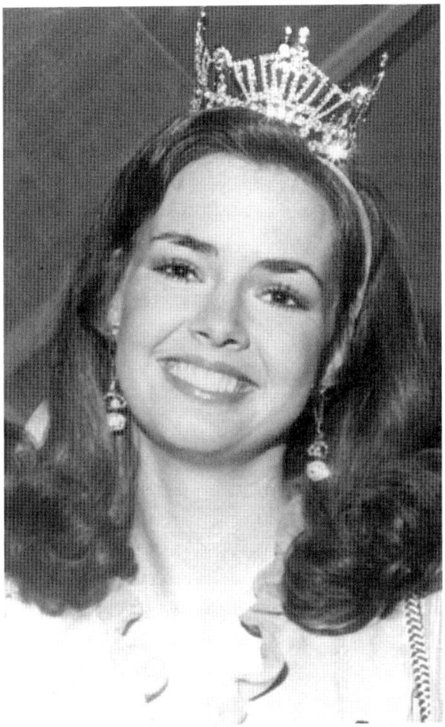

Miss New Mexico

Carlsbad has been home to six Miss New Mexicos. The earliest winner, Shirley Hughes in 1949, created a charcoal and chalk drawing titled *Cruising down the River* for her talent. Carolyn Adams Moore drew a caricature of a pageant celebrity in 1960, and Sandi Moore sang, "My Lover Has Gone" in 1963. Rosemary Brown, who competed as Miss Portales although she was from Carlsbad, sang "This is my Song" in 1967. Brown toured with the USO Troupe during the Vietnam War. Already mentioned as a sculptress, Wren Prather-Stroud won in 1972 after her unique performance of an upside-down tap dance to "Yankee Doodle Dandy." The most recent winner, Cyndi Ann Friesen, performed "Carnival" as her talent in 1982. Carlsbad is known for beautiful women, and this group certainly proves that point.

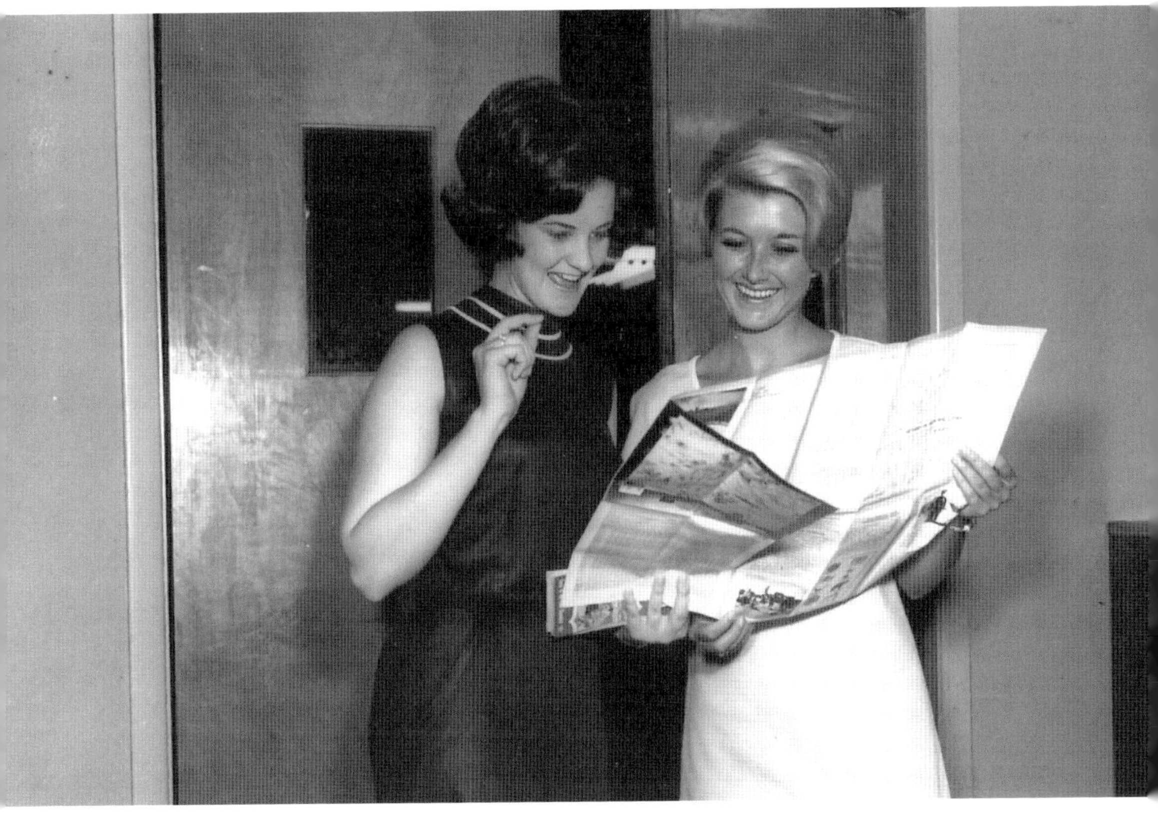

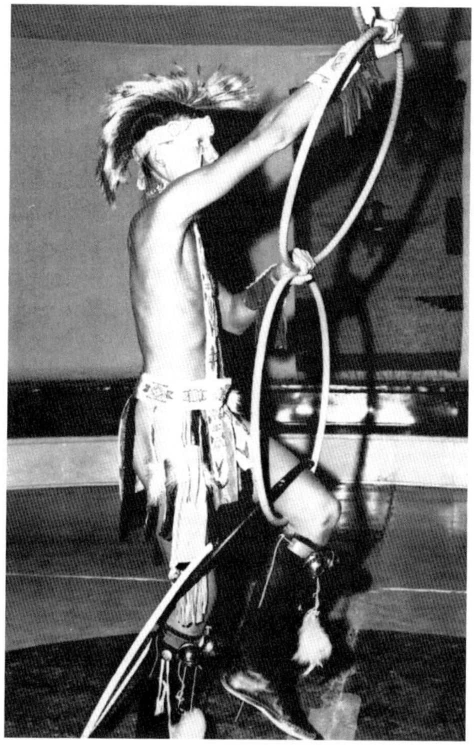

Thunderbird Indian Dancers
Always a highly anticipated act of local parades, the Thunderbird Indian Dancers (teen members of area Explorer Scouts), adorned only in breechcloths, feathered headdresses, and moccasins, would perform complex, traditional native dances. It was considered a great honor to be chosen as a Thunderbird, although the organization was originally started to help troubled boys. Chief Sunny Skies Hunt worked closely with the group to perpetuate authenticity.

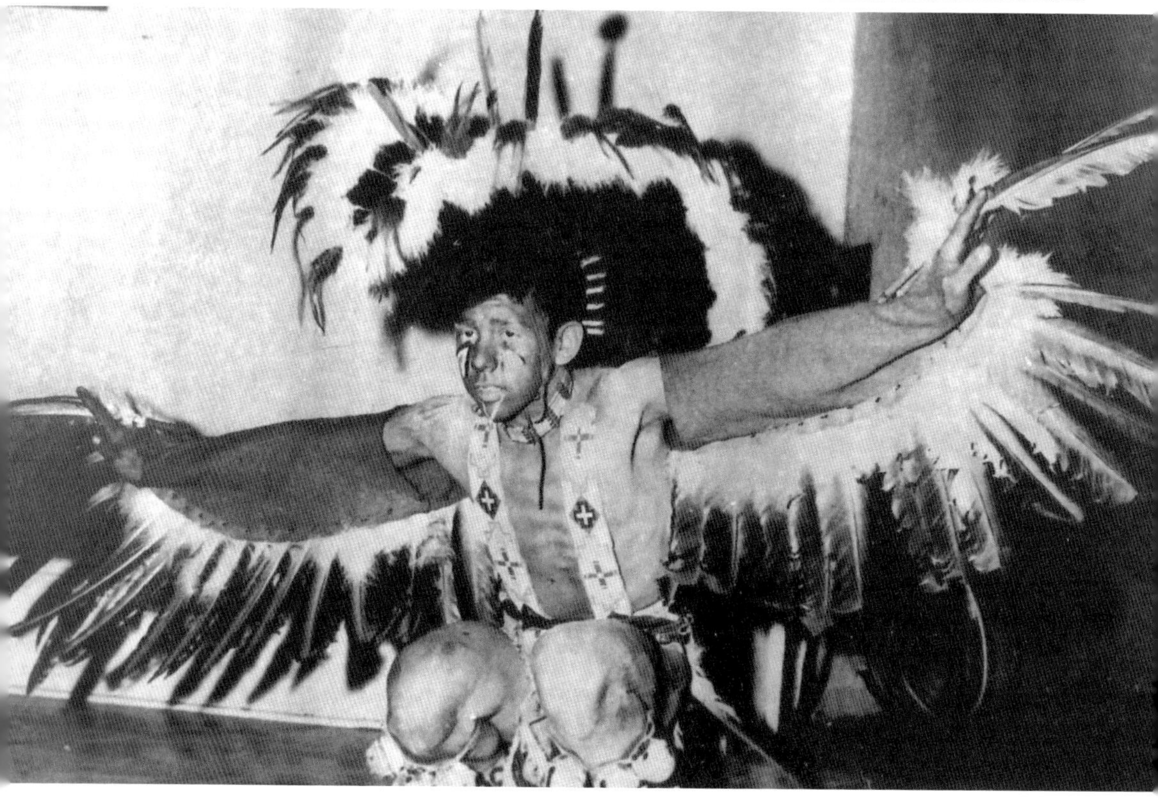

CHAPTER FOUR

Business Sense

Carlsbad was built on the largest promotional scheme known in its early days. Blessed with many silver-tongued promoters, the town saw the quick rise of many successful businesses in short order. Those savvy businessmen knew a good thing when they saw it; Carlsbad was ripe for the acceleration of commerce. Opportunity was everywhere, and all they had to do was capitalize on the idea.

The Carlsbad Spring was touted to have the same healing elements found in the mineral spas of Europe, so enterprisers decided to sell vials for $1 in 1899. It is not known how many were sold, but the spring was not as big of a draw as originally hoped.

However, the town saw progress in the building of the Schlitz Hotel, a three-story structure which stood out against the bare horizon. Once the Joyce-Pruit grocery store opened its doors, the demand for products grew quickly, and it expanded into the neighboring communities of Artesia and Roswell. Unfortunately, the building burned in 1904, putting an end to the business in Carlsbad. Yet, it was rebuilt and now houses the Candlewood Gift Shop, a retail store of Elaine Mead Murphy, the daughter of renowned artist Roderick Mead.

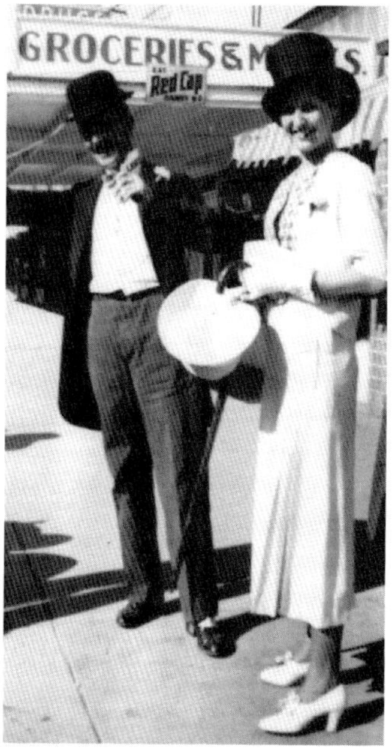

John R. Joyce

John R. Joyce, the first banker in Carlsbad, was quoted in 1912 as a witness to the *Titanic* tragedy as a passenger of the *Carpathia*. Joyce was full of life and tried to start traditions in Carlsbad that he had become accustomed to in New York City, such as the Easter Bonnet Parade. Joyce was co-owner of the largest grocery store in Eddy County, the Joyce-Pruit Store.

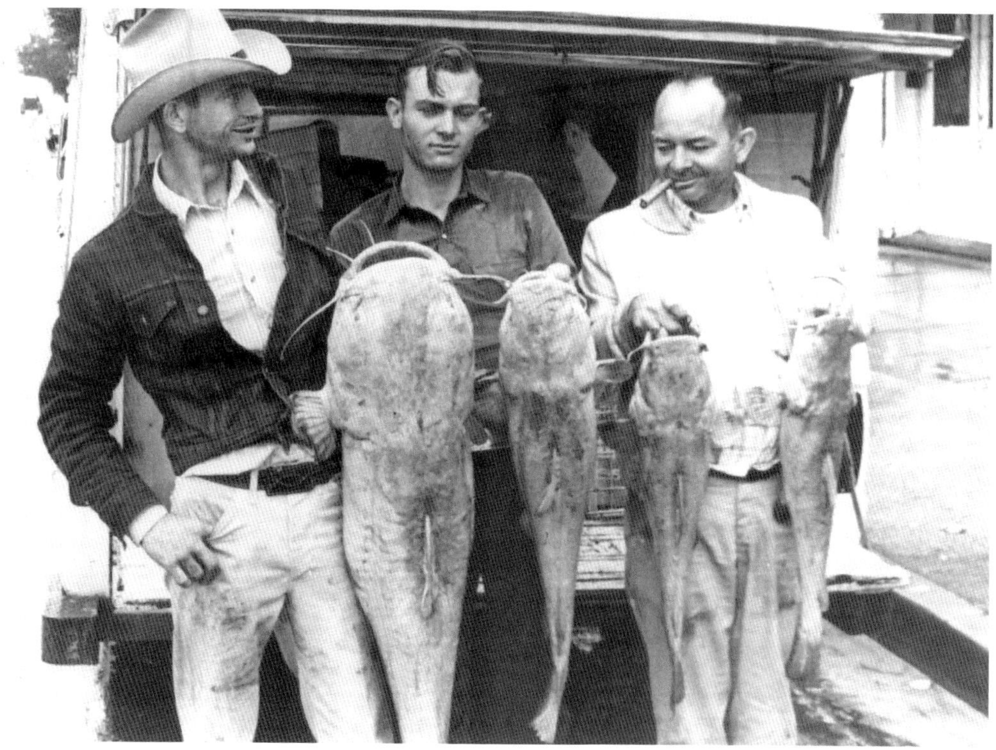

Charlie Beaver

Restaurant owner Charlie Beaver (shown on right) was also an accomplished singer, performing on the scared circle at the Grand Ole Opry. The Beaver family arrived at Carlsbad in 1947 to open and operate five restaurants; the latest was Beaver's Restaurant, opened in 1970 and closed in 2010. An avid fisherman, Beaver could be found with a pole in the water, catching some monster catfish.

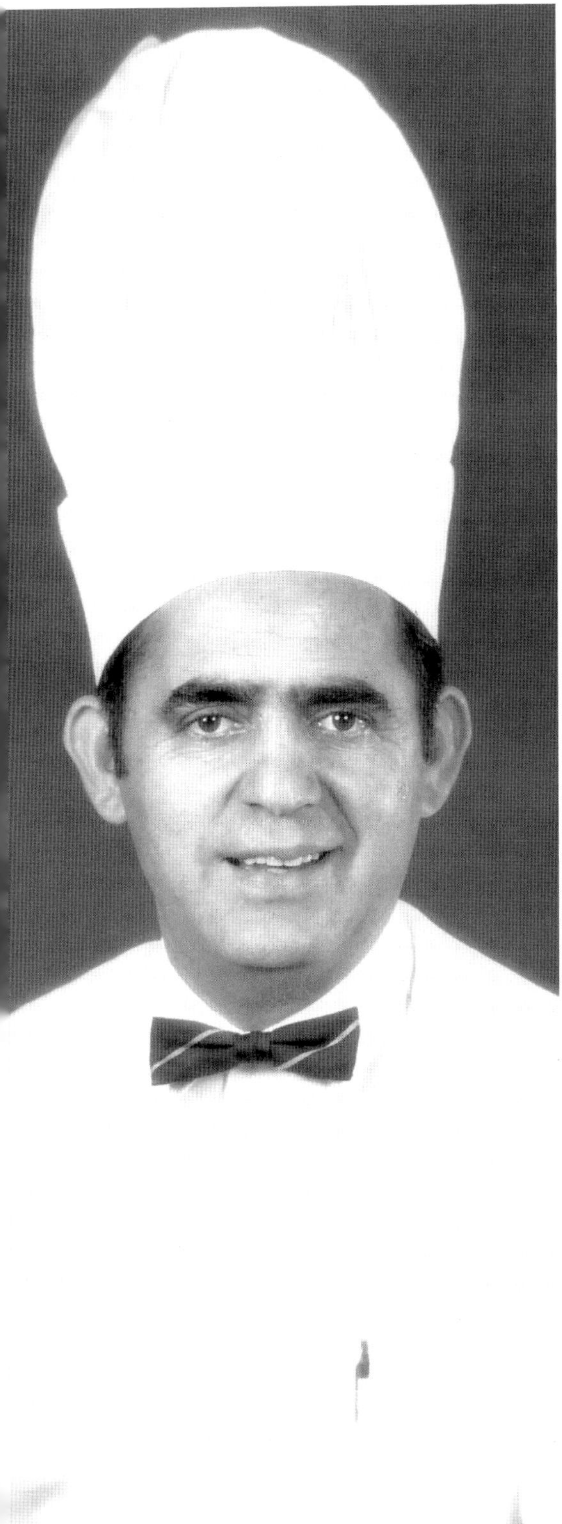

Pete Panagopoulos

Pete "the Chef" Panagopoulos's Deluxe Café was a fixture at the crossroads of Highway 285 and 62–180. Open 24 hours, the café was a favorite hangout after a night at the local bars. Panagopoulos never knew a stranger and helped those down on their luck by providing a hot meal and some sage advice. For 20 years, on Christmas Day, the café was opened for free turkey dinners, first for the laid-off potash miners and then for anyone who wanted a meal. In its heyday, upwards of 1,000 meals were served on Christmas. A philanthropist, Pete was a founding member of the International Goodwill Council, chairman of the Salvation Army, and member of the Carlsbad Chamber of Commerce and American Hellenic Educational and Progressive Association. Born in Greece, Panagopoulos came to the United States as a political refugee in 1951.

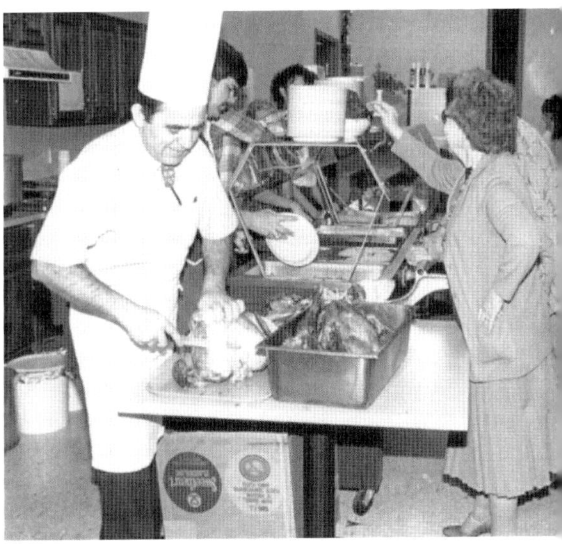

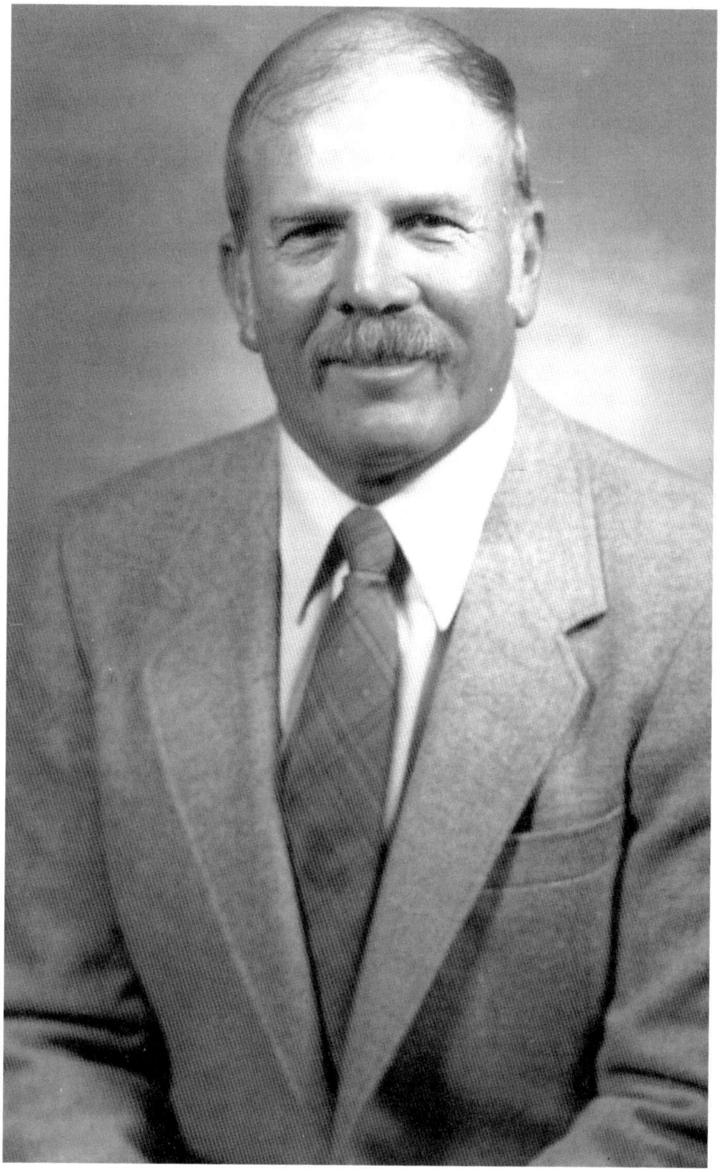

Bob Forrest

The Forrest family has long been involved in many aspects of Carlsbad, as business owners, sports leaders, political figures, and highly active community servicemen. Forrest Tire Company is a fixture along South Canal Street, providing tire services to not only Carlsbad but Hobbs, Roswell, and Artesia, New Mexico, as well as Lubbock and El Paso, Texas. Bob Forrest was instrumental in opening a caring and safe center for citizens with mental and physical disabilities, which has grown from a few housing units to two ranches with greenhouses, a recycling center, and thrift and retail shops. There has also been an integration of the citizens as a workforce for many businesses around town. Bob and his twin brother, Dick, left promising football careers to take on the family business. Bob would go on to become mayor of Carlsbad for 16 years and advocate for the Waste Isolation Pilot Plant, which was built east of Carlsbad. This resulted in an interview with *Forbes* magazine. Bob is still highly active within the community.

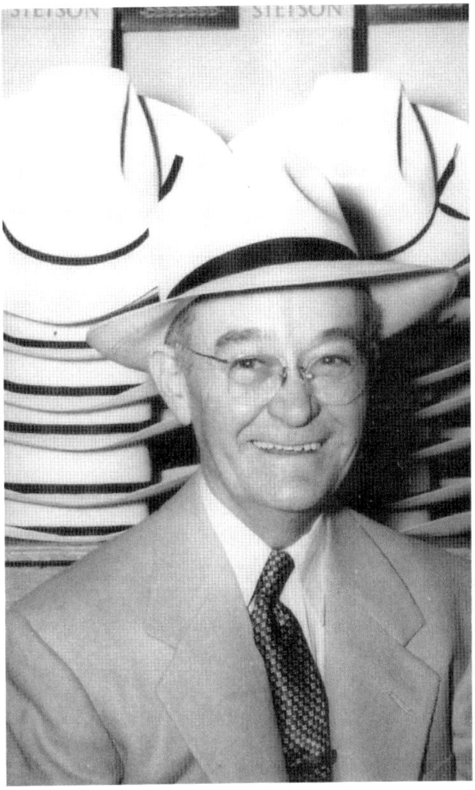

Collin Gerrells
Born in Indian Gap, Texas, in 1892, Collin Gerrells eventually moved to Carlsbad and worked for the Joyce-Pruit Company and then as a clerk for the Santa Fe Railway. Gerrells and his wife, Eula, opened Collin Gerrells Men's Store, which was a staple shop for the men of Carlsbad until his death in 1962. The store was then owned by his son, Walter, who was a longtime mayor.

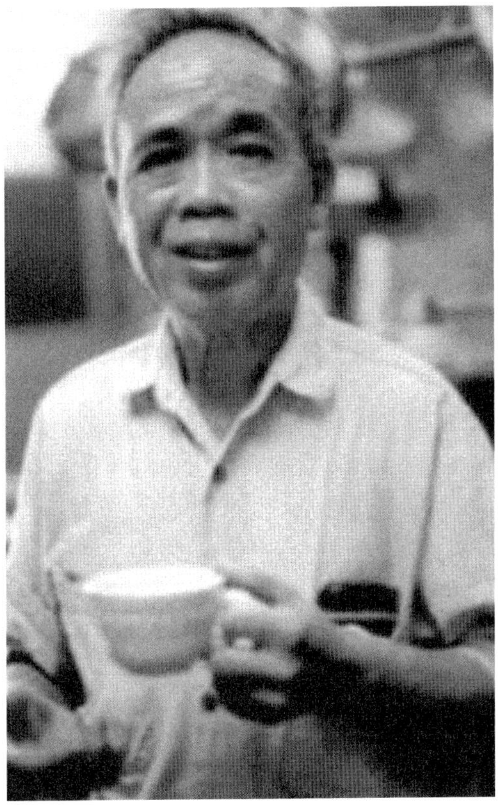

Ping Wong
Anyone who was a fan of almond chicken knew to go to Ping Wong's China Lantern. Funded by his mother, Wong and his older brother came to America at ages 14 and 16, respectively. Wong and his wife, Eva, operated the restaurant for 44 years before retiring. The China Lantern is still open and serves Chinese, Mexican, and American foods.

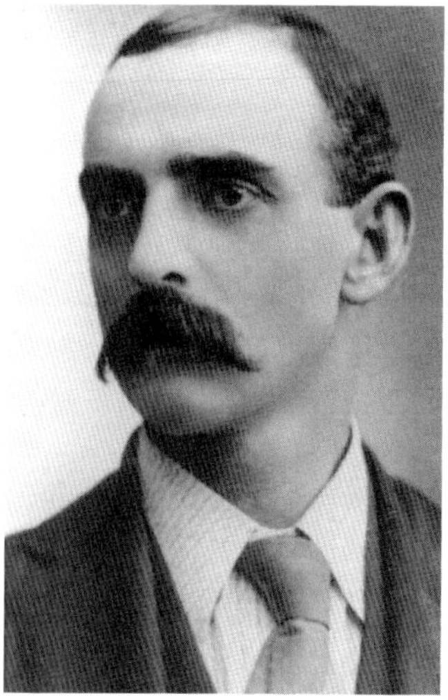

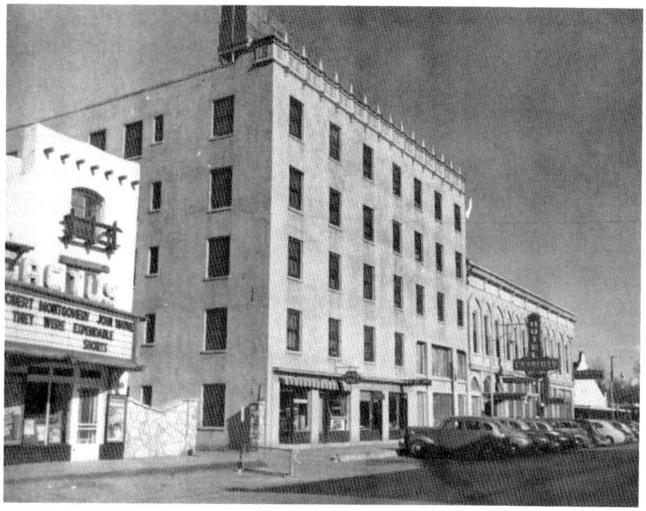

Abel Justus "A.J." Crawford

Labeled shrewd by his biographers, Crawford started life as a sheepherder who barely had enough to eat. He would turn this into a rags-to-riches story by becoming a self-made millionaire who owned luxurious hotels. He did this by becoming a representative for the area woolgrowers and negotiating large deals with out-of-state buyers. With these profits, Crawford quickly built his empire. Although he became rather miserly in his ways, he was very generous with several large endowments, one to the Carlsbad Foundation and another to the Carlsbad Memorial Hospital. The latter was eventually sold and the profit of $500,000 was returned to the fund. Each year, the Carlsbad Foundation presents the A.J. Crawford Humanitarian Award to a deserving citizen for his or her work in the community.

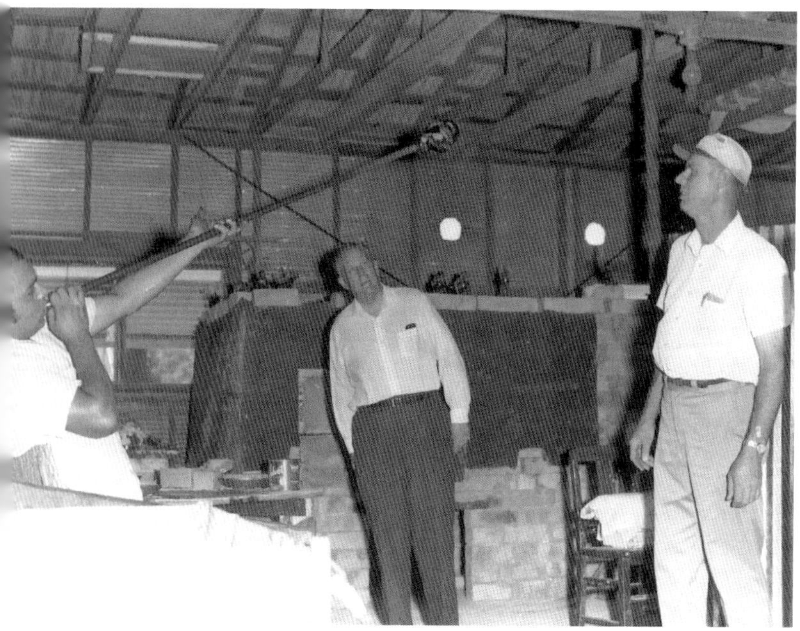

Enchanted Glass Factory

The quick work of the talented glassblower of the Enchanted Glass Factory was magical. The factory was owned by Jasper Evans (shown on right) and located in a converted garage. Delicate glass swan bowls, intricate baskets, tall vases, and small bird paperweights were produced. Glowing red ovens and orbs of glass starkly contrasted the beautiful swirled glass objets d'art that resulted. Some items are still for sale online.

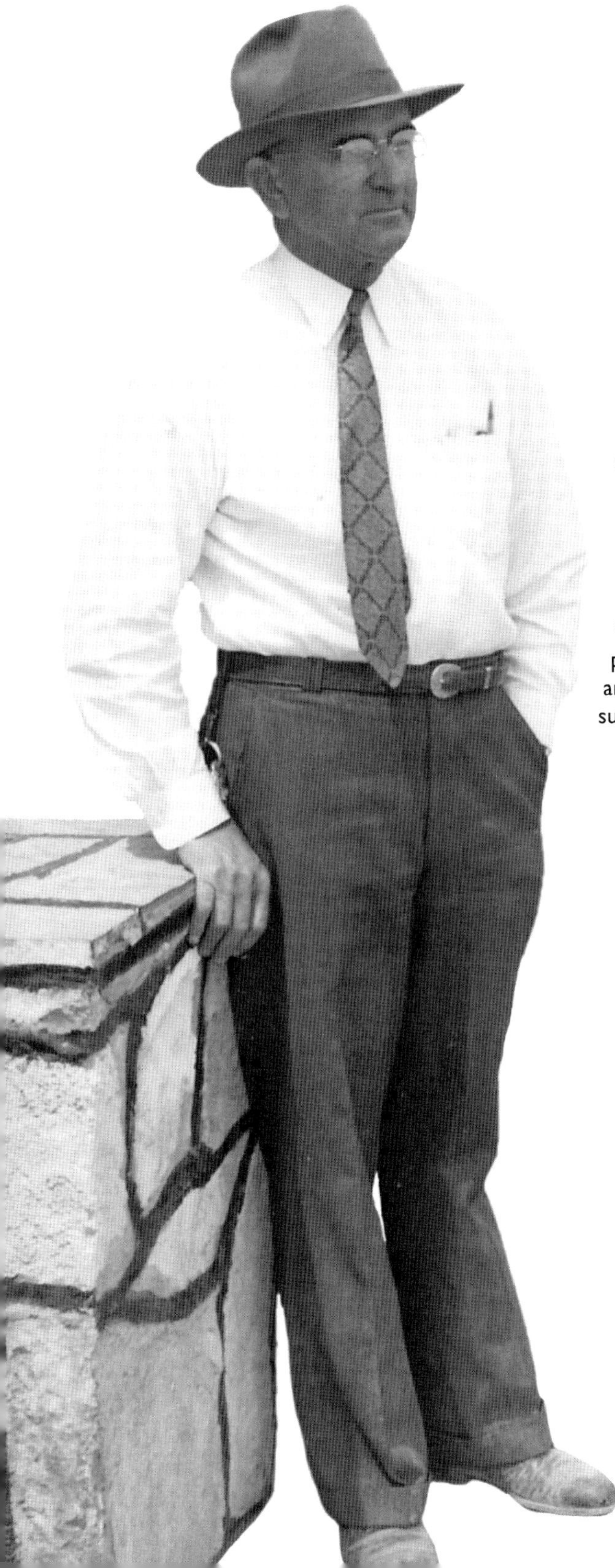

Charlie White

Arriving by train with fewer than $3, Charlie White came west for his health. Enduring two kitchen table family operations, White was glad to leave Kentucky. En route to the Carlsbad Caverns, he noticed the land where White's City now sits and filed a claim on the property. The Whites moved there in 1927, and were testimony to the healing powers of sun and fresh air.

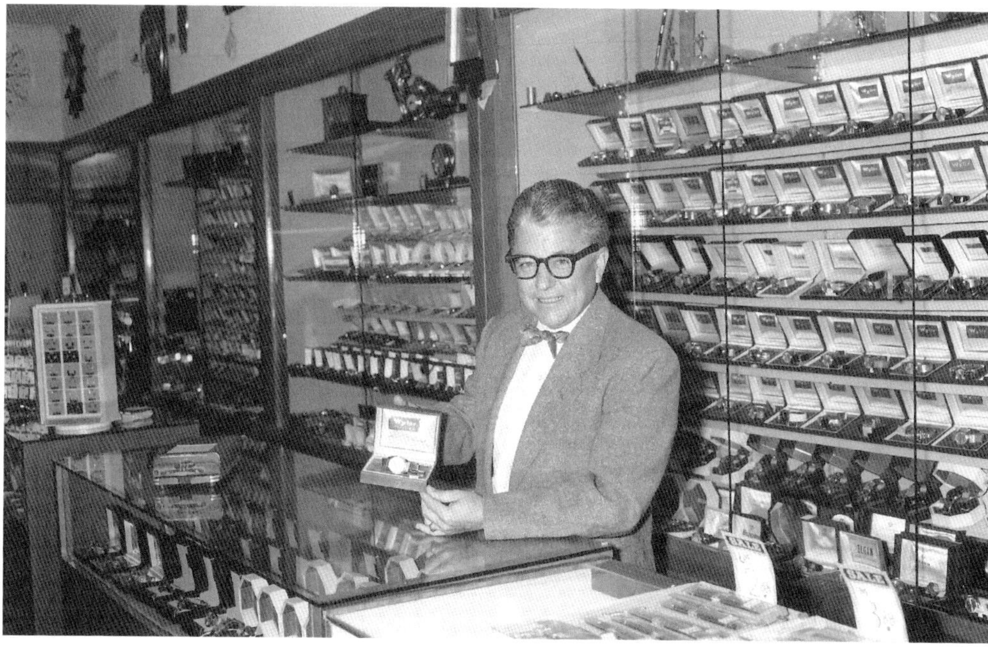

William Adair Gossett
As businessman, mayor, and civil defense official, Adair Gossett wore many hats. With initial display cases located in a local pharmacy, Gossett quickly grew and opened his own jewelry shop on Fox Street. Still operated by the Gossett family, it is the oldest retail jewelry store in Carlsbad. Gossett was instrumental in convincing state officials of the importance of bringing the Waste Isolation Pilot Plant (WIPP) to the area.

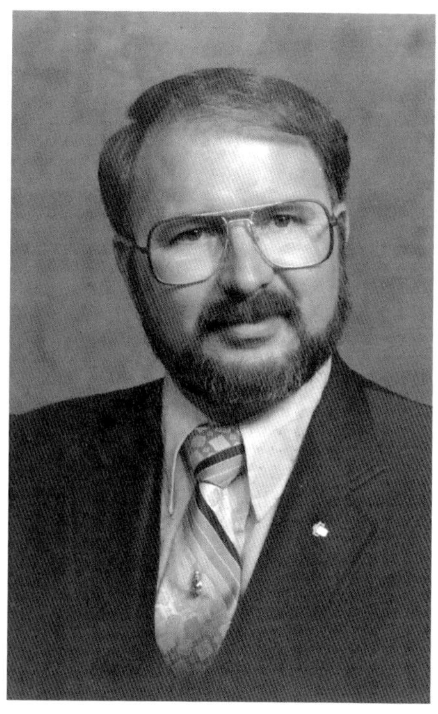

Jack White Jr.
Called "Mr. Carlsbad" by his contemporaries, Jack White Jr. was a consummate businessman, involved in numerous civic activities like serving as a regional ambassador. After graduate school at the University of Denver, he returned to White's City to manage the restaurant while his wife, Beverly, managed the motel. White was passionate about his communities and took every opportunity to talk them up.

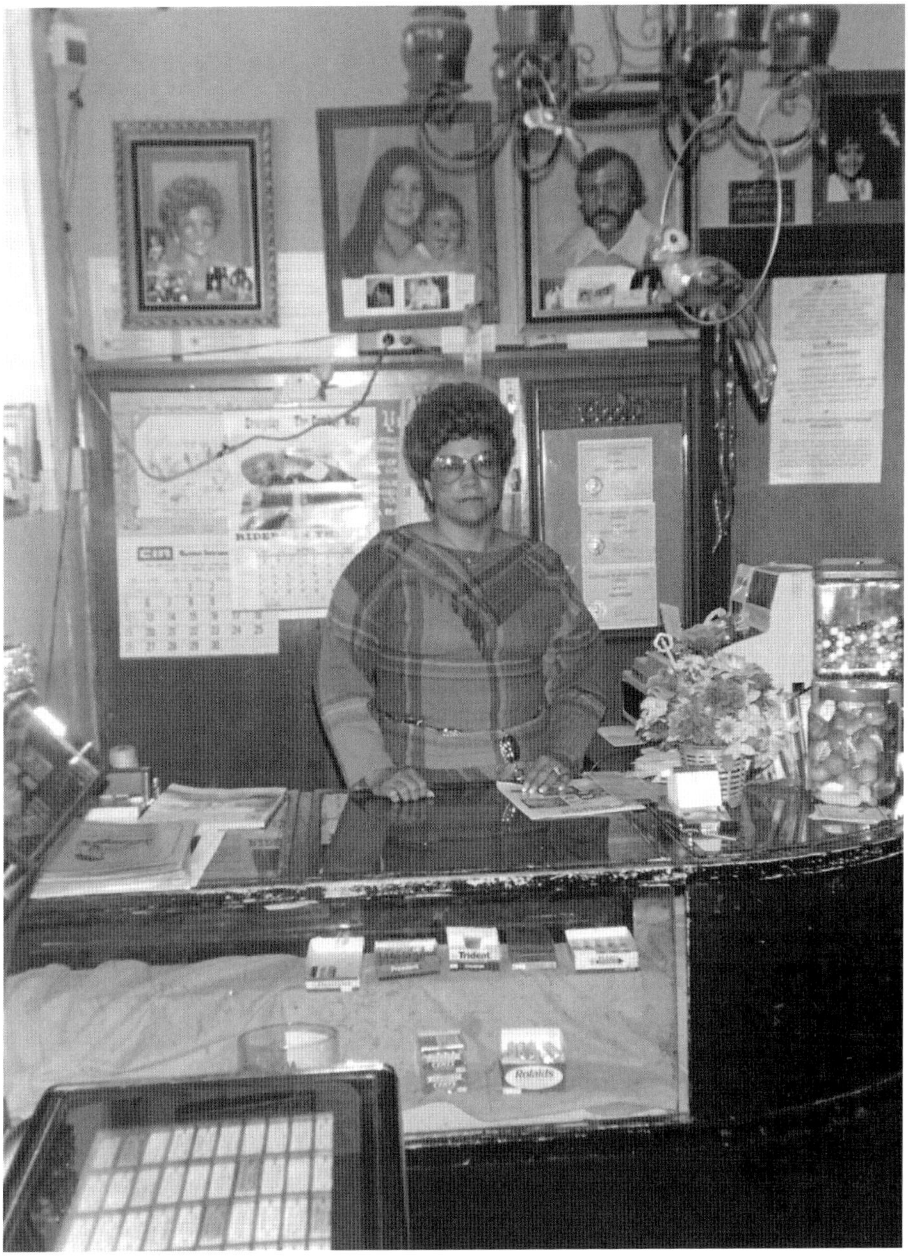

Lucy Yanez
A legend in the local restaurant business, Lucy Yanez has owned Lucy's Mexicali Restaurant since 1977. One of the biggest promoters of the Mexican culture, Yanez is known for her flamboyant dress and demeanor. She has branched out to two other locations in Ruidoso and Hobbs, New Mexico, while boasting to serve the best margaritas around. Yanez has been described by Mayor Dale Janway as "an outstanding citizen of Carlsbad, by making the city a better place in which to live." Yanez is certainly one of the most successful businesswomen in Carlsbad, with two restaurants across from one another. She started selling burritos and tamales as a child at the urging of her brother, Bobby, to help supplement her mother's meager income. The business grew from there—in a big way—and has not stopped since.

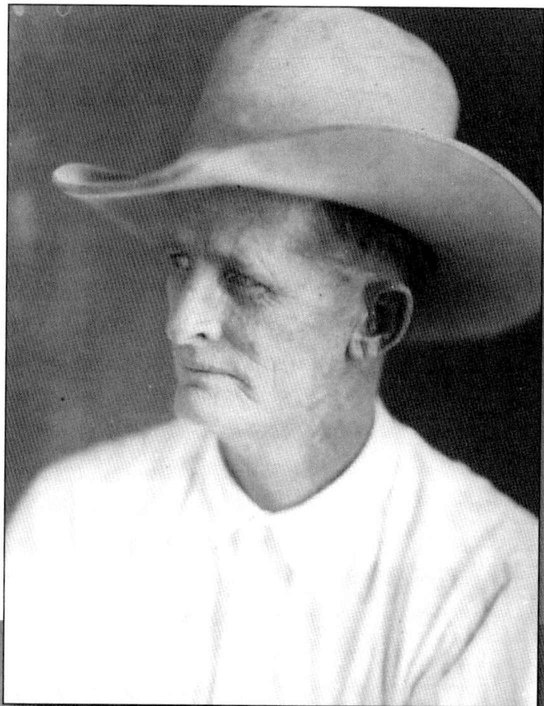

Jim White and the Carlsbad Caverns

Often touted as the discoverer of the Carlsbad Caverns, Jim White was not actually the first to enter the cave, though he was the first to widely explore and promote its rare beauty. Through the photographs of Ray V. Davis, the "Bat Cave" was first brought to light, and from there, White and his wife, Fannie, provided tours to the curious; Jim became the first park ranger. Displayed to the world for the first time in 1923 via stunning images taken by photographer Ray V. Davis between 1913 and 1915, the Carlsbad Caverns became a National Monument in a declaration signed by Pres. Calvin Coolidge. Carlsbad Caverns National Park was established in 1930. The cave formations were created by calcium carbonate deposited by drops of rainwater filtered through limestone over the course of 20 million years.

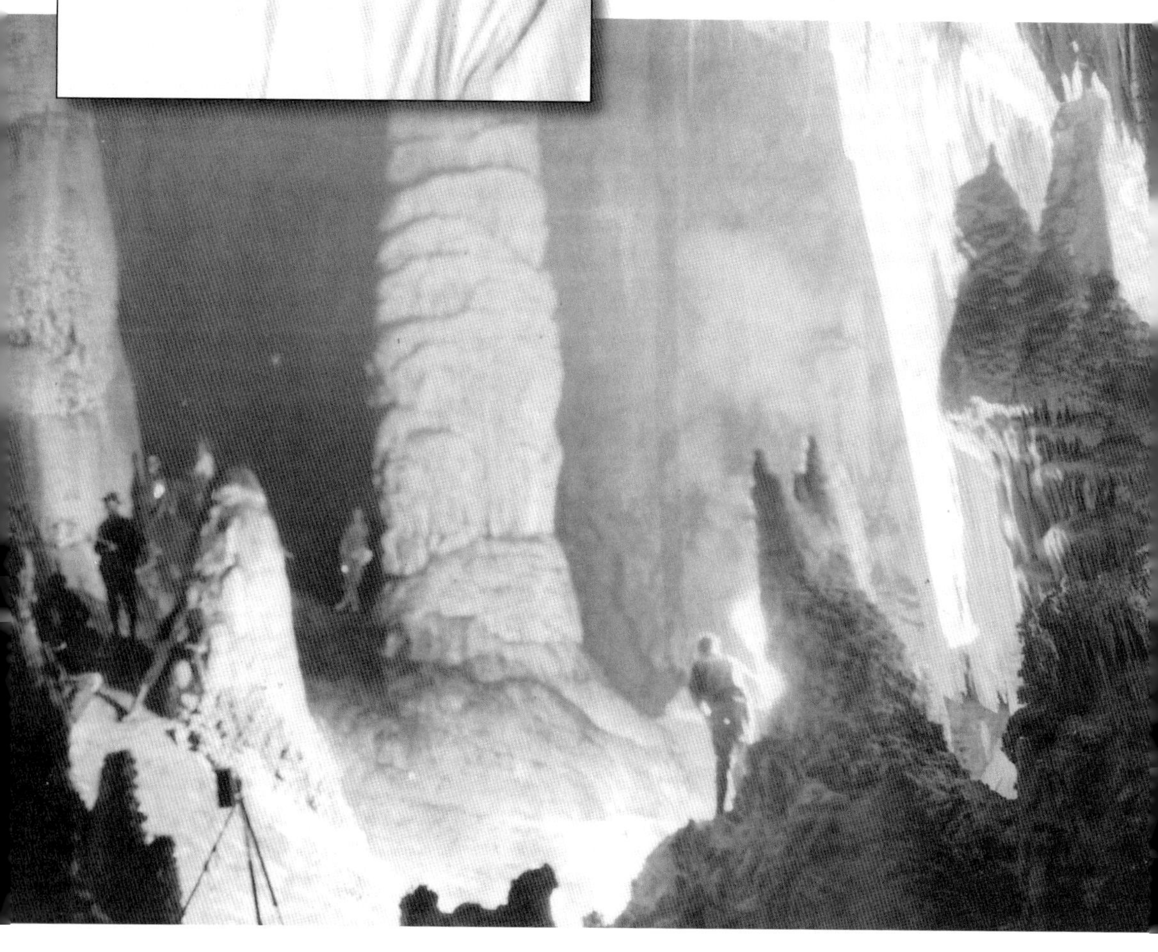

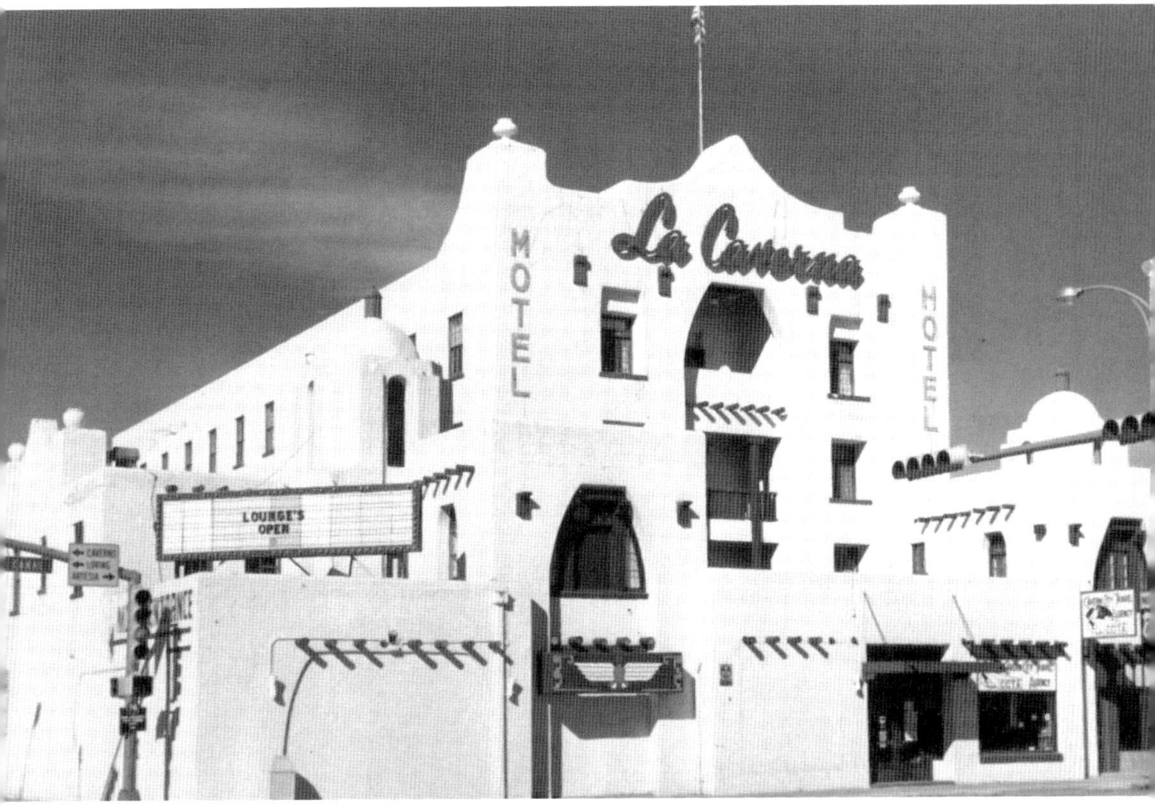

La Caverna Hotel
Although the La Caverna Hotel is a building, citizens of Carlsbad often refer to it as a legend. Built at the crossroads of two highways, the majestic southwestern style hotel once beckoned wary visitors to stay in Carlsbad a little longer (in one of the 125 air-conditioned rooms) and enjoy what the town had to offer. Dignitaries, movie stars, tourists, artists, and politicians all enjoyed the comforts of the large oasis. Owned by Miers and Rose Johnson, the hotel was taken over by their son Johnny, a Korean War veteran, after Miers's health failed. Artist Herndon Davis lended his talents to paint a huge historical map for the lobby in 1928; it is now housed at the Pecos Valley Conference Center. Many were devastated when a wrecking ball brought down the beloved hotel in 1981.

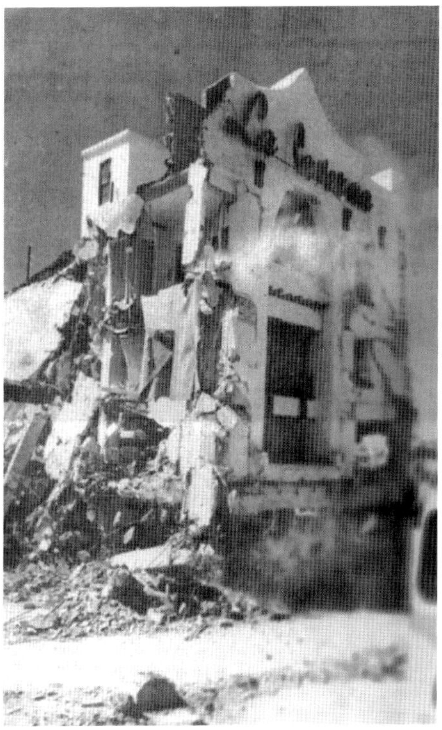

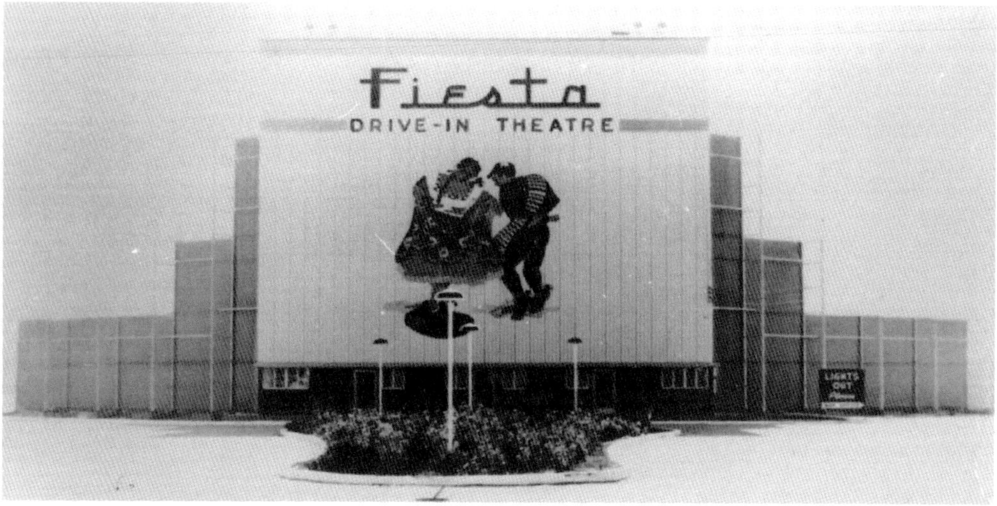

Fiesta Drive-In
One of a few remaining drive-in movie theaters in the country, the Fiesta Drive-In is still showing movies at its original location since 1948. Gone are the speakers you placed on your car window (and hopefully remembered to remove before driving off), replaced by a radio station. Recently remodeled by owners Zach and Sidney Rogers, the Fiesta is one of a dying breed that has recently seen a revival in the United States.

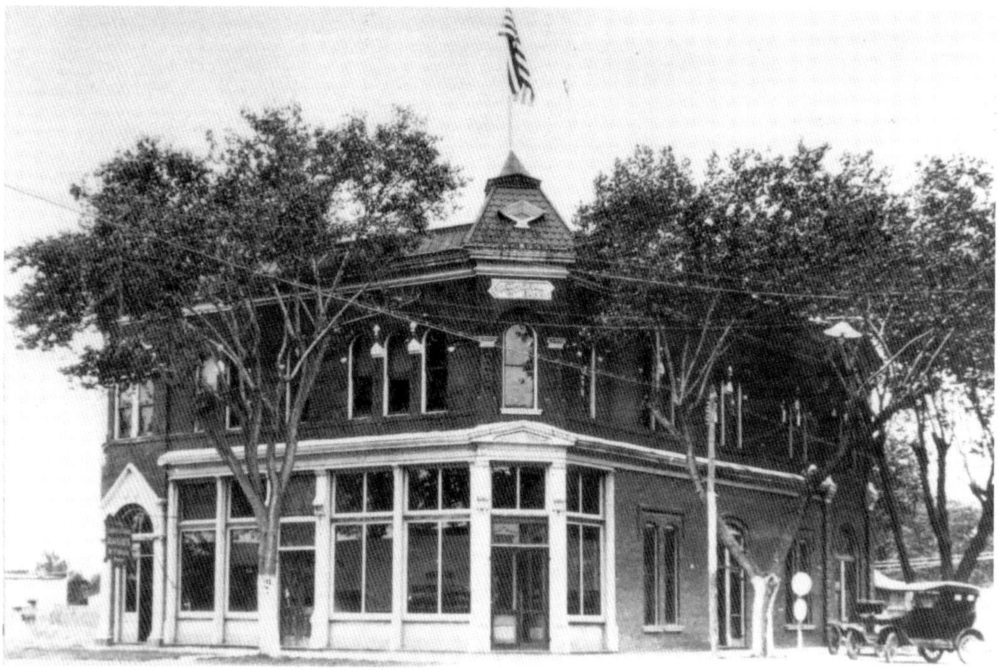

Trinity Hotel
Starting as the First National Bank in 1893, this stately building saw many tenants and changes; it housed a newspaper office, thrift store, and offices for the Carlsbad Irrigation District. Falling into disrepair, wrecking ball rumor flew, but through the efforts of wine-grower Dale Balzano and his three partners, the National Historic Landmark is now a boutique hotel and restaurant.

CHAPTER FIVE

Personalities Galore

Every town has its quirky residents, the ones that give flavor and excitement to an often mundane existence. Carlsbad is no different. The people featured in this chapter are just a drop in the proverbial bucket of big personalities that have resided along the winding Pecos River. Many who unfortunately were not able to be included due to a lack of photographic evidence, have livened up the region with their antics.

One such person was an African American cowboy who cooked for the various cattle outfits around Eddy. What made him special was the fact that he would cook barefooted in a woman's dress while singing. He was so well loved by the community that he was the first African American allowed to be buried in the city cemetery.

Others include the women who worked at Phenix, the tiny hamlet south of Eddy from 1892 to 1895, as bar jerks and ladies of the evening. Goldie Elliott would get into brawls with the other girls, and ended up with a beer bottle broken over her head. The bout went to trial, packing the small courthouse with residents who wanted to hear the juicy details.

Carlsbad has its fair share of colorful characters who add zest to life in the desert, and they are just a few of the people who have helped develop the city into a well-rounded environment.

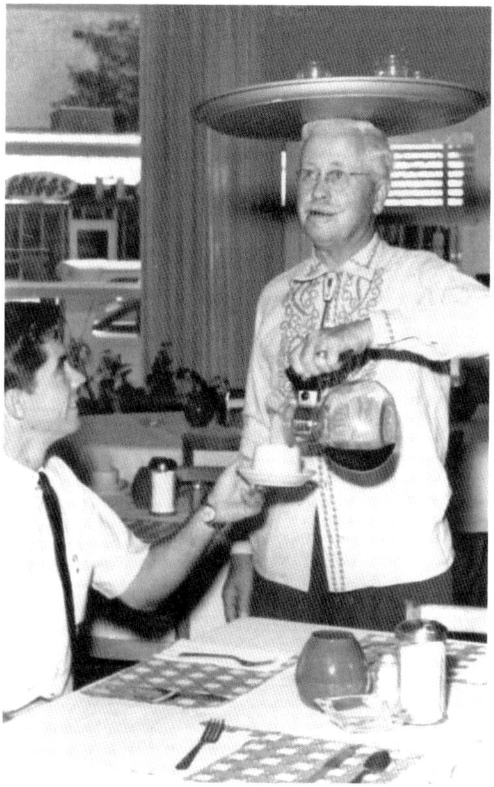

Frank Kindel

Known as the "Paperboy of the Guadalupes" and "Mr. Welcome," Frank Kindel delivered newspapers through a special-made chute in his airplane to ranches in the Guadalupe Mountains. Kindel was always forefront at any event in town, riding his big-wheel bicycle or unicycle. A daredevil and memorable for his red hair and freckles, Kindel defied death with stunts but met his demise in a fiery plane crash when something went terribly wrong with his *Piper Cruiser.* Carlsbad erected a memorial to Kindel at the crash site near Queen, New Mexico, and adorned it with his airplane propeller:

In Memoriam Frank A. Kindel
The Flying Paper Boy of the Guadalupes
October 30, 1892–May 31, 1964

> *Whatever propelled Frank A. Kindel through life left an undiminishing wake. Whether riding his unicycle in a parade, greeting and entertaining visitors to his community, or dropping newspapers from his Piper Cruiser to ranchers and hunters in these Guadalupe Mountains, he lived a life of service dedicated to his family, his community and his fellow man. On his last day in life, he flew the Rev. Willis E. Plapp to this site to conduct sunrise services for members of the Pecos Valley Trail Ride. The services were the last for Frank. He flew across the great divide into eternity when his plane crashed near this spot in the Lincoln National Forest.*

There is not enough space to tell all Frank Kindel has accomplished. Historian Jed Howard said, "We were all in shock when he was killed. It seems like that was the most appropriate way for him to die instead of quietly in a hospital. Kindel was a beloved Carlsbad resident and those who knew him could never forget him." His funeral service was broadcast over the radio, since no church was large enough to hold all of the mourners.

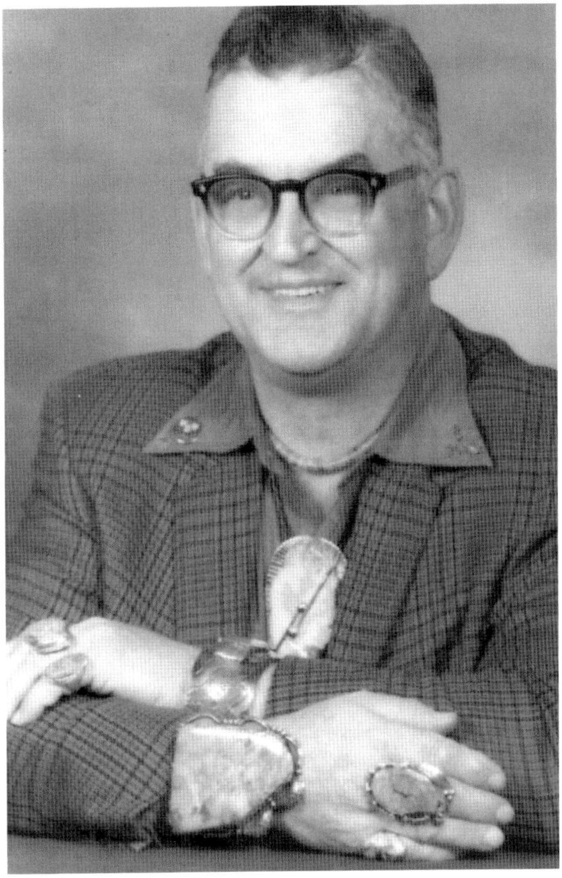

William "Bill" Balgemann
Known as the "Turquoise Kid" because of his love for wearing massive amounts of silver and turquoise jewelry, William "Bill" Balgemann wore many hats as an amateur archaeologist, paleontologist, naturalist, mentor, author, potash miner, curator of the Living Desert Zoo & Gardens, and historian. Without his detailed records, maps, and oral histories, most of the history of Carlsbad would have been lost to the winds. Carlsbad owes much to this humble man with a big heart. Balgemann's office bookshelfs at the Living Desert were filled with jars of "pickled" specimens of small animals, which he used as teaching tools for local youth groups who were lucky enough to get tours.

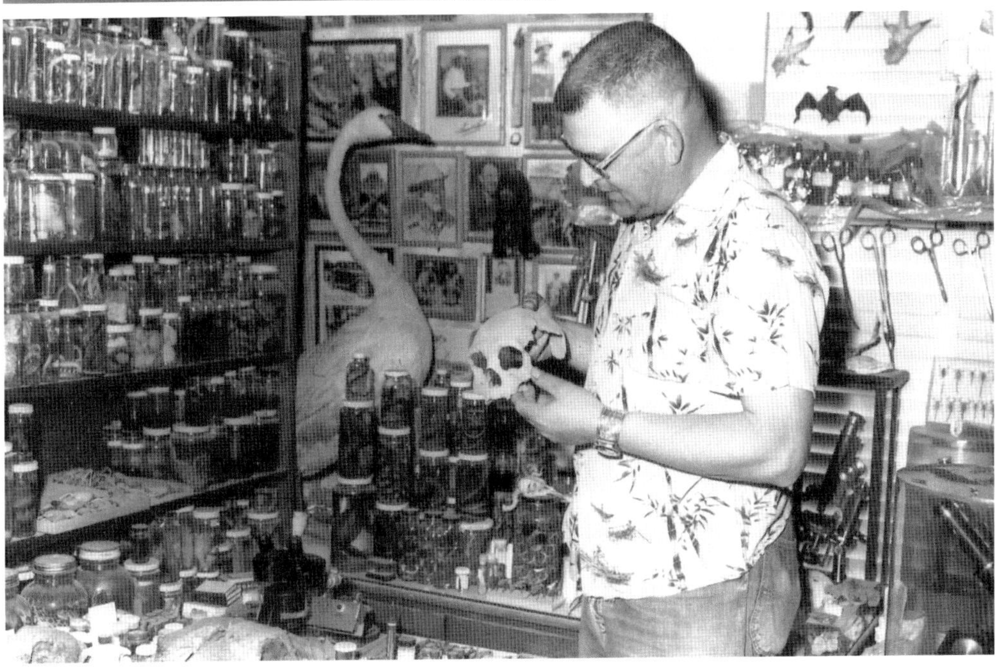

Michael Rosenberg

Carlsbad native Michael Rosenberg has lived a remarkable life. Rosenberg joined the Ringling Bros. circus as a promoter, served in the Vietnam War, and worked for New Mexico congressman Thomas G. Morris and New Jersey senator Harrison Williams. Through his skills as a promoter, Rosenberg represented celebrity clients like Hugh Hefner, recording artists Ashford and Simpson, Aretha Franklin, and Stevie Wonder, and ice skaters Dorothy Hamill and Tonya Harding.

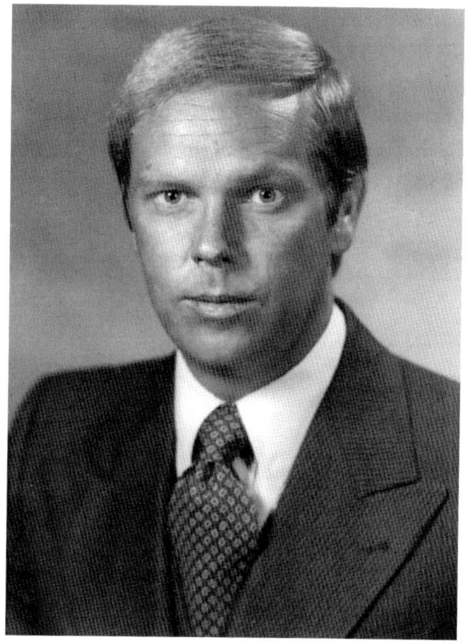

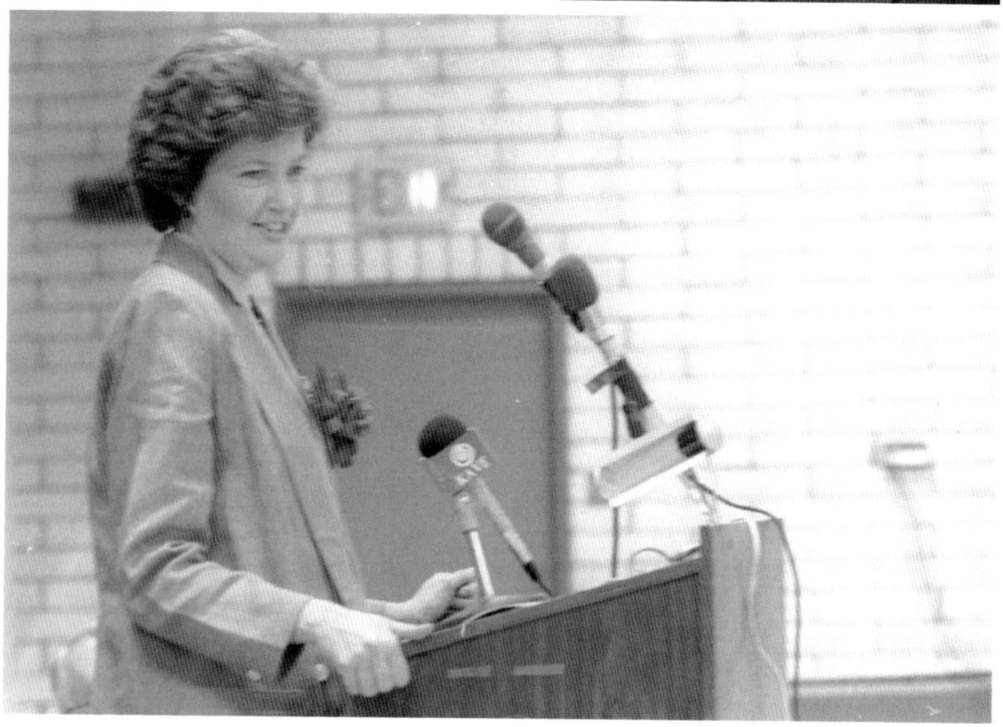

Linda Wertheimer

NPR's senior national correspondent, Linda Wertheimer, grew up in Carlsbad. Nnamed one of the top 50 journalists in Washington, DC, she received the honor of being named one of America's 200 most influential women in 1998. A Wellesley College graduate, Wertheimer received its highest honor in 1985, the Distinguished Alumna Achievement Award. Wertheimer also holds honorary degrees from Colby College, Wheaton College, and Illinois Wesleyan University.

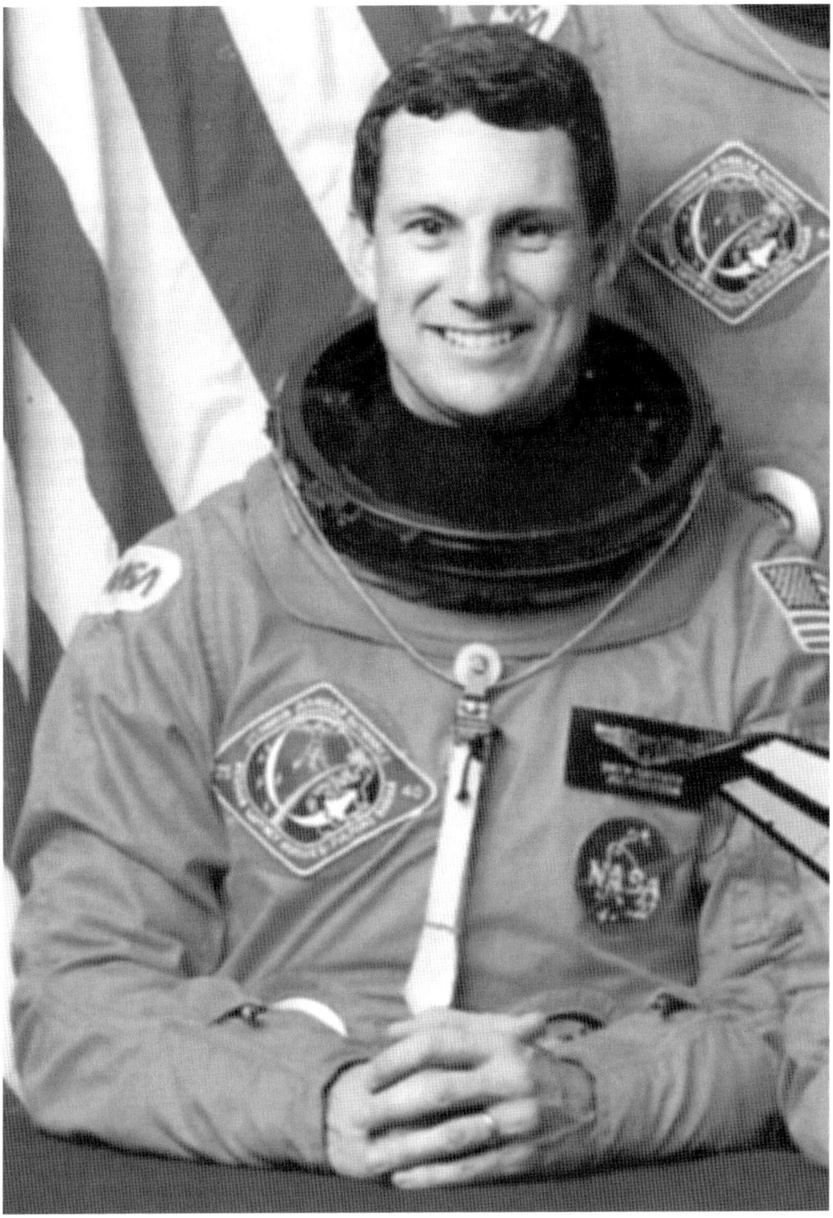

F. Drew Gaffney

Dr. Francis Drew Gaffney served as payload specialist No. 1 for the Spacelab Life Sciences (SLS-1) Mission STS-40 aboard Space Shuttle *Columbia* on May 22, 1991. Gaffney's fellow crew members included Millie Hughes-Fulford, M. Rhea Seddon, James P. Bagian, Bryan D. O'Connor, Tamara E. Jernigan, and Sidney M. Gutierrez. This mission included a couple of firsts: first mission dedicated solely to biomedical studies, first mission to have three women crew members, and first time in space for four of the seven crew members, including Gaffney. The nine-day journey was the 11th launch of *Columbia* and had the Space Lab Module as its payload. The crew was able to bring back more medical data than any other mission to date. Gaffney then became a professor of medicine, specializing in cardiovascular disease at Vanderbilt University in Tennessee. (Author's collection.)

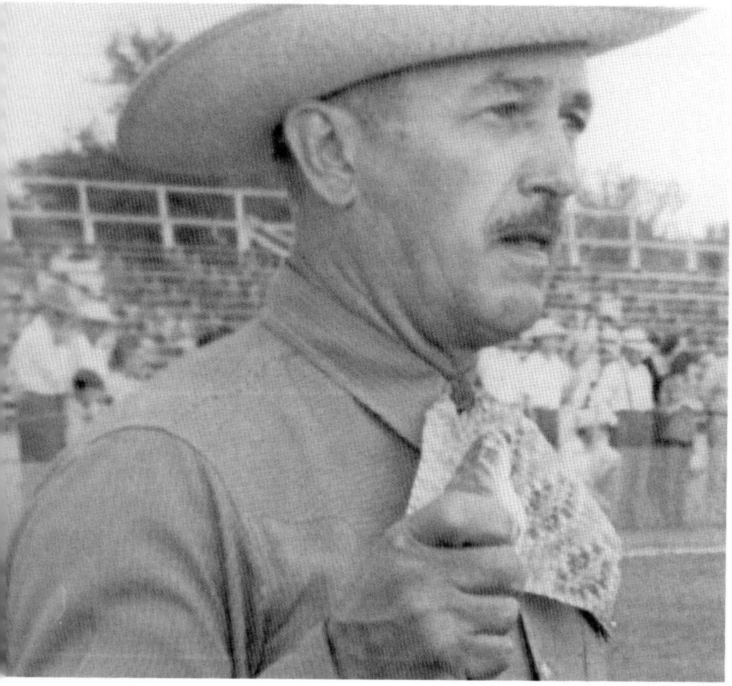

Merwin "Snakey" Campbell
Coordinator for the Rattlesnake Derby, Merwin Campbell earned his nickname, "Snakey," in 1934. The snake race brought competitors from many locations and became a regular celebration at the Fourth of July, complete with barbeque, rodeo, fireworks, and a dance. Spectators were said to have risen from 2,000 in 1934 to 25,000 in 1936, with the addition of water carnivals and the expansion to a three-day event.

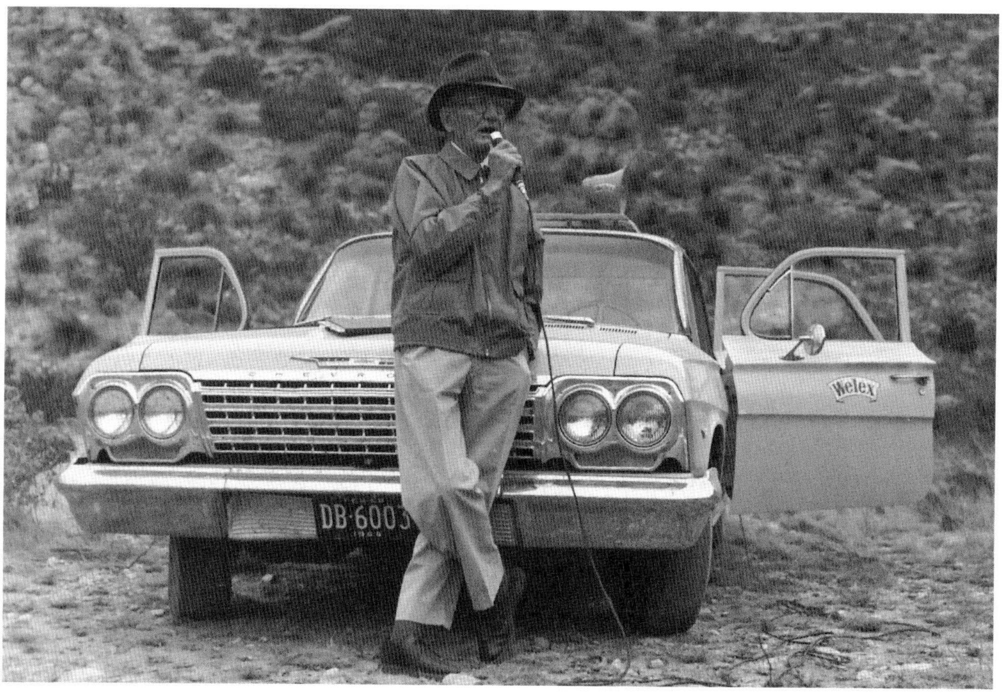

Wallace Pratt
Geologist Wallace Pratt was fascinated by the Permian Reef, which is the foundation of the Guadalupe Mountains. He could often be found speaking to tour and school groups about his beloved mountains. As the owner of famed McKittrick Canyon, Pratt selflessly donated his beautiful land to the National Park Service for the enjoyment of others.

Etienne de Pelissier Bujac

Those who speak of Colonel Bujac still do so highly. Known in Carlsbad, as well as the world, as a great orator, fine attorney, and an outstanding soldier, Bujac would cut a dashing figure with his movie star good looks as he strolled downtown. Born to affluent parents, Bujac grew up in Baltimore County, Maryland, on his father's estate. After entering the workforce at age 12 at his local post office, Bujac earned a law degree at age 29. Two years later, Bujac entered into the Spanish American War as the captain of Company H of the 1st US Volunteer Infantry in Cuba. He then served in the Philippines and China before moving to Carlsbad in 1902. While in Carlsbad, Bujac became the voice of the underdog and was said to have brought his opponents in courts to tears with his impassioned orations. Bujac lived and died on his own terms, creating a huge wake behind him.

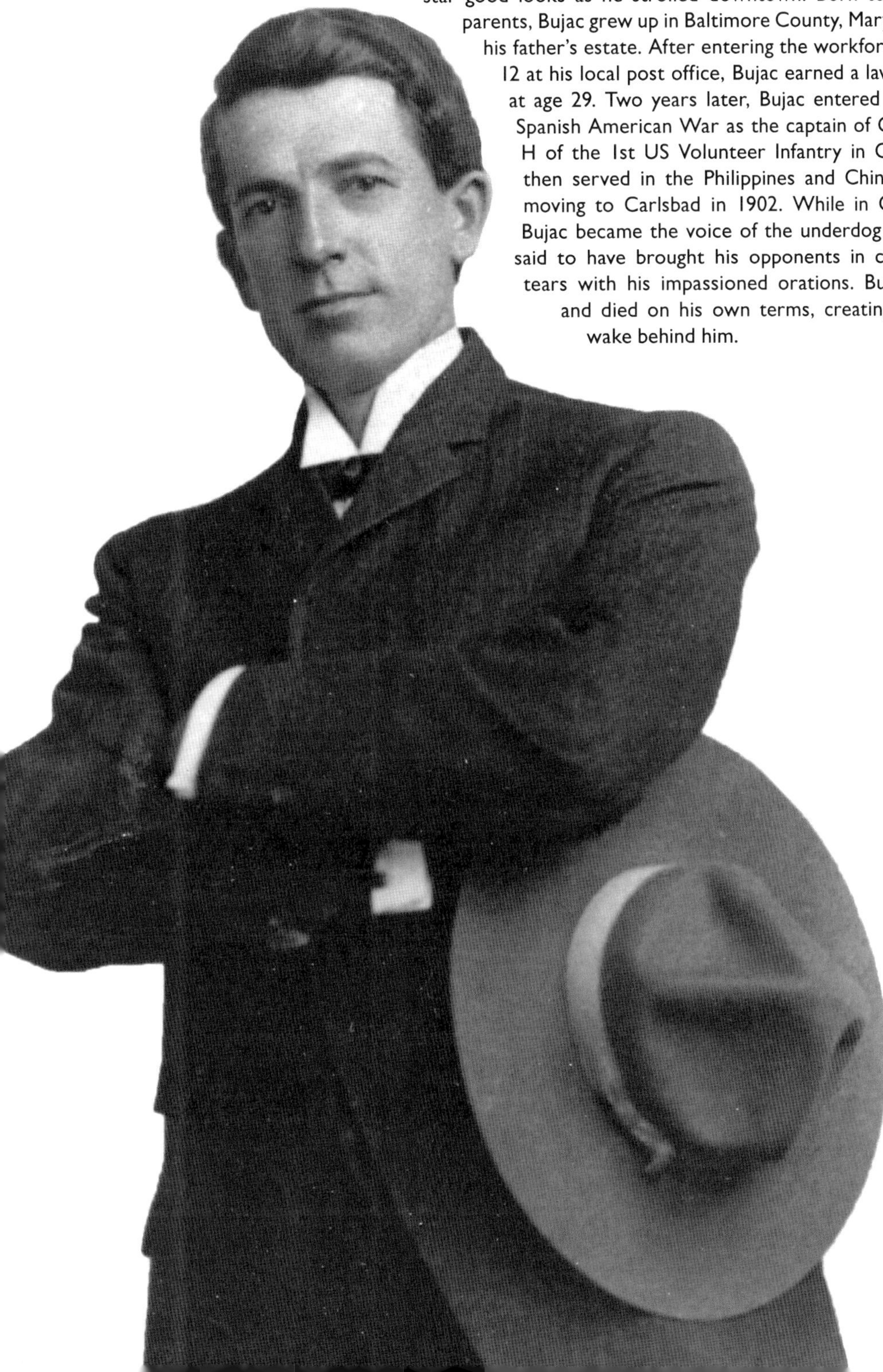

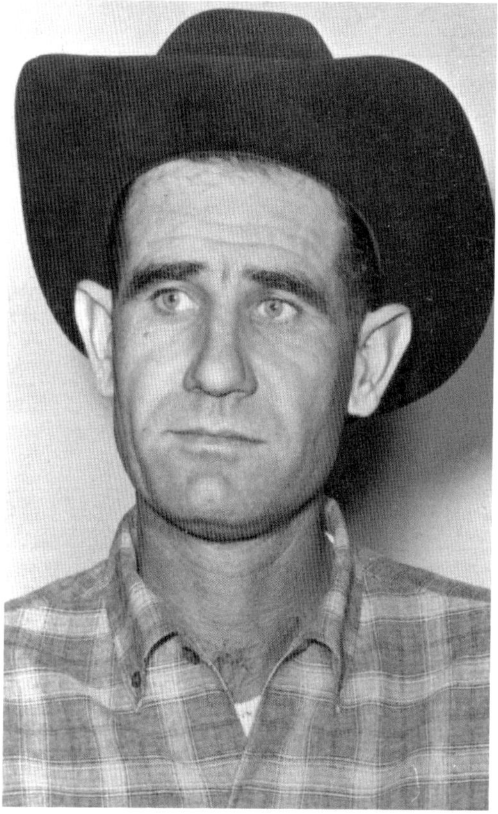

Noel Kincaid

Foreman for the Hunter Ranch, Noel Kincaid was known for his quick humor and cowhand skills. Kincaid knew the Guadalupe Mountains like the back of his hand and conducted tours for politicians and celebrities who wanted to experience the rugged mountains. It is joked that Kincaid's skills as a biscuit maker may have been the deciding factor to the completion of the negotiations for the Guadalupe Mountains National Park.

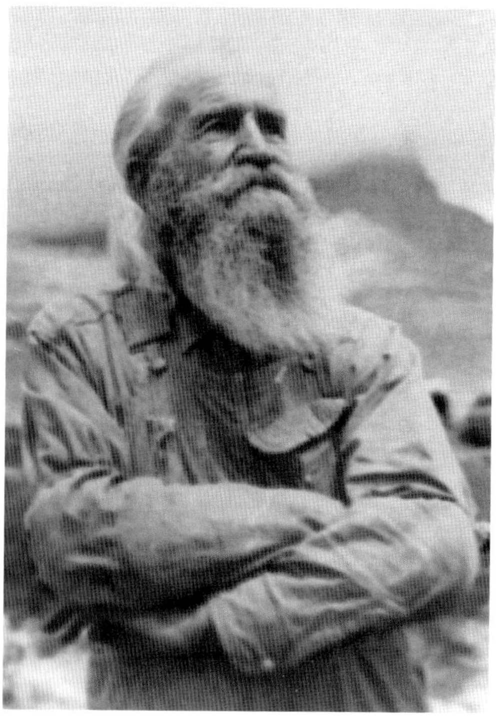

Ben Watson

Striking figure Ben Watson, with a hook for a hand, worked his way into history as a prospector in the Guadalupe Mountains. From Odessa, Texas, Watson visited Carlsbad and would often stay for months. His haggard horse and buggy became a common fixture on the city streets. Claiming to find a gold mine, Watson only told one person its location; this man died before revealing Watson's secret.

CHAPTER ONE

A Salute to Our Military Heroes

Sons and daughters of Carlsbad have long participated in the many wars the town has witnessed during its history. Beginning with battles with the Apache and Comanche tribes and progressing to the Spanish-American War, Mexican-American War, Punitive Expedition (in pursuit of Pancho Villa), World Wars I and II, Korean Conflict, Vietnam War, Operation Desert Storm, Operation Iraqi Freedom, and the War in Afghanistan, members of the community have a long history of participating in preserving our freedom.

The valor shown by the military men and women of Carlsbad is second to none. The United States owes a huge debt of gratitude to the soldiers who, faced with unimaginable odds and circumstances, exhibited nothing but pure heroism—many of whom paid the ultimate price with their life.

Host to the Carlsbad Army Airfield during World War II, the community played a large role in training bombardiers, both domestic and foreign; there were two classes of Chinese National Airmen trained at the base. Over 1,600 servicemen and women (members of the Woman's Army Auxiliary Corps) served at the CAAF base, which also housed the top-secret Norden bombsight. It was said that with the use of this device, the pilots could "drop a bomb into a pickle jar."

The Carlsbad Veterans Memorial Park is a touching, ongoing tribute to the veterans who served in all branches of the US military. The American flag flies proudly in their honor, especially on Memorial and Veterans Day.

Carlsbad residents have given their best to protect the United States and the world, and through great sacrifices, have forged and protected freedom. The community is forever grateful and humbled by their bravery.

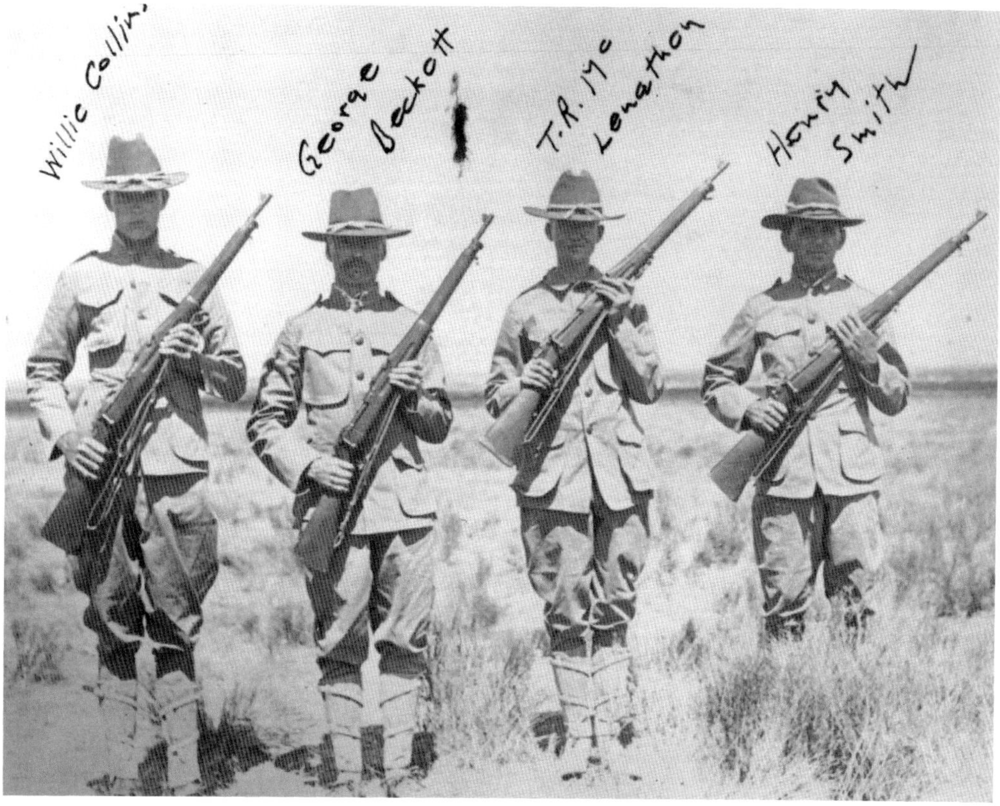

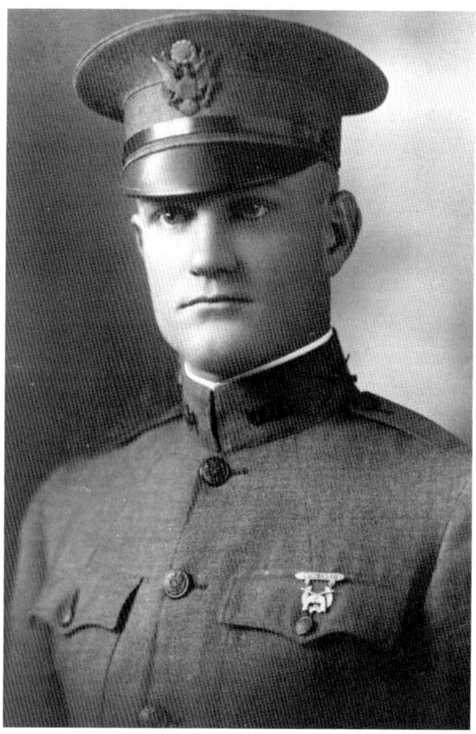

Company B

Company B of the 1st Regiment of the New Mexico National Guard, commanded by Col. Etienne Bujac, was sent to Columbus, New Mexico, to thwart Mexican revolutionary "Pancho" Villa in 1916. Many of the troops sent from Carlsbad to Columbus were still in high school at deployment. These men returned to Carlsbad to answer another call to arms in the "war to end all wars," World War I.

Bryan Mudgett

Carlsbad's first casualty of World War I was 2nd Lt. Bryan Mudgett, who served with the 357th Infantry Regiment, 90th Division of the American Expeditionary Forces (AEF), near St. Mihiel, France, during World War I, fresh from the Punitive Expedition, where he served as a first sergeant in Company B. Mudgett earned the Distinguished Service Cross for extraordinary heroism during the advance on September 12–13, 1918.

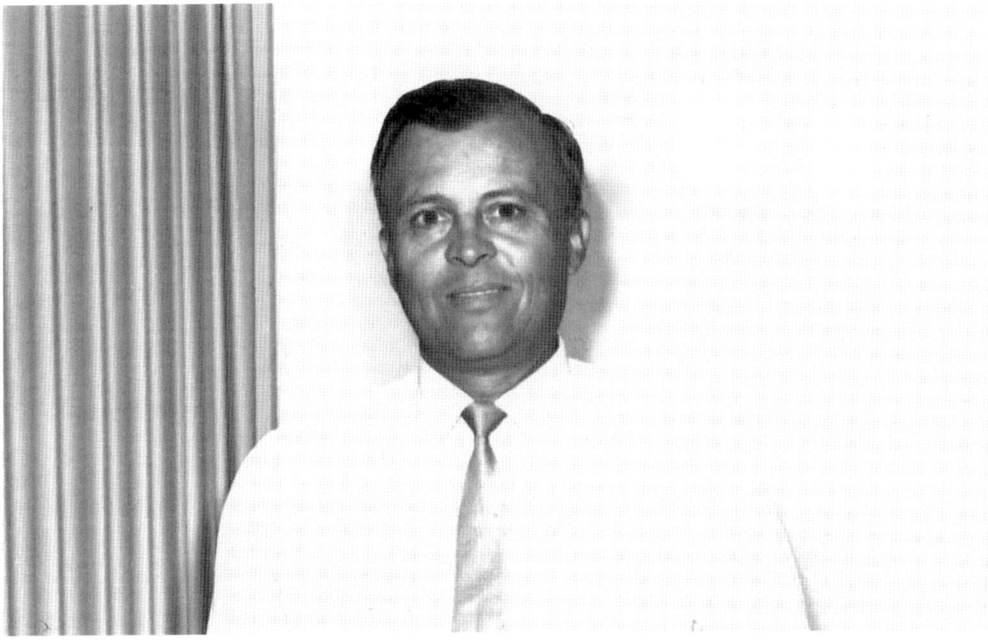

Calvin Graef

Another survivor of the Bataan Death March, Calvin Graef was a Japanese Prisoner of War for three years as a member of the 200th Coast Artillery. He narrowly escaped death when the prison ship in which he was riding was bombed; it was one of only seven to survive. His amazing, heartbreaking story was immortalized in *Ride the Waves to Freedom*, a book by Melissa Simpson Masterson.

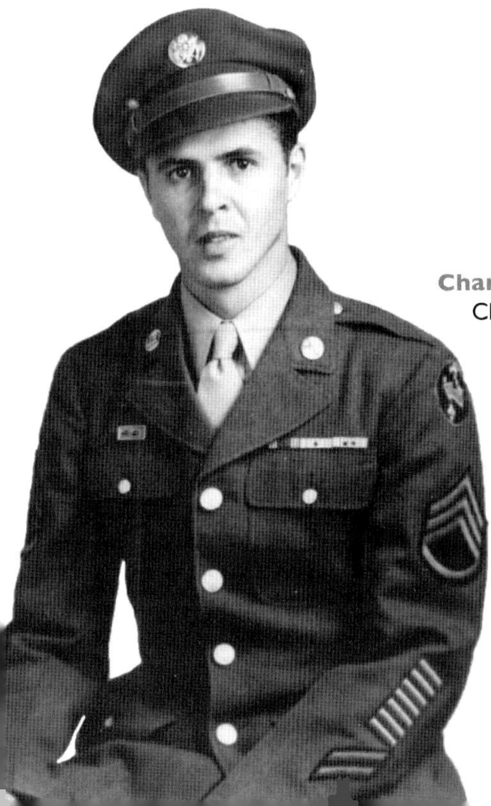

Charles James

Charles James is a Bataan Death March survivor and Japanese Prisoner of War in a forced labor camp. James was liberated in 1945 and given a Purple Heart and Bronze Star for his service. He worked hard to keep the memory alive, and his daughter, Joanna Sieberg, participates in the grueling 26.2 mile Bataan Memorial Death March at White Sands Missile Range each year in his honor.

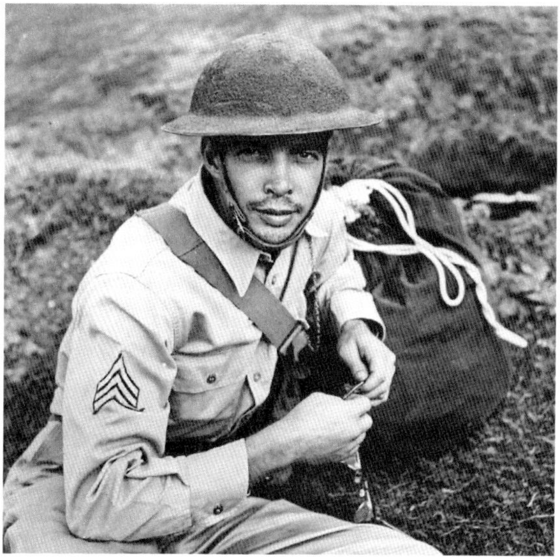

Joe Stanley Smith (ABOVE)
Held in horrible conditions for four years, Joe Stanley Smith was a survivor of the Bataan Death March and a Japanese prisoner-of-war camp. Congress heard Smith's statements taken from other survivors on the mistreatment they received while prisoners in order to get increased aid for Bataan veterans. Tragically, Smith's life was cut short at age 32, when he died in an airplane crash with 27 other people in Dallas, Texas.

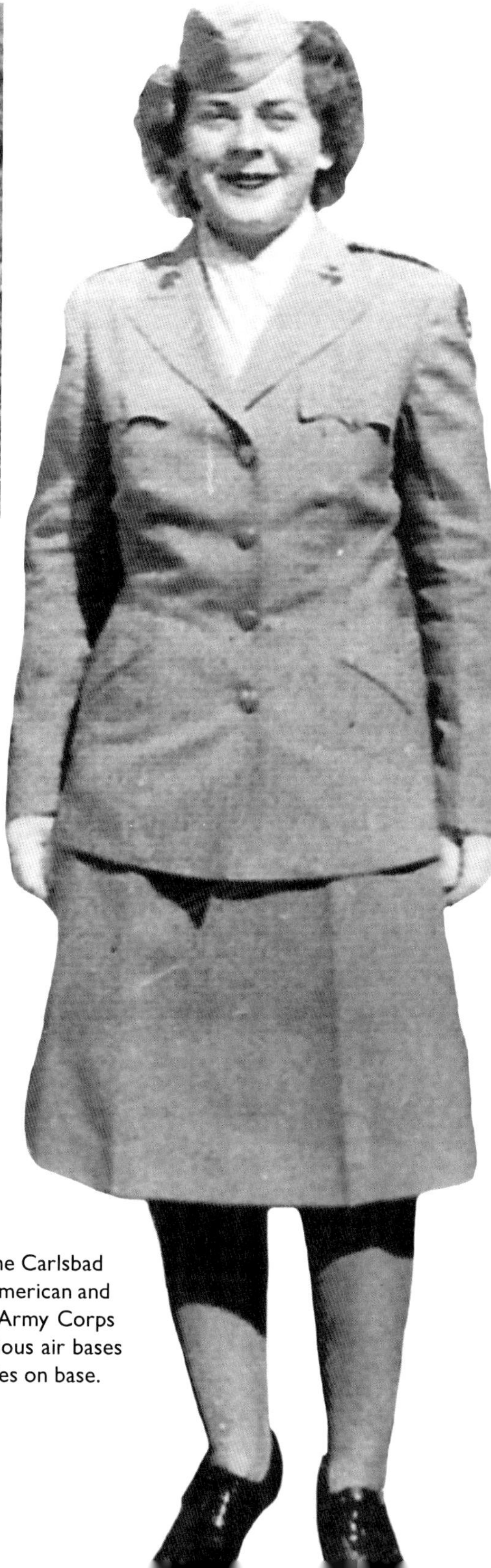

Marilyn Haynes (RIGHT)
Carlsbad played host to over 1,600 men and women at the Carlsbad Army Air Base, which housed bombardier cadets (both American and Chinese) as well as Marilyn Haynes with the Women's Army Corps (WAC). These women would transport planes from various air bases to Carlsbad during World War II and perform other duties on base.

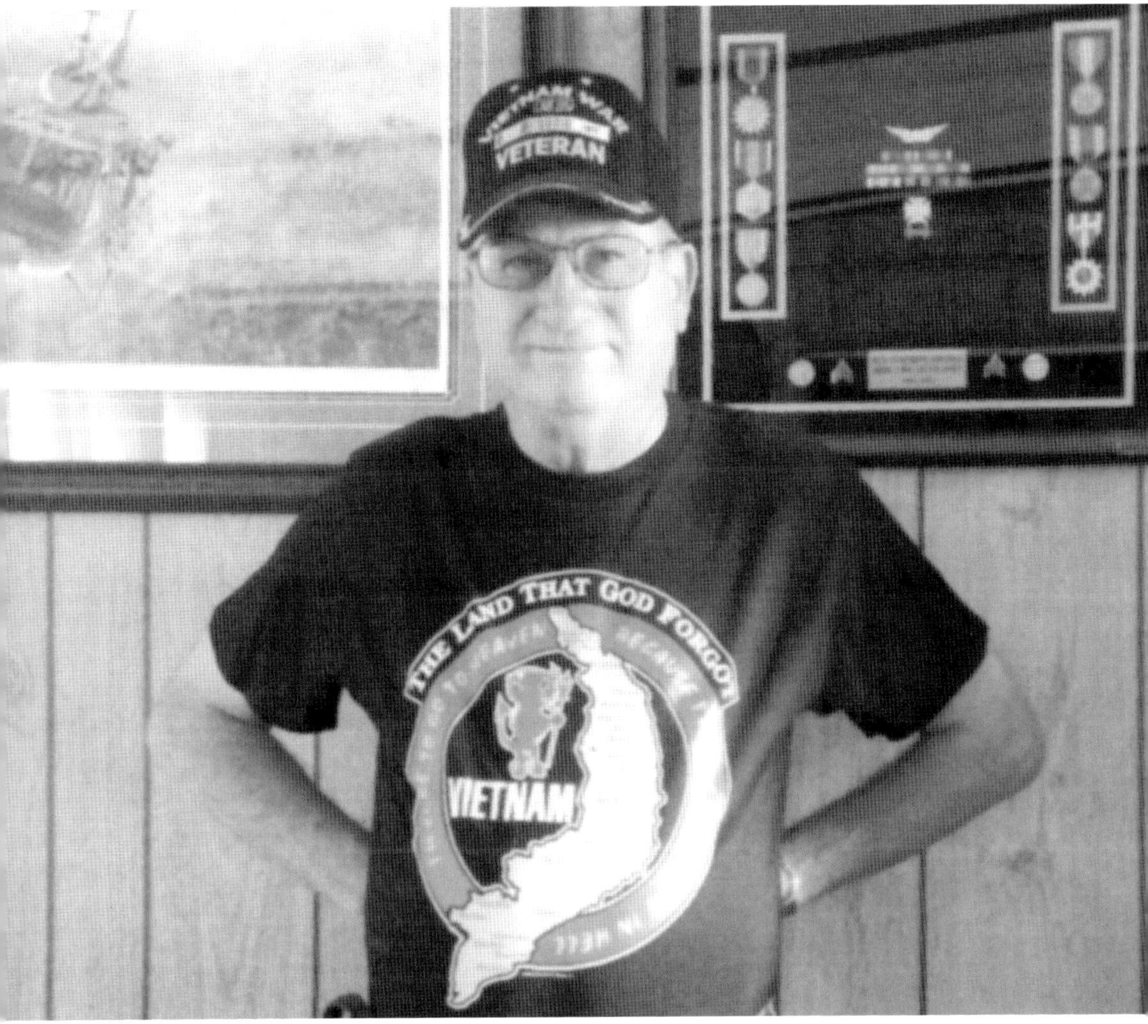

Steve Angell
Huey helicopter crew chief Steve Angell can be best described as a quiet hero. He served four tours in Vietnam and was stationed at Can Tho in the Mekong Delta. Feeling others were hurt worse than him, Angell refused a deserved Purple Heart, stating that he was just doing his job. Sergeant Angell saw combat, survived several aviation crashes, and was awarded the Commendation Medal while with the 1st Aviation Brigade. Angell's unit saw action during his time in country, and as with many veterans, the horror of these encounters are remembered but rarely spoken about. Returning to the United States was difficult, since his service was not well received at that time; the servicemen would change out of their uniforms as quickly as possible to avoid being spat upon. (Courtesy of Carye Lou Angell.)

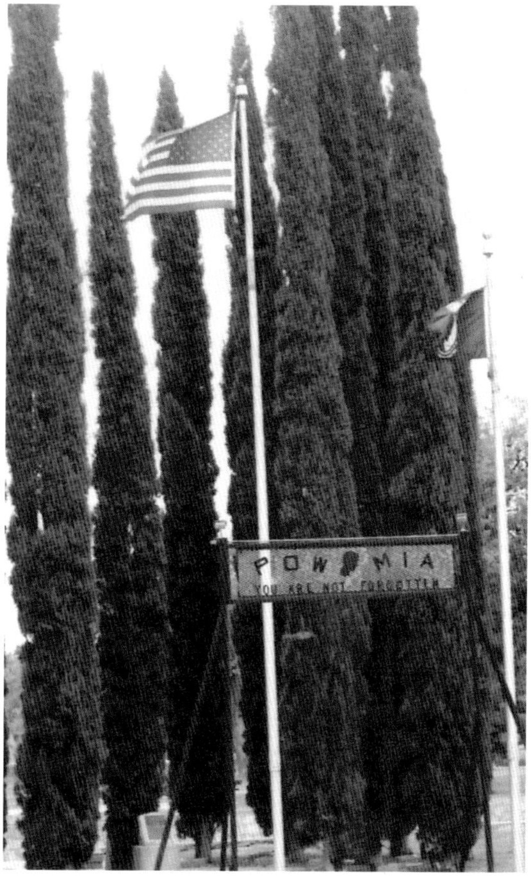

POW/MIA Memorial Grove

In every war, some brave souls never return. The Atwood family honored the Missing in Action (MIA) and Prisoners of War (POW) soldiers by creating a grove of Freedom Trees in their memory. Soldiers include Maj. Calvin W. Maxwell, Sp. Ricardo G. Davis, Max Coleman Simpson, and Andres Garcia, all from the Vietnam era. This is a solemn memorial, which quietly reminds onlookers that freedom is not free. (Author's collection.)

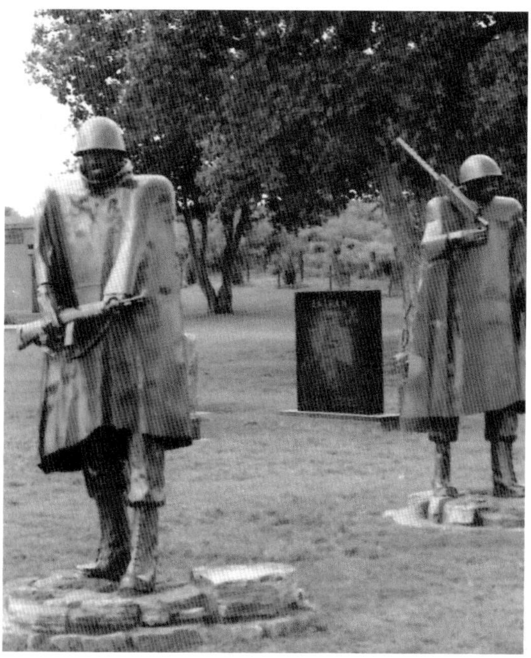

Carlsbad Veterans Memorial Park

Grown from a small memorial plaque, the Veterans Memorial Park proudly honors all of the Carlsbad veterans with sculptures of soldiers created by Frank Westfall, monuments, a vault that housed the Norden bombsight, and a Duster Tank. Seven years in the making, Chairman Joe Epstein stated that the memorial was created without funding; 90 percent of the memorial was donated by local businesses and the public. (Author's collection.)

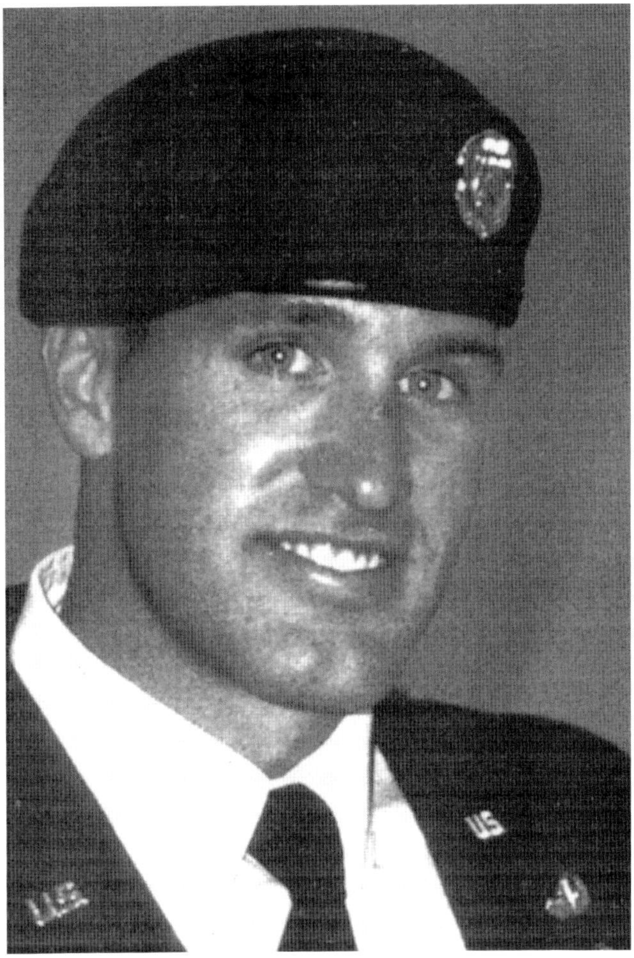

Jason Dean Cunningham

Sr. Amn. Jason Cunningham, a pararescueman and combat medic with the 38th Rescue Squadron, was the epitome of a true hero. During the bloodiest day in the Afghanistan War (March 4, 2002) in the Battle of Robert's Ridge, supporting Operation Anaconda, a chain of events led to the deaths of seven valiant men, including Cunningham. Although mortally wounded, Cunningham saved 10 of his team members after the Chinook MH-47 helicopter in which they were riding was shot down over Afghanistan. The team was en route for a rescue mission of American soldiers, including Navy SEAL PO1 Neil Roberts, who had fallen out of the helicopter and was pinned down by Al-Qaeda. Remaining in the burning fuselage of the helicopter, the airman treated the wounded, despite close mortar rounds and enemy gunfire. Cunningham fearlessly relocated his patients out of harm's way three separate times. It was then that the medic received at least two deadly gunshot wounds to the lower body, but he continued to direct patient care and successfully delivered 10 team members for lifesaving treatment and made it possible for seven others who were killed to come home. Cunningham was the first casualty from Carlsbad and the first pararescueman to be killed in battle since the Vietnam War. Cunningham's family members were not surprised by his extraordinary heroism. Cunningham was presented the Air Force Cross and Purple Heart posthumously for his uncommon valor. At his funeral service in Albuquerque, Cunningham's wife, Theresa, read a moving letter from her husband, who said he died happy because he had his wife and children in his life and was able to do what he wanted to do. (Courtesy of Carlsbad City Hall collection.)

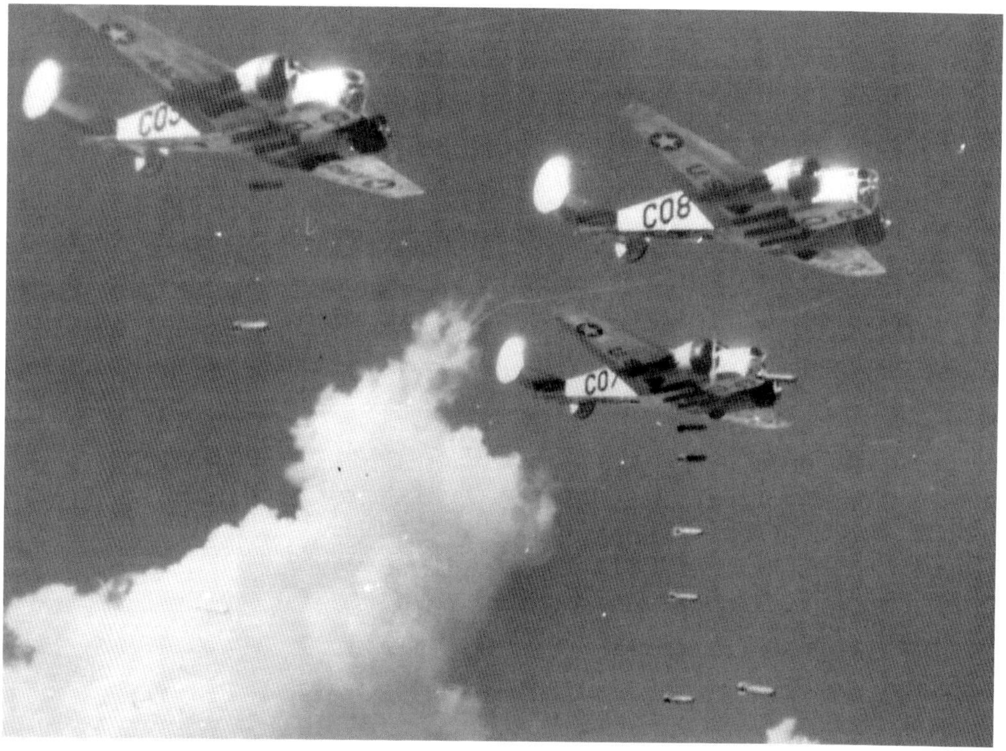

Carlsbad Army Airfield

During World War II, air bases were utilized to train bombardiers for service overseas. Built in 1941, Carlsbad Army Airfield played host to over 16,000 service men and women. The 1,678-acre airfield consisted of barracks, mess hall, commissary, chapel, theater, training facilities, clubs, library, weather station, motor pool, and many support buildings. The base trained pilots for the AT-11 bomber, B-17 and B-24 Liberators. The pilots were able to tell the wind direction and speed by the enormous American flag atop a 75-foot pole in the center of the base. Carlsbad was host to the highly secret Norden and Sperry bombsights, which arrived by a heavily armed convoy. After closure in 1945, many of the buildings were moved to Carlsbad. (Norden Vault photograph courtesy of the author.)

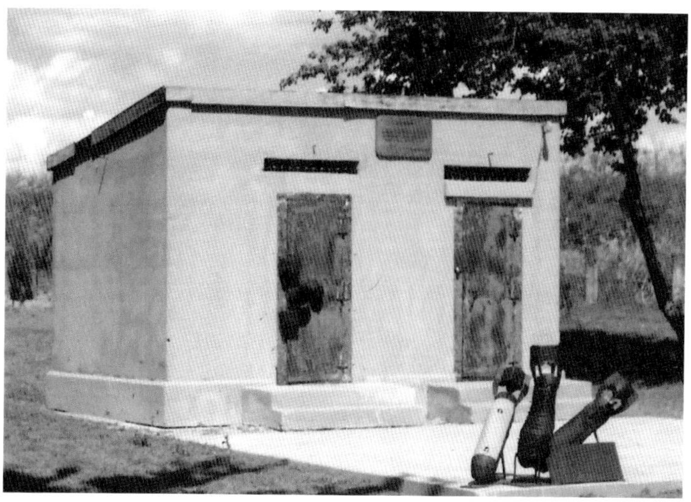

CHAPTER SEVEN

Sports Legends

Although Carlsbad is big on all sports, football is the king and baseball the prince of the Pecos Valley. County rivalries liven up Friday night skirmishes for a year of bragging rights. Early sports in Carlsbad revolved around the current trends of the day, which included bicycling and sailing, but these would give way to a sport that stemmed from the major occupation of the day—rodeo. Competition was fierce in the valley for the honor of the best ranch hand in the county. Steer roping and riding, bronco riding, and calf roping were featured events of the rodeo, and many champions emerged from the rowdy sport to represent Carlsbad.

Carlsbad High School produced many professional sports players whose stories are in these pages, but one person who should be included but was not due to lack of images is Frank Giddens from the Class of 1977. Giddens was the six-foot-seven-inch, 330-pound tackle who played for the Philadelphia Eagles for two years and was described as a "packing crate with feet" that anchored offensive lines and was known as "Big Frank" by his teammates. It is unfortunate that his size would ultimately lead to his untimely death at age 45. Frank was a gentle man who loved his family and was one of 10 athletic children.

The sports programs offered by the Carlsbad school system are some of the best in the state of New Mexico and have the records to prove it. The people illustrated here are only a few of the great athletes of many diversified sports who show that you can come from a small town in the New Mexican desert and achieve greatness.

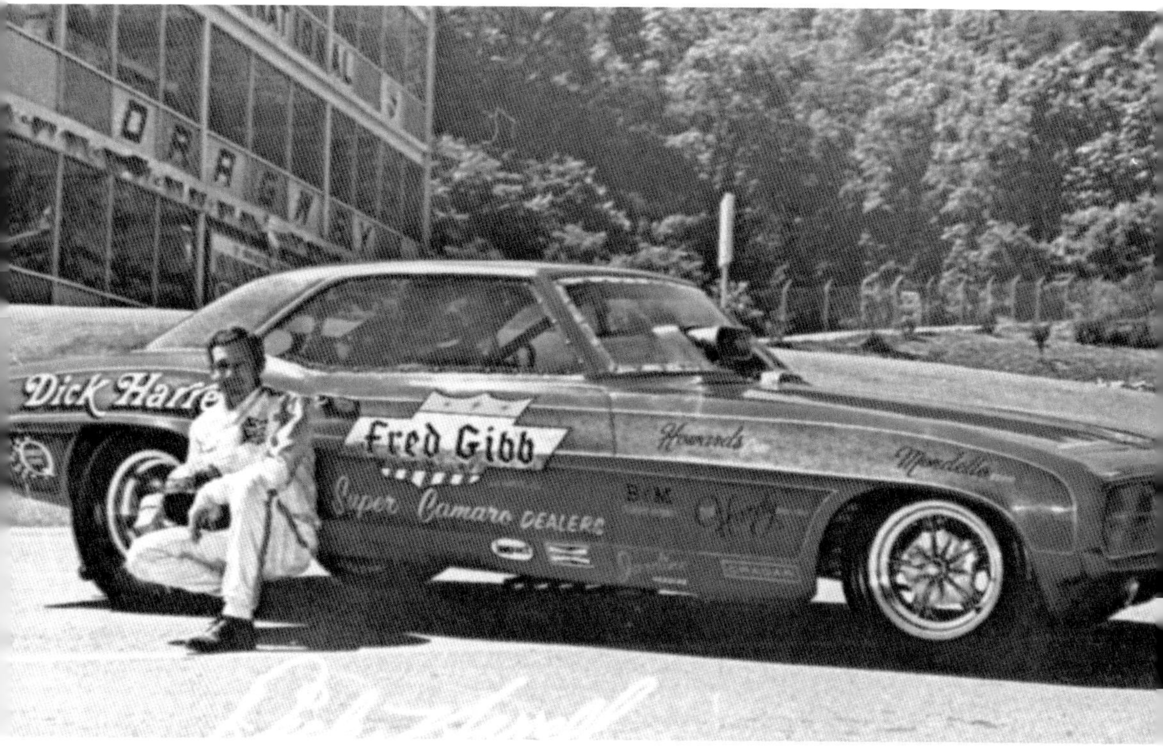

Dick Harrell

Dick Harrell, known as "Mr. Chevrolet," drove professional stock and drag cars. Harrell began his racing career at age 14, when he drove sprint cars at the Carlsbad racetrack. A drag race pioneer, Harrell was well respected by those who raced against him. Actor Dan Blocker, who played "Hoss" Cartwright on *Bonanza*, was proud to call Harrell his friend. Named Driver of the Decade in 1970, Harrell tragically lost his life behind the wheel of his Top Fuel Camaro Funny Car in Toronto, Canada, on September 12, 1971. Harrell's daughter, Valerie, is continuing her father's legacy as the owner of the Dick Harrell Performance Center and still spends most of her time at the racetrack around the machines she was raised around and loves. Harrell was inducted into the International Drag Racing Hall of Fame in 2010.

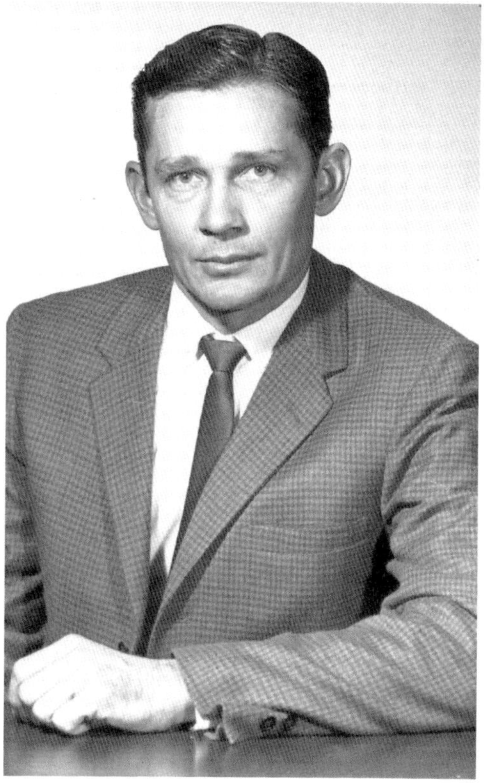

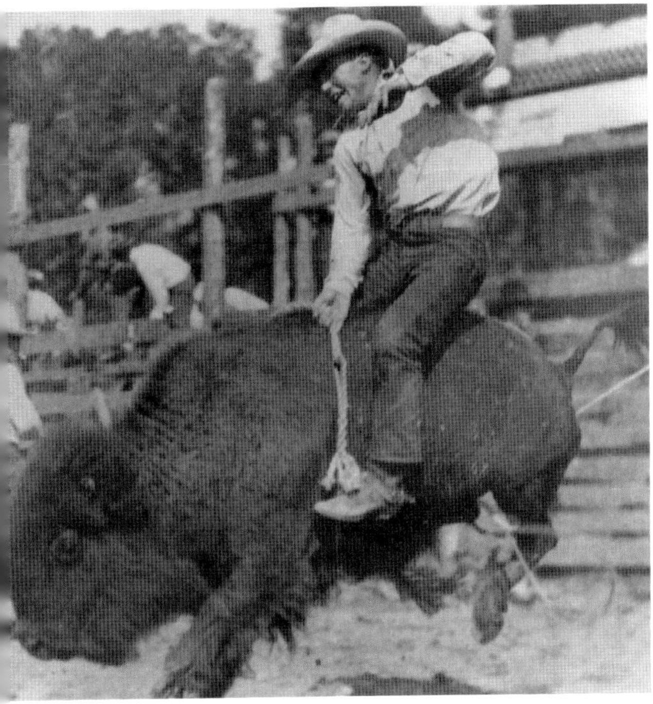

Elmer Hepler

Rodeo champion Elmer Hepler knew how to thrill audiences. He and his brothers were founding members of the American Quarter Horse Association. Hepler was the proud owner of Shue-Fly (shown here), the world champion quarter running horse in the 1940s, who was inducted into the American Quarter Horse Association Hall of Fame in 2005. Hepler traveled to London with Tex Austin's rodeo in 1934, where he rode bucking broncos. When he returned home, he became interested in horse racing and found great success with his famed quarter horses, including Little Joe the Wrangler, whose father, Joe Hancock, was inducted into the Quarter Horse Hall of Fame in 1992. Hepler died at age 72 in 1978 after many years in the Rodeo Association as an official with Floyd "Skipper" Rigdon and Jim Derrick.

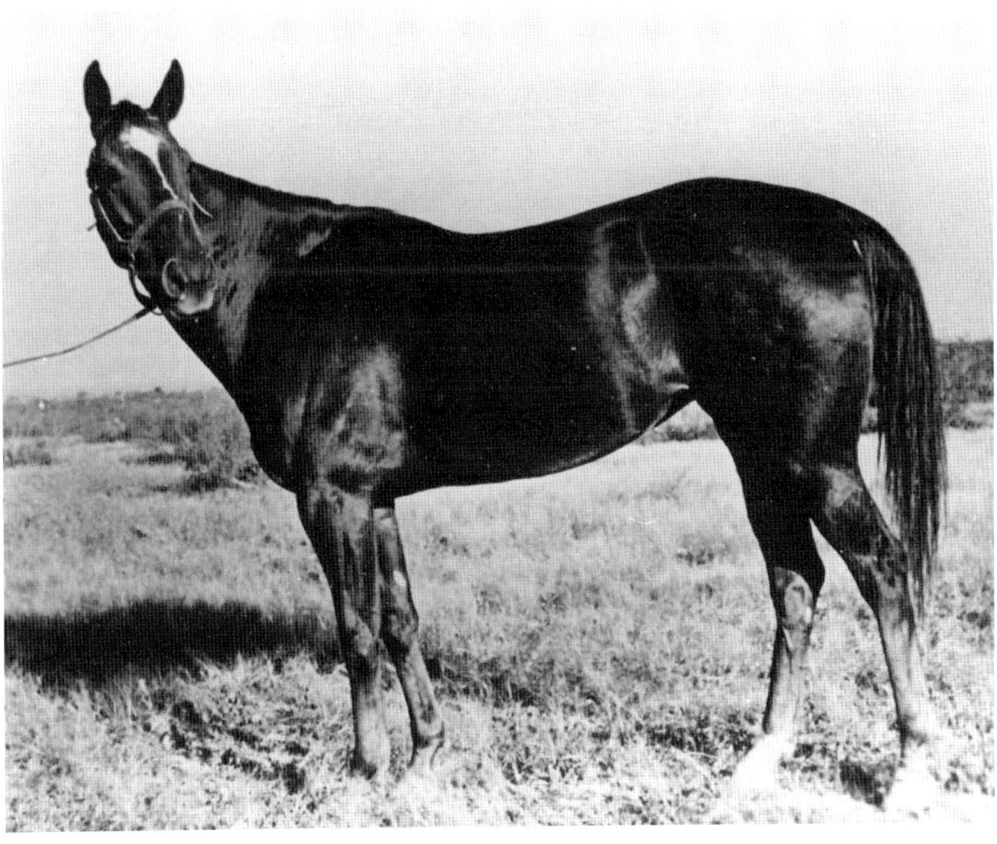

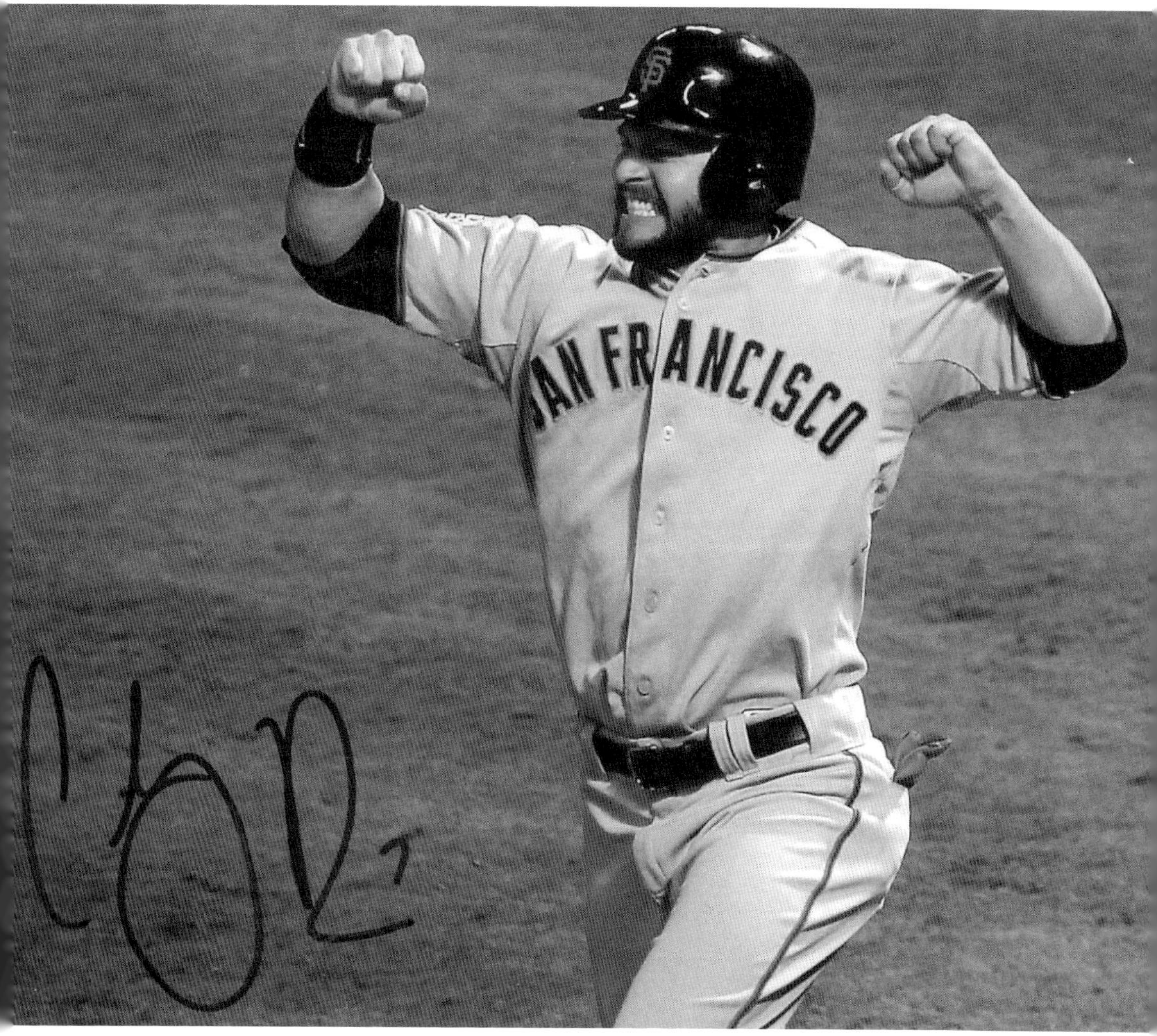

Cody Ross

Voted the Most Valuable Player of the 2010 World Series while playing for the San Francisco Giants, Cody "Smiles" Ross returned to Eddy County a true sports hero. Ross began his sports career with the baseball program at Carlsbad High School. There, he was not given much encouragement, given his small stature, but he went on to prove the naysayers wrong in a big way. Ross grew up around the rodeo and watched his father, Kenny, ride bulls professionally. He became a proficient roper while roping "cats, dogs, and anything that moved," according to his mother, Janet. As a child, Ross wanted to be a rodeo clown, but as he grew, football won out. A broken leg in the eighth grade ended that dream, so baseball took over. Even after the many injuries that Ross suffered over the years, he maintains a positive attitude while pushing forward. It is this "never quit" attitude that keeps him in the books as an all-star. (Author's collection.)

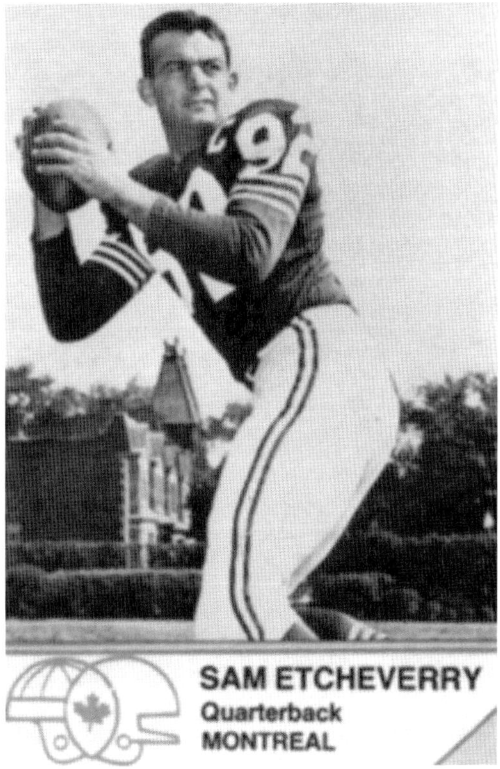

Sam Etcheverry
Sam "The Rifle" Etcheverry, born to immigrant Basque sheep farmers, became a star in the Canadian Football League. As quarterback for the Montreal Alouettes, Etcheverry was named the Canadian Football League Most Outstanding Player in 1954 and inducted into the Canadian Football Hall of Fame in 1969. Starting his football career at Carlsbad Senior High School, Etcheverry played for the University of Denver before going to Canada. (Author's collection.)

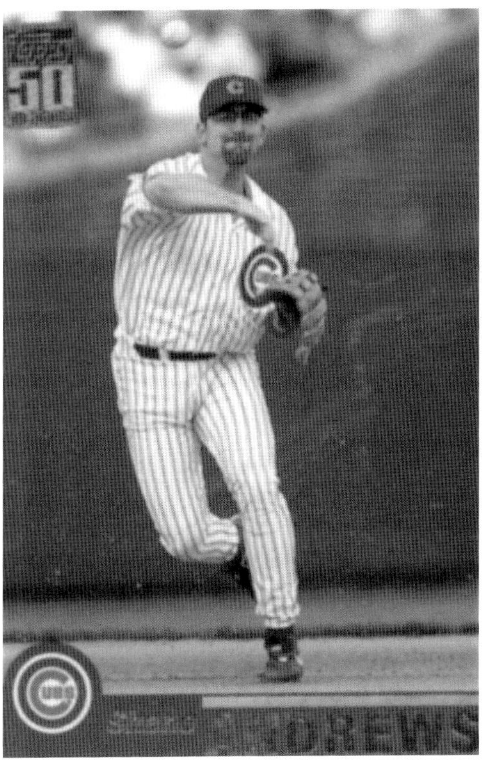

Shane Andrews
Carlsbad native Shane Andrews became the 11th overall draft pick in 1990, picked by the Gulf Coast Expos and leading the South Atlantic League with 25 home runs and 107 walks. Andrews then played for the Montreal Expos from 1995 to 1999. He ended his seven-season baseball career with the Boston Red Sox in 2002, batting an average of .220 with 86 home runs and 263 RBIs in 569 games played. (Author's collection.)

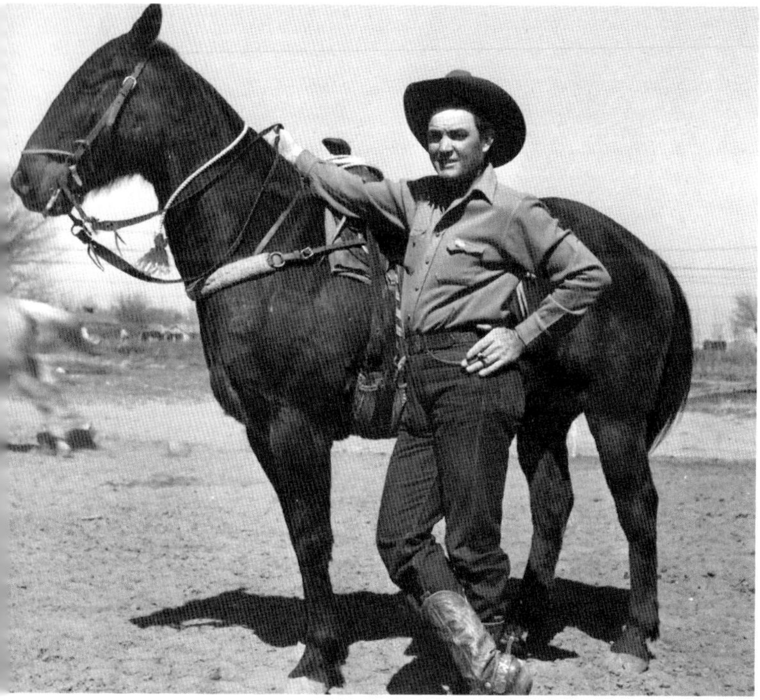

Joe "Tuffy" Welch
World champion cowboy Tuffy Welch earned many belt buckles and saddles during his career. He was known to be a tough contender for most titles. Welch thrilled audiences in Reno, Nevada, with his attempt to ride an unridden buffalo named Sunny Jim, who got the better of him. Welch was inducted in the Cowboy Hall of Fame in 1991 as a champion calf and steer roper.

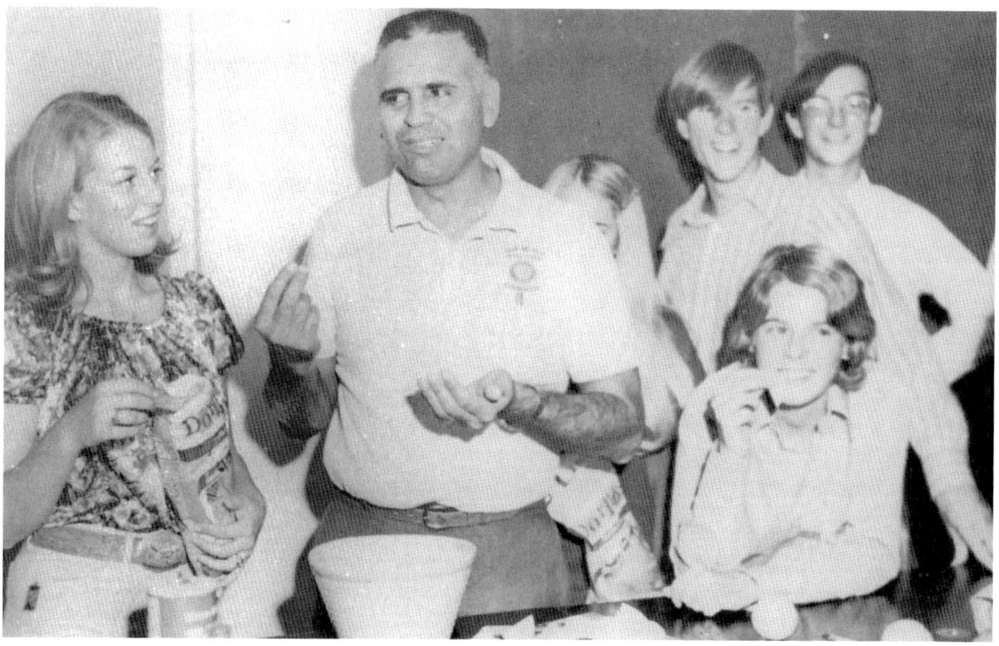

Porfirio R. "Porky" Leyva
Any student who had Porky Leyva as a biology teacher will certainly remember the "digestion labs" resulting in delicious guacamole. Leyva taught for 30 years at Mid-High School—the same school which bears his name today. After serving with the US Marine Corps in Korea, Leyva returned to New Mexico at attended the University of New Mexico on a football scholarship, receiving a bachelor's and master's degree.

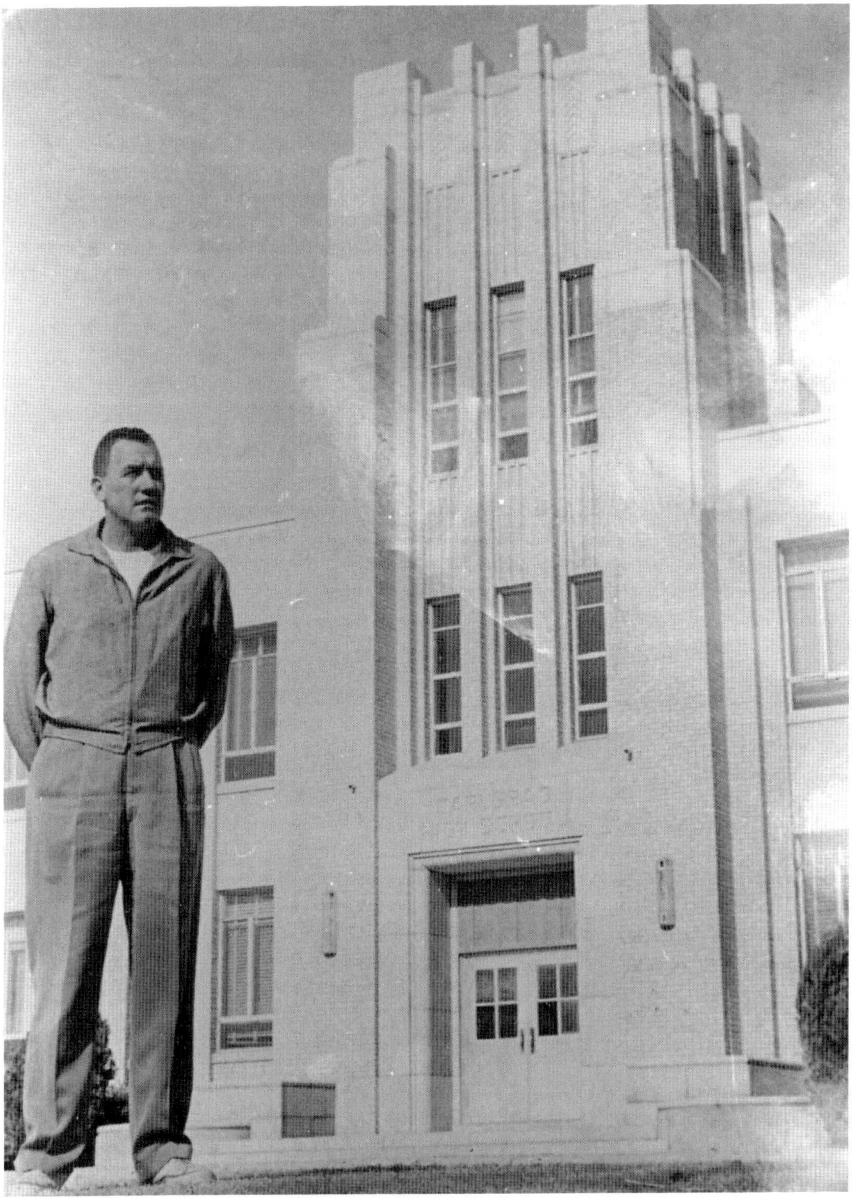

Ralph Bowyer

The Carlsbad High School football stadium bears the name of Ralph Bowyer to honor one of the most valued coaches in Cavemen history. Known to be a practical joker, Bowyer enjoyed pranking his team members and faculty. At his 2005 memorial service, Bowyer instructed that plastic spiders be placed on all the pews as one last joke. The school song, "Onward Cavemen," was sung to honor the revered coach. Bowyer was known for his fairness, equality, and love of life. It was more than just about the scores and records; his athletes mattered. He coached three sports in Carlsbad for 24 years. Described as "everyone's mentor and a role model who had very high morals" by lifelong friend Joe Zeni, "no matter where you went, Bowyer would draw a crowd. Everyone wanted to talk to Ralph Bowyer." Bowyer was highly respected by all who played for him, and players worked extra hard to please their coach. As a child of the Depression, Bowyer never wanted riches; it was all about his players and integrity.

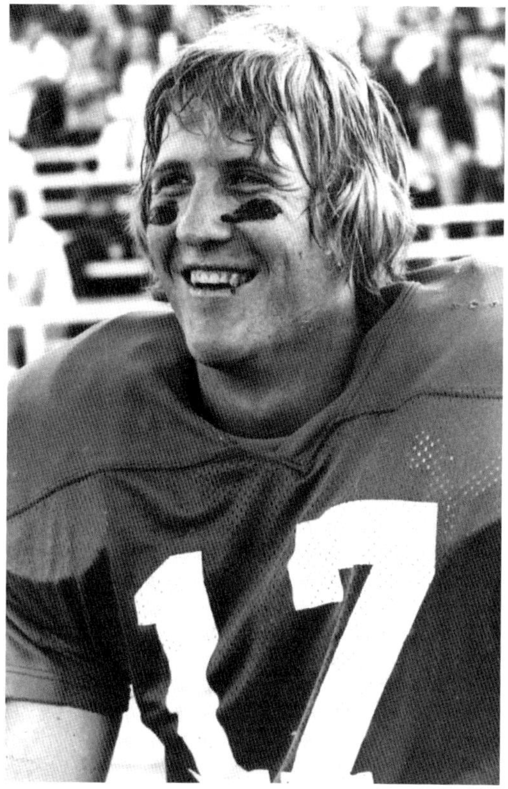

Mark Jackson

After leaving Carlsbad High School as a winning quarterback, Mark Jackson went to play for the Baylor University Bears from 1974 to 1976. He then went on to play six seasons in the Canadian Football League as quarterback for the Montreal Alouettes (1977), Toronto Argonauts (1979–1980), and Winnipeg Blue Bombers (1981–1983).

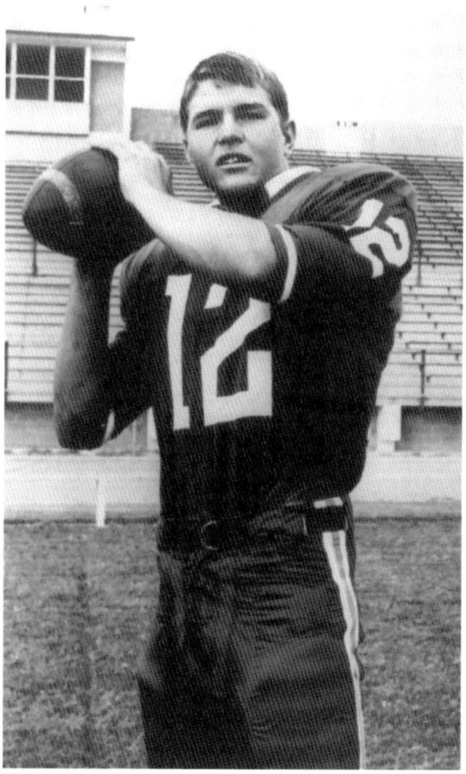

Kenny Ross

Said to be Carlsbad's first standout athlete, Kenny Ross was a six-foot-three-inch football player who could "run like the wind." Ross, who went on to play college football at the University of New Mexico, was also a professional bull rider who would bring his youngest son and future baseball legend, Cody, to the rodeos.

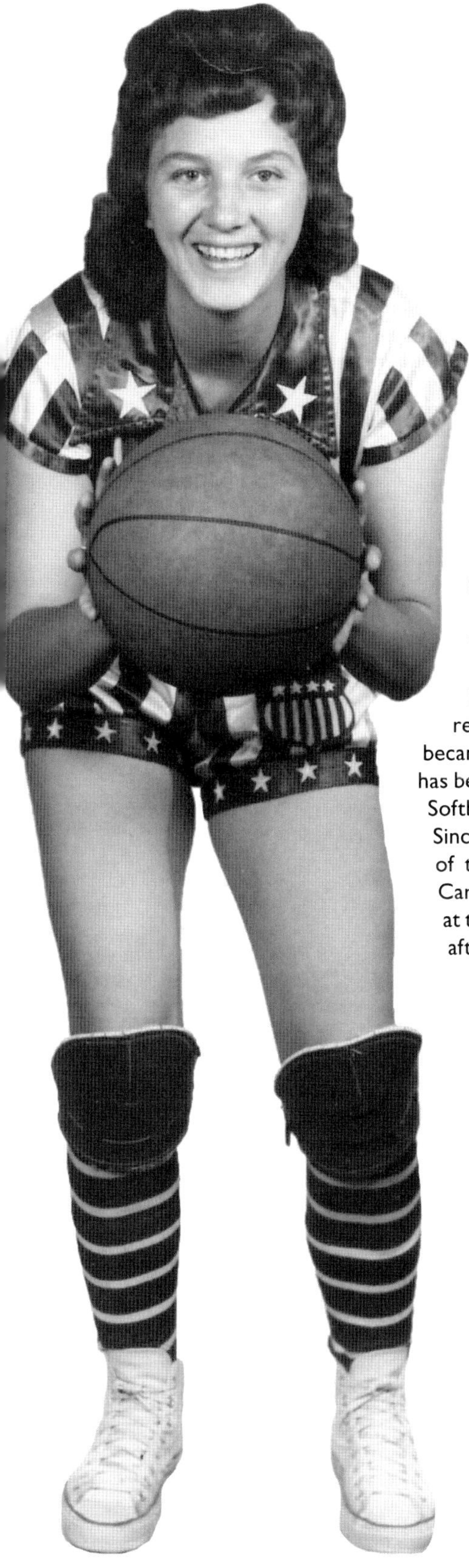

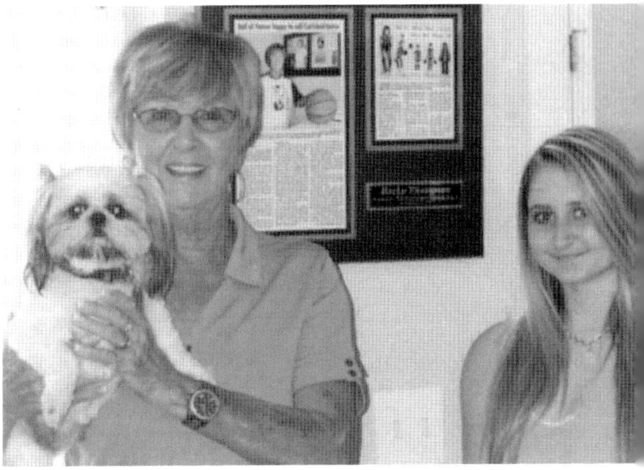

Becky Thompson

Known for both her business sense and softball skill, Becky Thompson (shown here with her 14-year-old granddaughter, Lexie) was the longtime owner of the Sportcenter and the much-loved, still-in-operation Becky's Drive-In. Thompson was also a star member in one of the world's most successful professional women's basketball leagues, the All American Red Heads, illustrated by this 1960 image. Thompson, a blonde, was told to dye her hair red or to get back on the bus; she joked that this is when she became a redhead. Originally from Texarkana, Texas, Thompson has been inducted into the Amateur Softball Association National Softball Hall of Fame and the Women's Basketball Hall of Fame. Since retirement, Thompson has become the first female coach of the Shorthorn Little League and continues to work as a Carlsbad community youth volunteer basketball coach. A field at the Carlsbad Bob Forrest Youth Sports Complex was named after her. (Author's collection.)

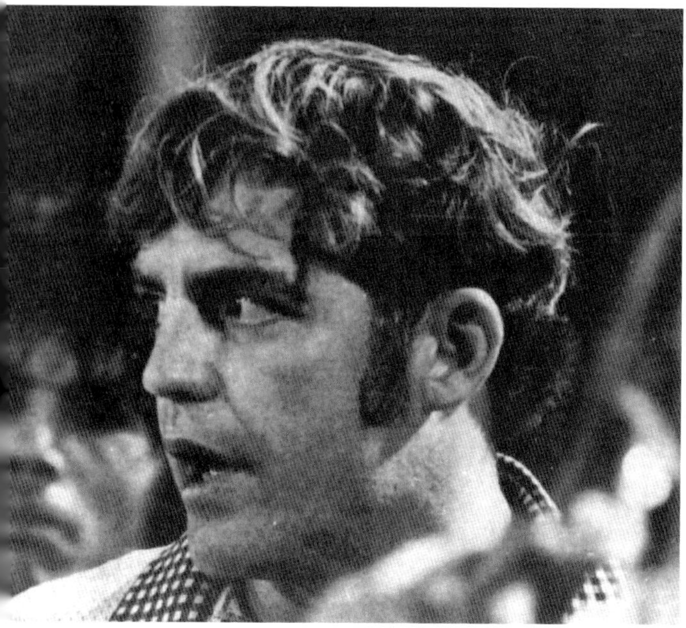

Dave Perini

Dave Perini is known as one of the best Carlsbad coaches. Taught by Ralph Bowyer, Perini learned patience, an understanding of the game, and the importance of getting to know and teach individual players. Retiring from coaching in 1980, Perini opened his own oil and gas company.

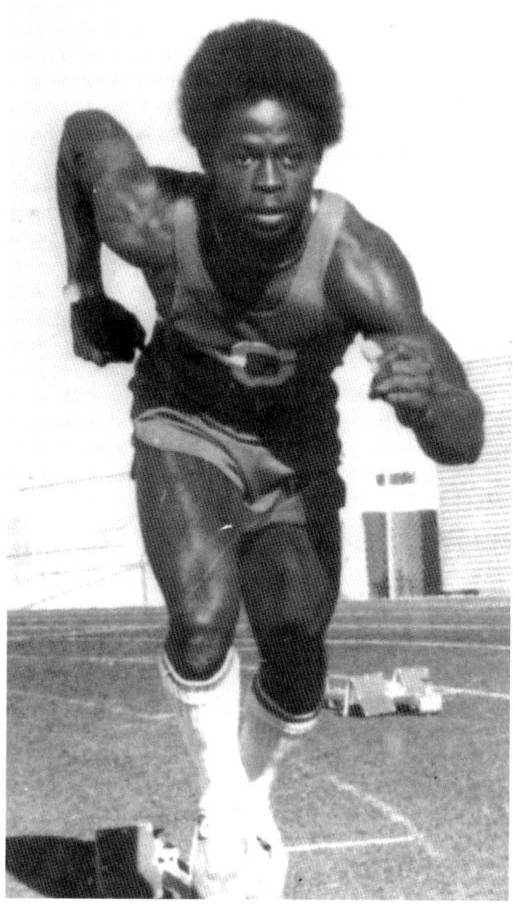

Kelley Johnson

All-star wide receiver for the Cavemen, Carlsbad football player Kelley Johnson drew the attention of professional football teams while attending the University of Colorado. In 1987, the Indiana Colts drafted Carlsbad football player Kelley Johnson; he played there for one season. Johnson went to the Canadian Football League with the Ottawa Rough Riders and then the United States Football League with Denver Gold (1985–1987) and the Detroit Lions (1989).

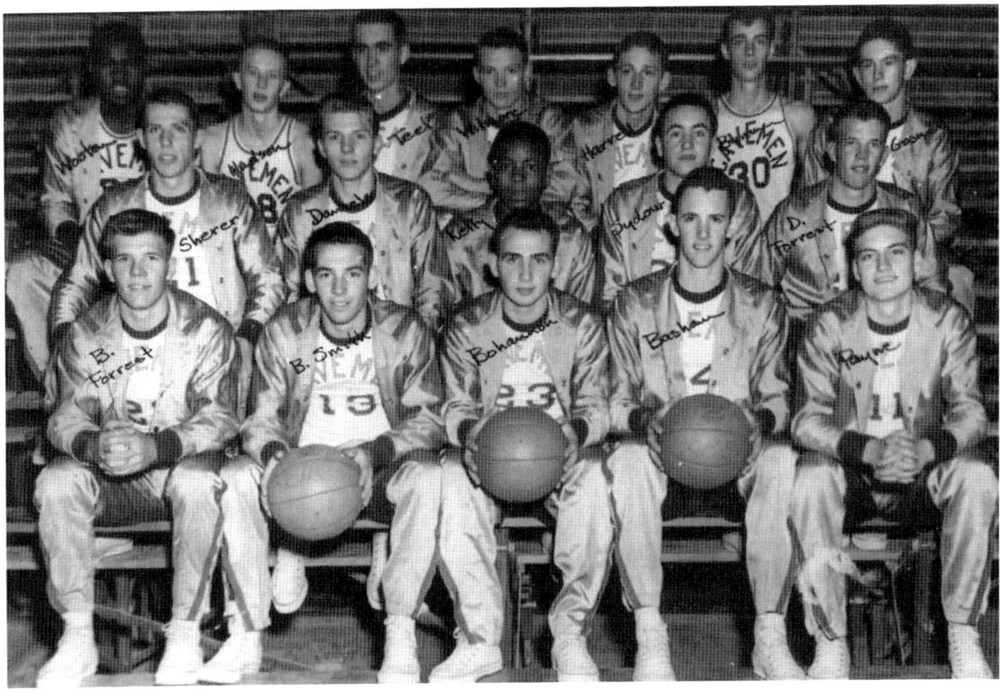

John Wooten

John Wooten (pictured in the top left corner) of Riverview, Texas, played football in 1952 for Carlsbad and then for the University of Colorado, where he became the second African American in the university's program history. Wooten graduated with a bachelor of science and was inducted into the College Football Hall of Fame in 2012. Wooten played professionally for the Cleveland Browns (1959–1967) and the Washington Redskins (1968).

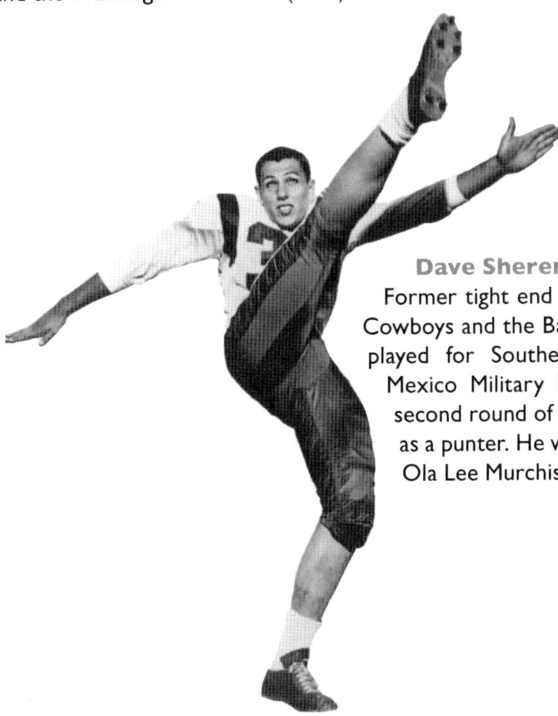

Dave Sherer

Former tight end and punter in the NFL for the Dallas Cowboys and the Baltimore Colts, Dave Sherer originally played for Southern Methodist University and New Mexico Military Institute. Sherer was drafted in the second round of the 1959 draft by the Dallas Cowboys as a punter. He was released in 1961 to make room for Ola Lee Murchison of the San Francisco 49ers.

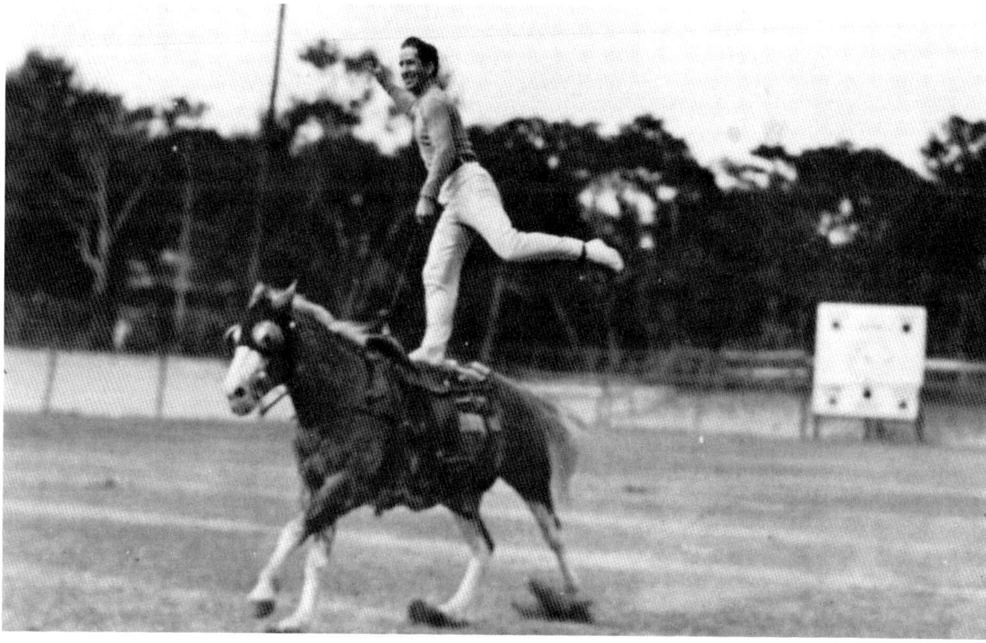

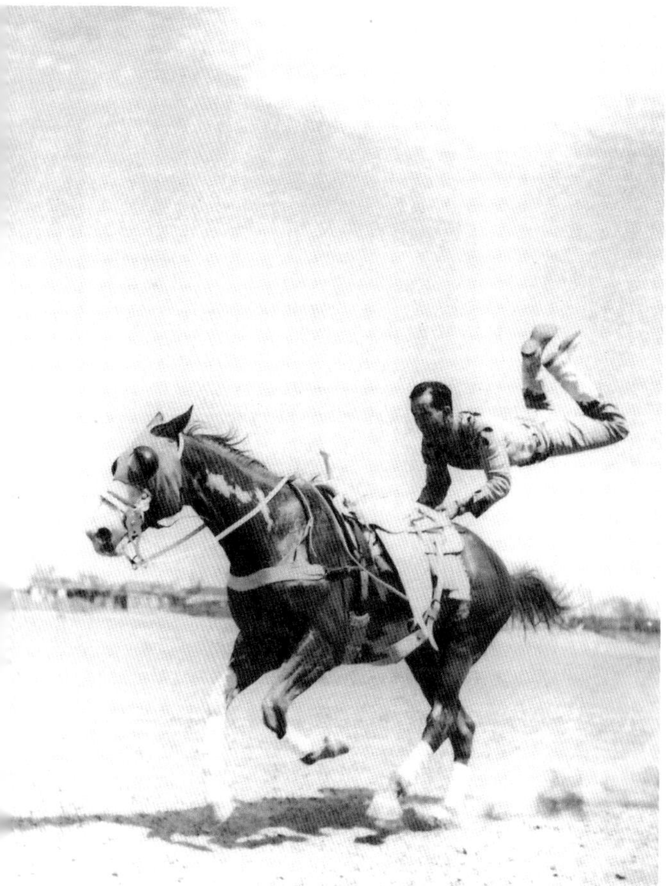

Paul Bond

Born on December 19, 1915, in Seminole, Texas, Paul Bond grew up on his parent's ranch, east of Carlsbad. A legendary cowboy, Bond could be found riding bareback broncos and bulls as well as trick riding and Roman riding on the rodeo circuit. He became a stuntman for movie star clients such as Gene Autry, Rex Allen, and John Wayne. As a young man, Bond met and married Joyce Roberta Ramsey, who also came from a family of trick riders. Bond later became a custom boot maker, featuring distinctive stitching patterns. He attracted the attention of many celebrities, like Montie Montana and Monty Hall, but his greatest satisfaction came from the boots he made for cowboys. The boot shop was a way to supplement his rodeo income, and Bond treated all of his clients—celebrity or cowboy—the same. Bond was inducted into the Rodeo Hall of Fame in Oklahoma City in 1992 and received many accolades from *True West* magazine as Bootmaker of the Year.

CHAPTER EIGHT

Public Servants

Every community has the worker bees—the people who give more of themselves than others—and Carlsbad is no exception. The community has a high degree of volunteerism, participation, and pride. Although not all deserving individuals are listed here, it is clear that Carlsbad has an extraordinary large group of citizens who go above and beyond for their town.

Carlsbad is in an isolated part of New Mexico, which can cause travel issues. This factor makes citizens and officials work a little harder to be heard. The state of New Mexico and the United States benefit from their grit and tenacity.

This chapter highlights a scant few of the truly outstanding public servants who have forged ahead and allowed Carlsbad to progress. While some reveled in the spotlight, others were happiest in the shadows. Yet, all made their community the great place it is today.

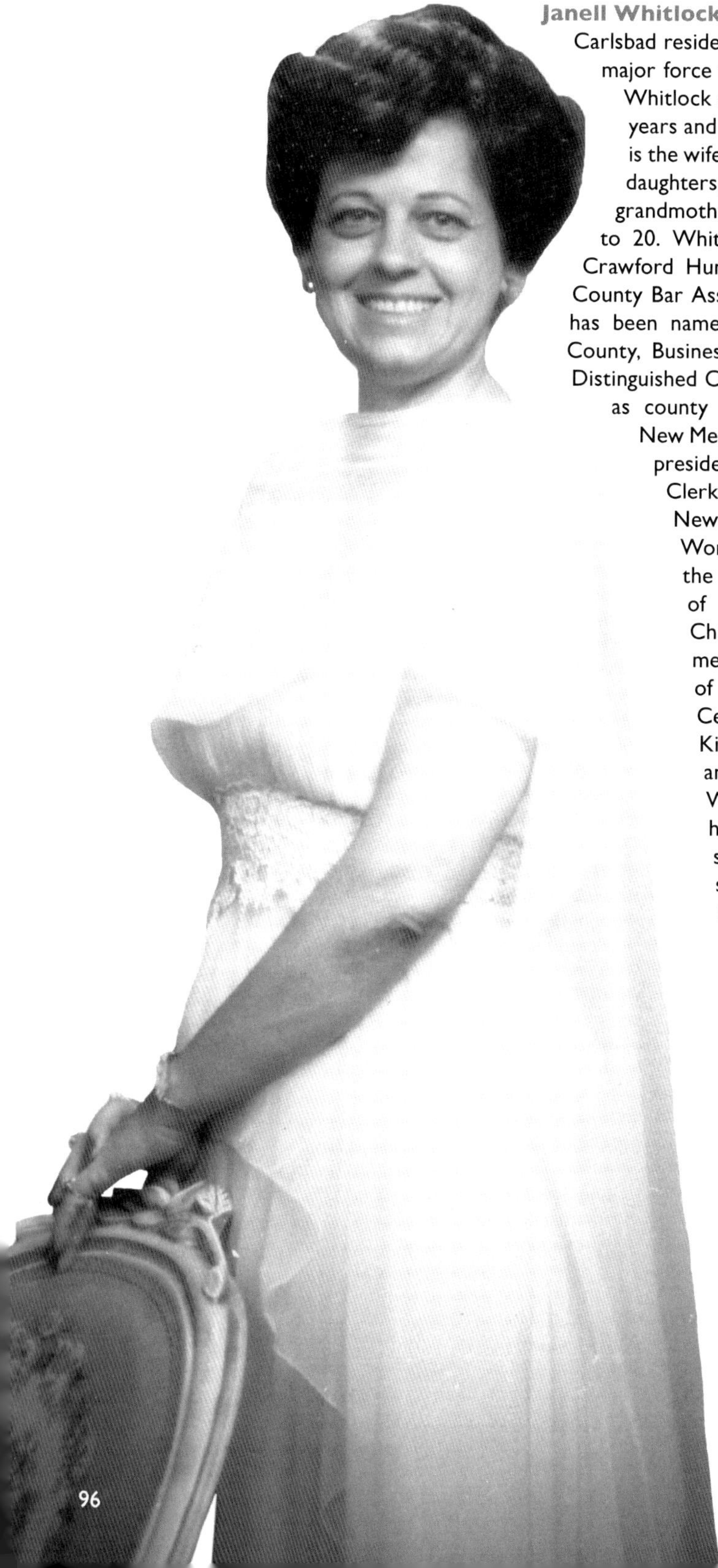

Janell Whitlock

Carlsbad resident since 1957, Janell Whitlock is a major force to be reckoned with in Carlsbad. Whitlock served as a municipal judge for 18 years and councilwoman for four years. She is the wife of a state senator, mother to two daughters, stepmother to three daughters, grandmother to 13, and great-grandmother to 20. Whitlock has received the 2014 A.J. Crawford Humanitarian Award, and the Eddy County Bar Association Liberty Bell Award. She has been named Outstanding Woman of Eddy County, Business Woman of the Year, and Elk's Distinguished Citizen of the Year. She has served as county commissioner, president of the New Mexico Municipal Judges Association, president of the New Mexico Court Clerks Association, president of the New Mexico Business and Professional Women's Organization, president of the Carlsbad Altrusa Club, director of retirement for the Carlsbad Chamber of Commerce, and as a member of the board of directors of Permian Basin Regional Training Center. Memberships include the Kiwanis, the Carlsbad Rotary Club, and the Mental Health Task Force. Whitlock sets the bar extremely high for everyone else and is a shining example of what public service is supposed to look. She is well known for her incredibly kind heart and classy demeanor and, on top of everything else, established homeless shelters in the community.

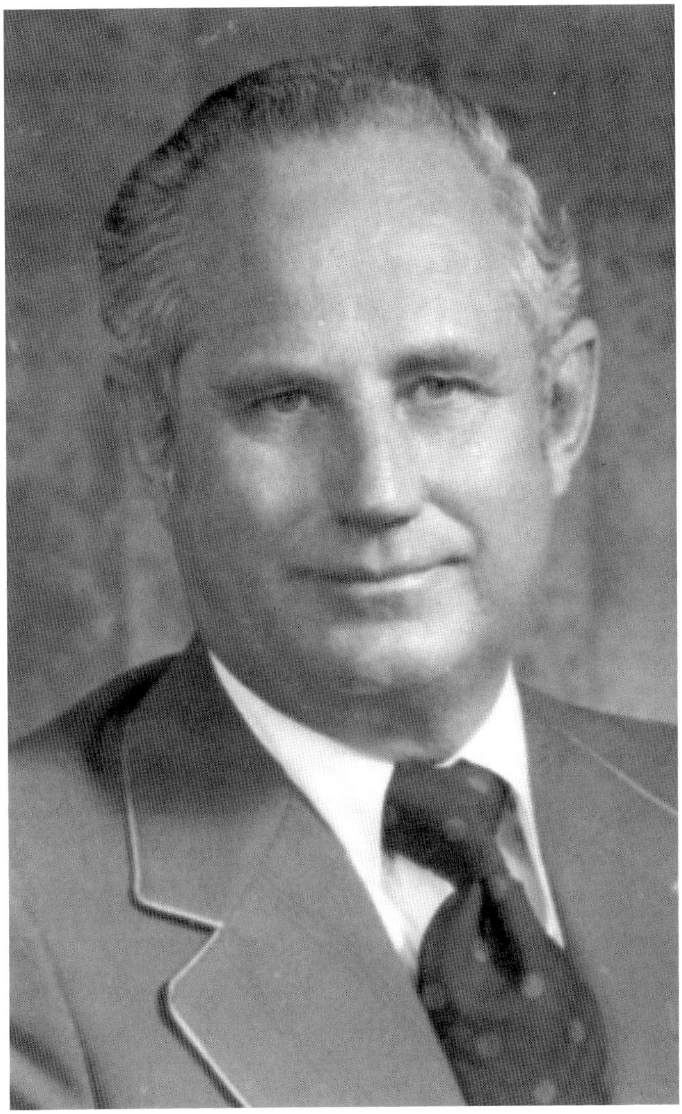

Louis Whitlock

As a young man, Louis M. Whitlock served in the US Army Air Corps in the South Pacific during World War II. Moving to Carlsbad to start work for the Federal Aeronautics Administration (FAA), Whitlock would immediately delve into local politics and become executive director of the Carlsbad Chamber of Commerce for a total of 21 years. He was also a state senator from 1989 to 1992. Whitlock was a member of the initial support of the Waste Isolation Pilot Plant (WIPP), a nuclear waste repository now located east of Carlsbad; he remained a stanch supporter of this project to see it to fruition. He continued his love for the environment by serving as New Mexico commissioner of the Pecos River Compact Commission, and funding promoter for the Living Desert Zoo and Gardens State Park and Brantley Dam project. Whitlock was also a wing commander of the New Mexico Civil Air Patrol, founding member of the New Mexico Amigos and chairman of the following: Radioactive and Hazardous Commission, Eddy County Democratic Party, State Democratic Finance, and State Highway Commission. Whitlock enjoyed water skiing, swimming, and gardening. He was married to Janell Whitlock, and the pair was known as Carlsbad's power couple.

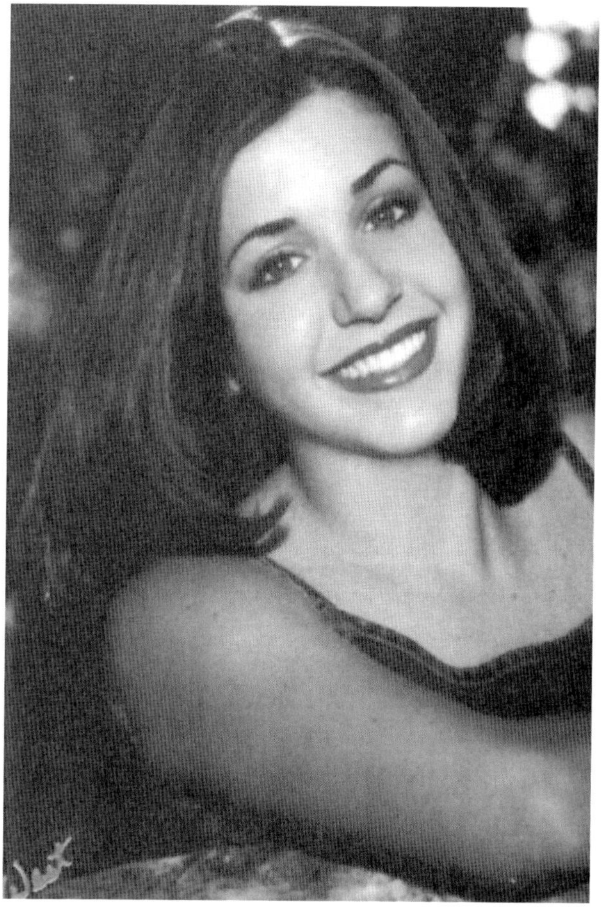

Kathryn "Katie" Sepich

Katie's Law would result from every parent's nightmare—the brutal death of their child. On the early morning hours of August 31, 2003, 22-year-old Kathryn "Katie" Sepich of Carlsbad walked a five-block route back to her home in Las Cruces, New Mexico, where she was attending college as a graduate student. Reaching the safety of her house, Sepich attempted to climb in a window, since she had forgotten her keys and did not want to awaken her roommate's mother. Unknown to Sepich, she had garnered the unwanted attention of a Mexican national, who had followed her home. Claiming he "lost it" when he saw the student struggle to get into her window, the 27-year-old man approached, strangled, and raped Sepich in her own yard. He placed Sepich in his truck, drove to an abandoned city dump, and doused her with alcohol in an attempt to burn her body. Sepich did not go without a fight; skin and blood DNA evidence was found under her fingernails. Frustrated with the inability to determine Sepich's killer from the evidence provided, parents Jayann and Dave Sepich, in shock and in unimaginable pain, worked tirelessly to pass a law known as the Katie Sepich Enhanced DNA Collection Act of 2010. The bill provided funding to implement minimum and enhanced DNA collection processes for felony arrests. In 2006, three years and three months after her murder, it was through DNA that Sepich's killer would finally be brought to justice. To save other families from having to face what they did, the Sepichs have traveled the United States, promoting the bill in every state in the nation; so far 28 have implemented the law. Jayann always speaks of one of the last conversations with her oldest daughter, in which Katie stated that she did not really know what she was going to do in her life, but she knew she was going to be famous and make a difference in the world. No truer words spoken. (Courtesy of the Sepich family.)

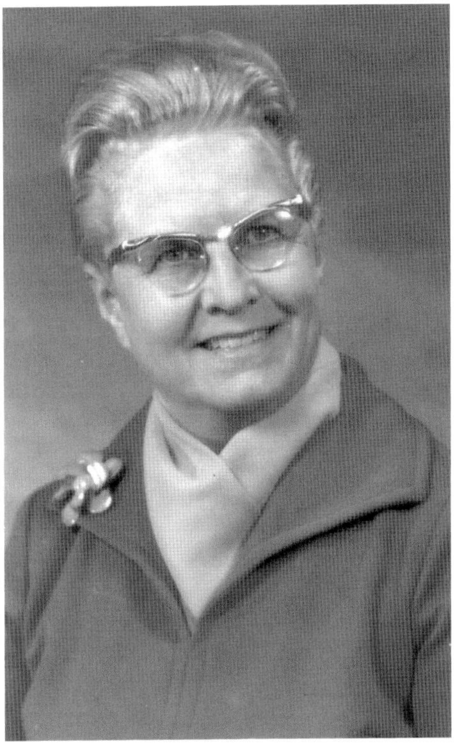

Helen Bond Melton

Helen Bond Melton looked like the quintessential librarian; she was petite, well groomed, stealthily quiet, and donned sensible shoes. Her career at the Carlsbad Public Library started in 1940 and spanned to even after her retirement in 1990. Melton dealt with many unpleasant circumstances during her career, ranging from library remodeling to staffing issues. She treated these with grace and poise but was tenacious when dealing with city officials who even remotely threatened the security of her library.

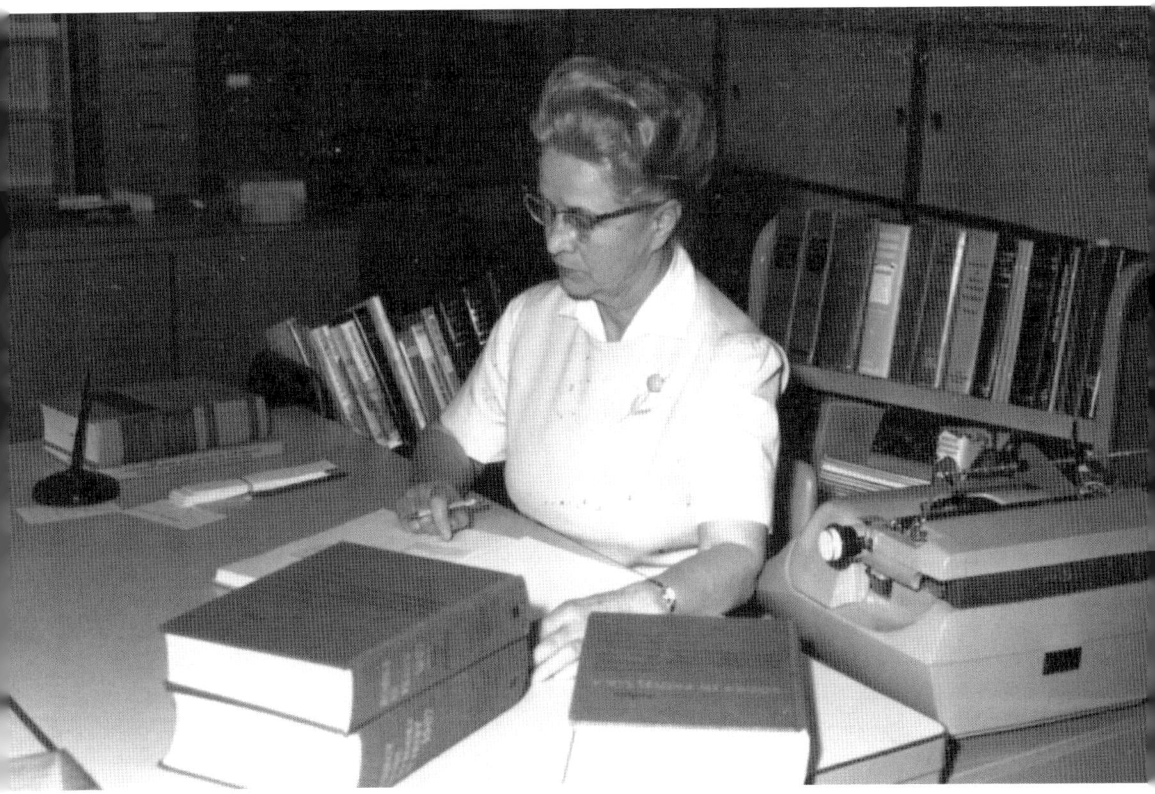

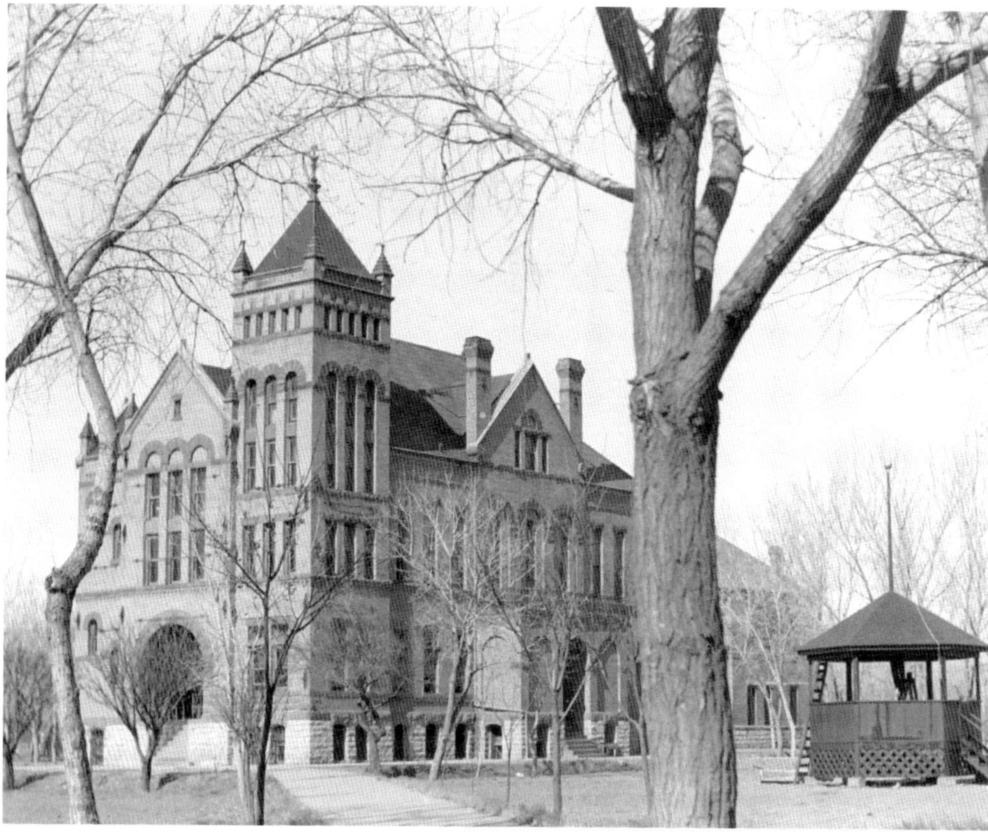

Eddy County Courthouse

Originally, the Eddy County Courthouse was a stately 1891 Victorian structure made from local bricks and located on a plot of land known as Block 3, which was deeded to the county by Charles B. Eddy. Over the years, the bricks were found to be unstable, and remodeling took place in 1938. A terrazzo floor covered the concrete, a 15-bed dormitory was built on the fourth floor to house court juries, and the current Pueblo Revival style architecture was adopted. In 1940, regional cattle brands were etched into the west-facing door frame to create a unique feature. Air-conditioning was not installed until 1953. When recently remodeled in 2002, a well was discovered under the parking lot and was displayed as a simulated river in the redesigned portico named Pioneer Plaza.

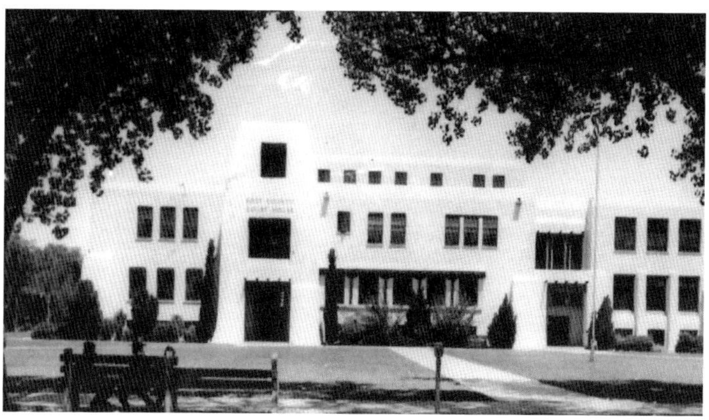

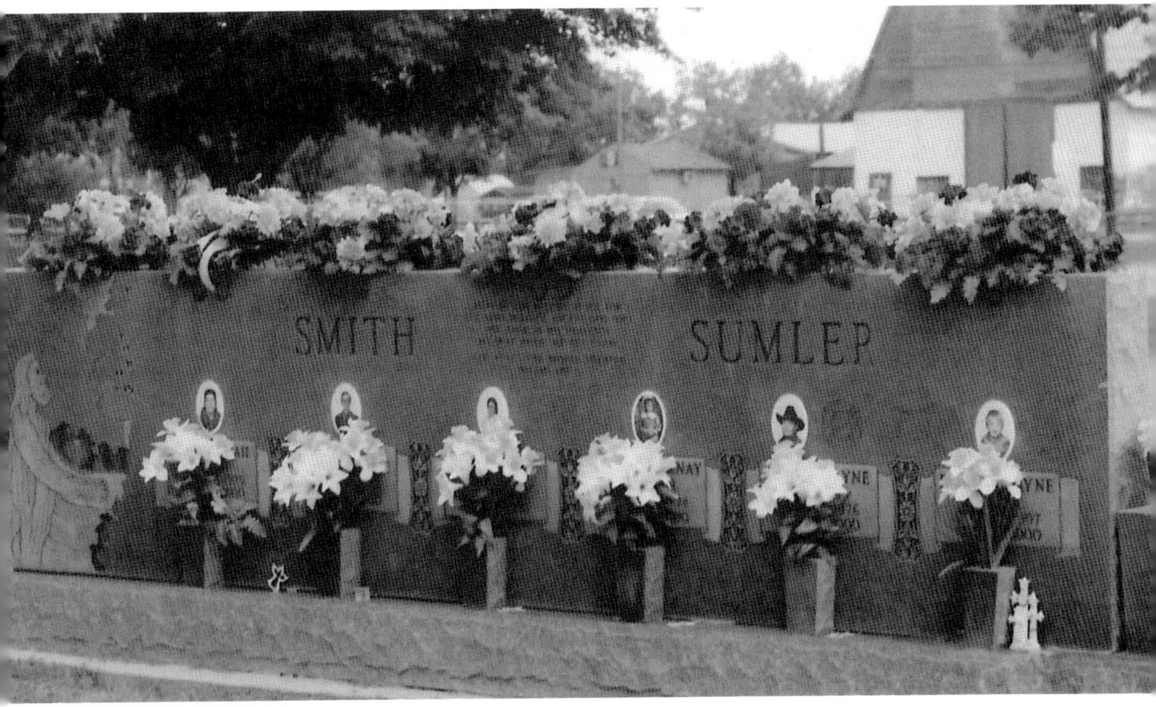

Martha Chapman

In the early morning hours of August 19, 2000, the worlds of the Heady, Smith, and Sumler families were rocked when the explosion of a 30-inch gas pipeline took the lives of 12 family members (six headstones are shown). Included in this tragedy were three small children and twin infants. First responders stated that the scene was the worst they had ever seen. Surviving family member, Martha Chapman (Nana), was awarded a large settlement from the El Paso Natural Gas Company; she put $10 million toward founding the Permian Basin Training Center, a firefighter training facility in Carlsbad that is used by all first responders to train for any scenarios. Chapman has been extremely generous to Carlsbad. Wanting to do something for the children, she founded Nana's Fire & Safety School, which shows children what to do in a fire to potentially save their lives. (Author's collection.)

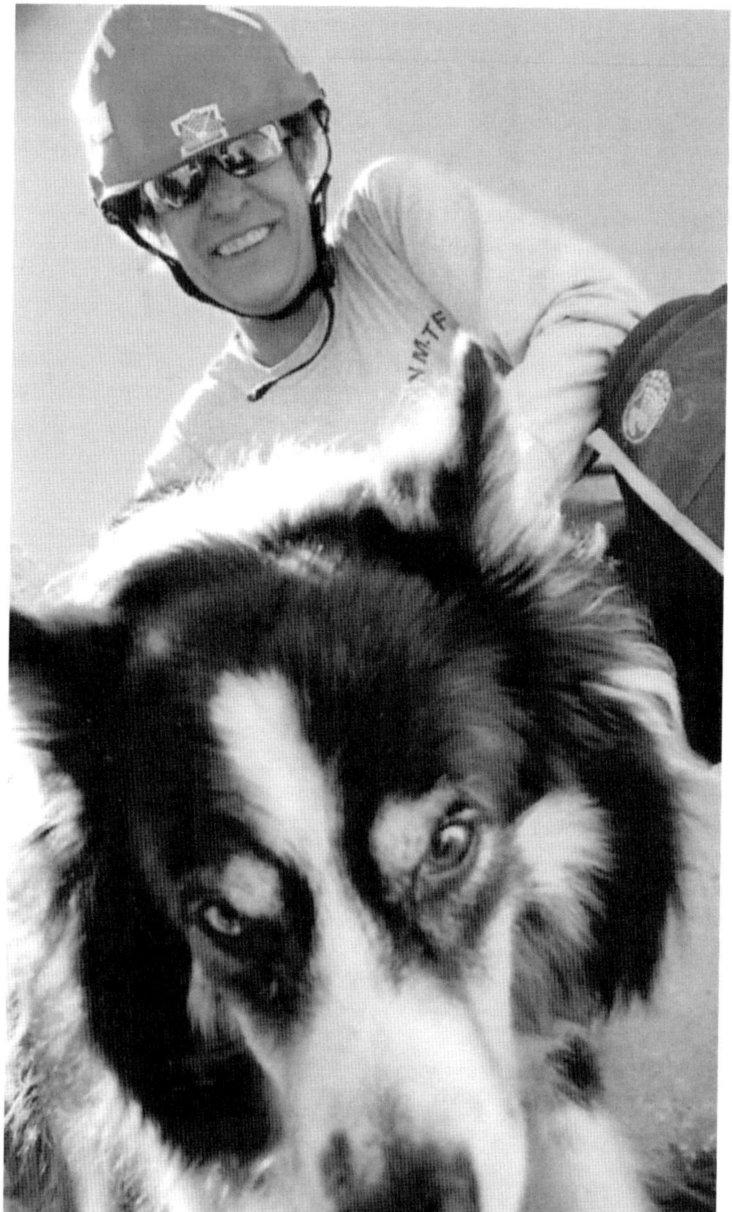

Kim Lark

The horrible events of 9/11 rocked the United States and changed our nation forever. Dr. Kim Lark was part of a FEMA team, utilizing canine search and rescue. Lark and her four-legged heroes were deployed to the Pentagon in a search capacity as well as a mental health role by providing a friendly stress relief to the rescue workers who faced the horrors of these events. Through Lark, the dogs, and her team, New Mexico played a part in efforts to provide closure to the families. Spearheading K-9 Search and Rescue, Lark and her dog Boot train at the 95-acre Permian Basin Training Center on two piles of rubble used in part as an agility course. "It is all about the dogs," says Lark. Her Border Collies are amazing to watch as they navigate the rubble. Lark loves what she does and is passionate about training. (Courtesy of Kim Lark.)

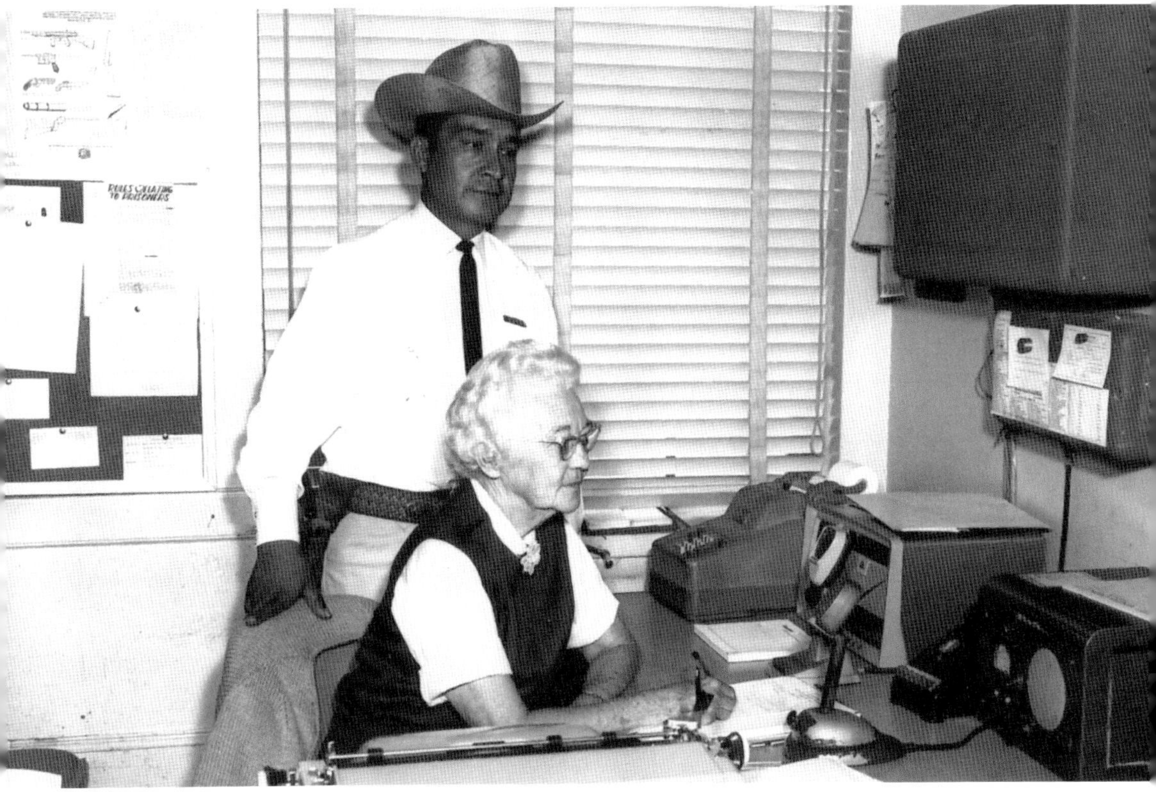

Ray Anaya
As an Eddy County sheriff and juvenile detention officer, Ray Anaya has seen the dark side of Carlsbad. Anaya built his life in the community by working at West Funeral Home for three years before enlisting in the Army. After his honorable discharge in 1958, Anaya was the first Hispanic to be elected sheriff in Eddy County in 1965; this was an honor he did not take lightly. Cofounder of Christmas Anonymous in 1963, Anaya collected new toys and clothes so that disadvantaged children would have a Christmas memory. The words written in his 2013 obituary said it best. *Ray loved people . . . all people. He treated people with dignity and respect. If you needed a hand, Ray was there to offer it. He sowed the seeds of his legacy in all the people he encountered with his compassion and love. It would be his greatest wish to see that legacy grow through all the good deeds of all those he has left behind.*

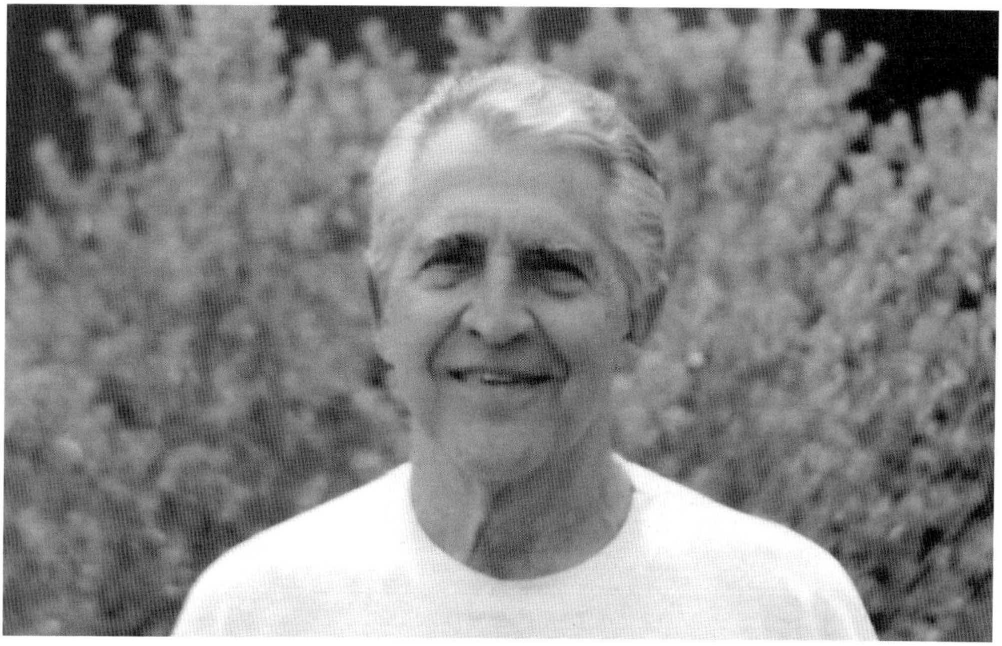

Joe Epstein

Since he could fit into many categories in this book, Joe Epstein is hard to pigeon hole into just one. Epstein came to Carlsbad as the general manager of Westinghouse for the Waste Isolation Pilot Plant and soon became a well-known public figure. As an activist for local veterans, Epstein has been instrumental in developing the Carlsbad Veterans Memorial Park at Lake Carlsbad. He sang as a second bass in the Carlsbad Community Chorale and was in the San Jose Choir. He also taught classes in tinwork at the Carlsbad branch of New Mexico State University and supported the Boys and Girls Club, Carlsbad Community Development, Mayor's Nuclear Task Force, and the Coalition Against Drugs. (Author's collection.)

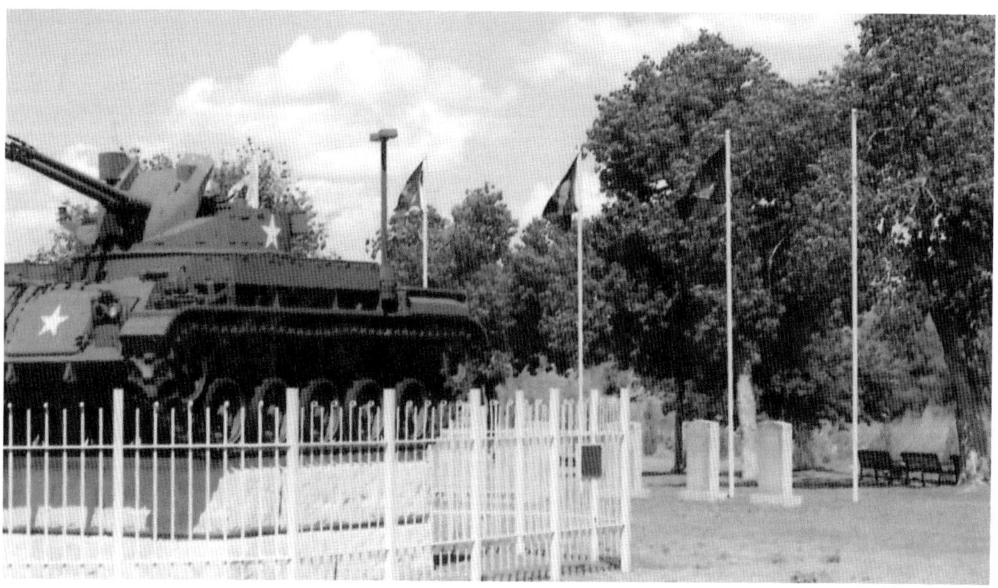

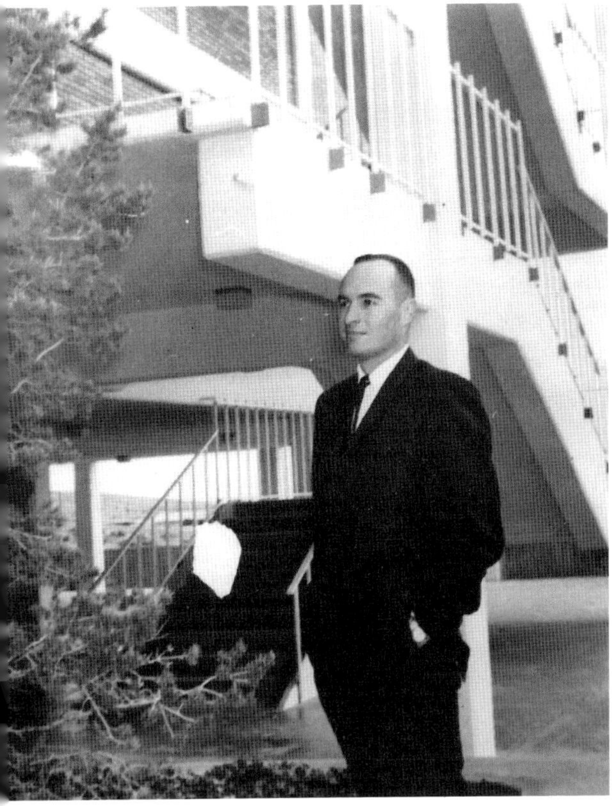

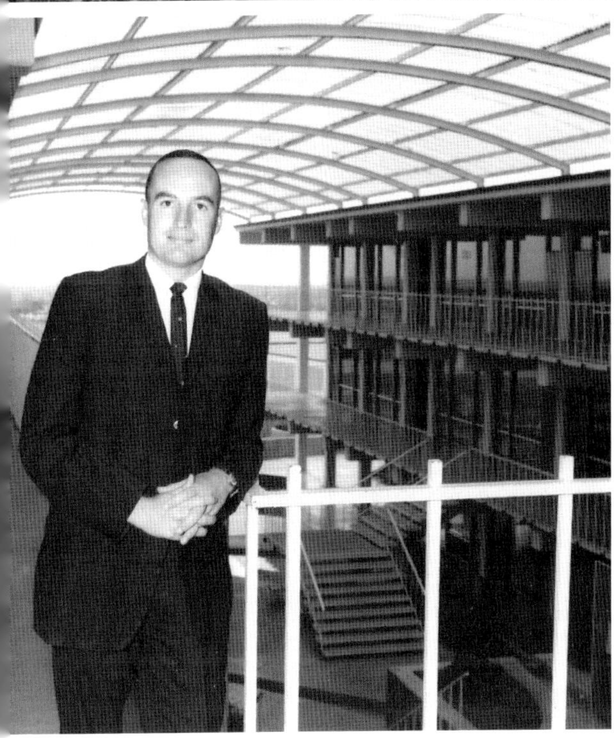

Jared "Jed" Howard

Jared "Jed" Howard is best known as a Problems of American Democracy (PAD) teacher at Carlsbad High School. His ingenious system, which involved card catalogs, magazines, and carbon paper was a vivid memory for his former students. While interning at a local photography studio, Howard became interested in the old images and wanted to preserve them for future generations. Howard continues to inspire by working tirelessly to save the photographic history of Carlsbad, serving as the archivist for over 400,000 items stored in the Southeastern New Mexico Historical Society's climate-controlled vault. It is through his phenomenal efforts that this book is possible. As the go-to person for historical facts, Howard is well respected and extremely knowledgeable. One of his greatest efforts is his website, which exposes the world to the images of Carlsbad.

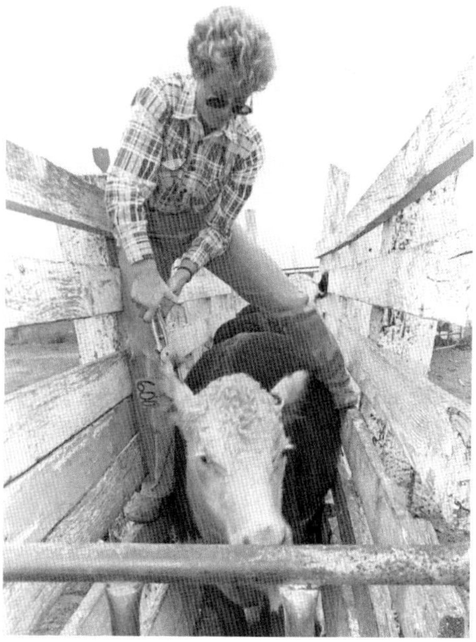

Alisa Ogden

Daughter of a local cattle rancher, Alisa Ogden is a strong advocate for the ranching industry and was named 2014 Cattleman of the Year by the New Mexico Cattle Growers Association. Ogden was described by her peers as "one-of-a-kind, knowledgeable, hard working and committed to the future of our [cattle] industry." Ogden was the first female president of the New Mexico Cattle Growers Association from 2010 to 2011, a position her grandfather held 50 years prior.

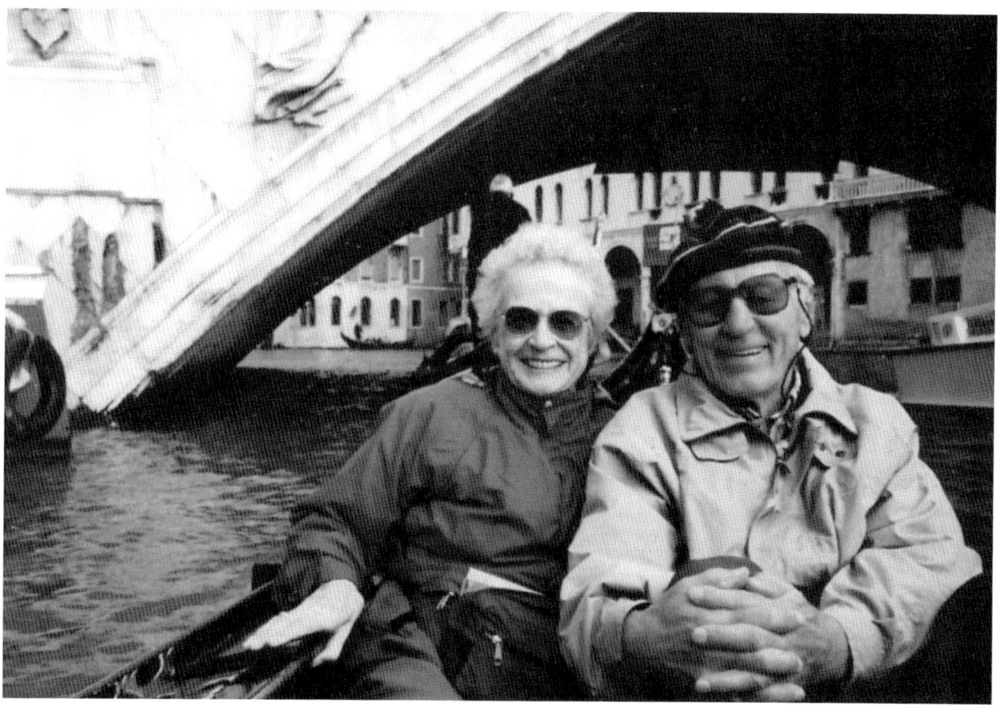

Barbara and Norman Meyer

Philanthropic couple Barbara and Norman Meyer were champions of many causes around Carlsbad, especially the Living Desert Zoo and Gardens State Park because of their love for science and the outdoors. Barbara had a master of science in zoology and worked as a teacher and librarian. Norman was one of the earliest Eagle Scouts and in the Navy during World War II. The pair volunteered at numerous organizations.

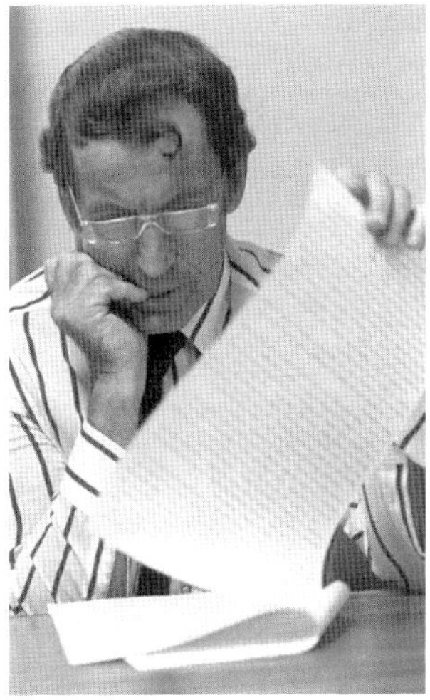

Robert Light

On the list as one of New Mexico's richest men, oilman Robert Light has known great joy and tragedy in his life. Light provided the land for some of Carlsbad's most prominent landmarks, such as the Living Desert Zoo and Gardens State Park and the campus of New Mexico State University. Light was a House Representative for the 55th District and an Eddy County commissioner in his illustrious career.

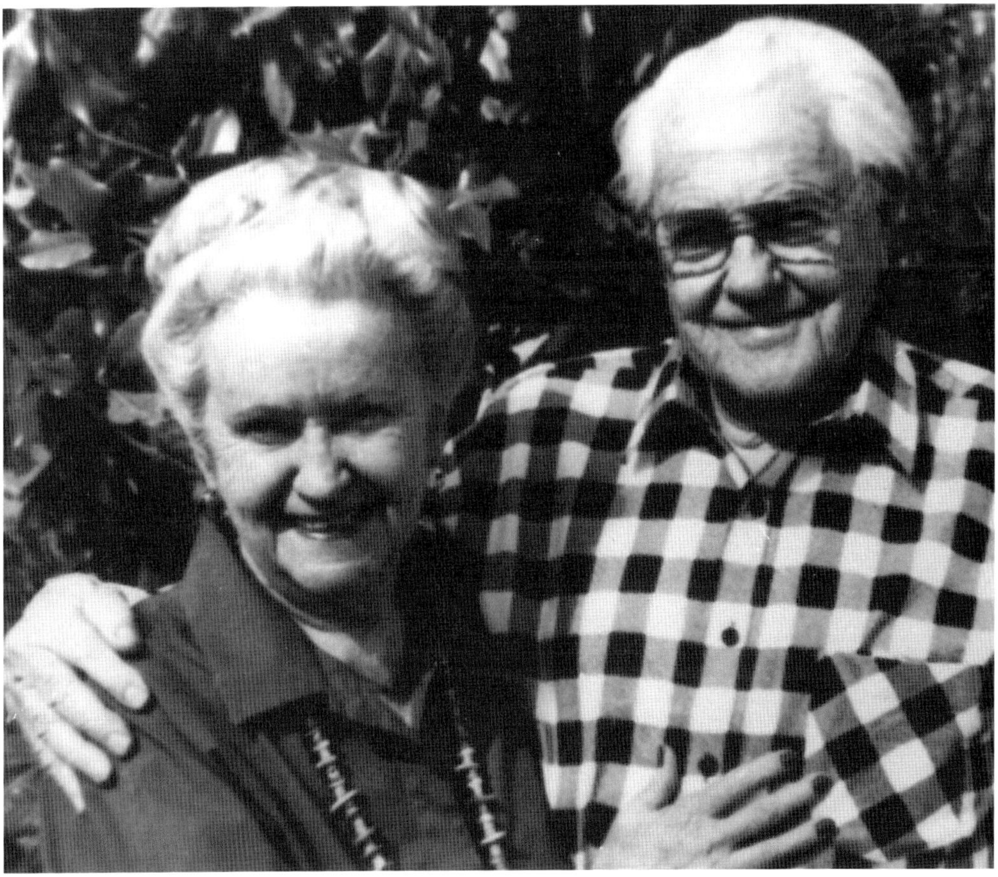

William "Bill" McAdoo

Avid collectors of the founding works of the Taos Society of Artists, pharmacist William McAdoo and his wife, Christine, amassed some of the best representations of famed Taos Ten artists, such as Joseph Henry Sharp and W. Herbert Dunton, in the state of New Mexico. This collection is now proudly housed at the Carlsbad Museum and Art Center in the McAdoo Room.

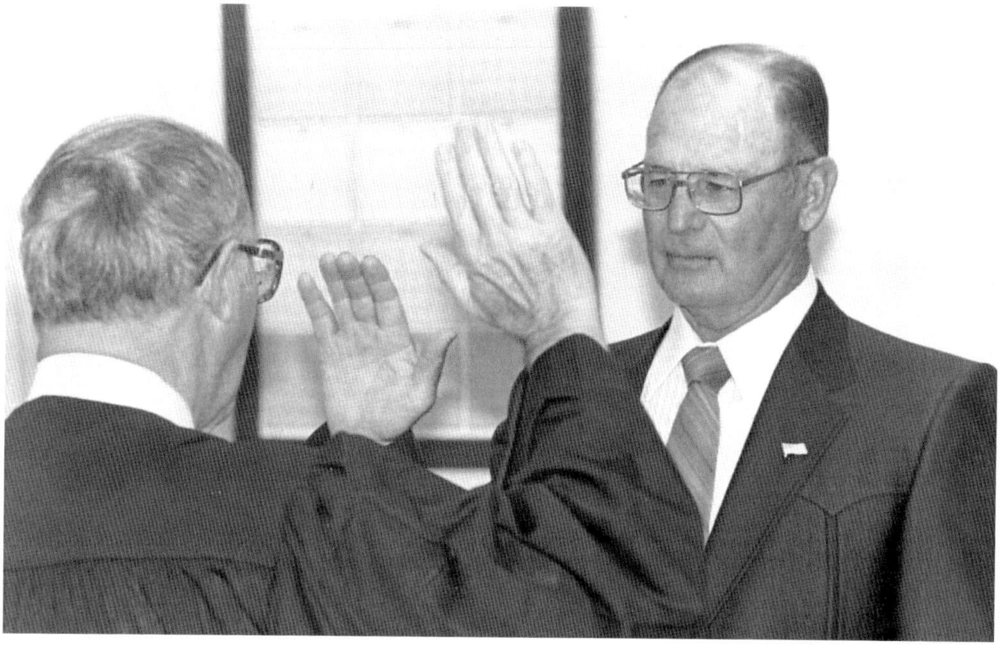

Joe Stell

As a former coach, teacher, principal and politician (20-year state representative) and current rancher, Joe Stell has served his community in many capacities. Stell is now hard at work on his newest endeavor—the preservation of history. As a native of the Carlsbad area, Stell has firsthand knowledge of this history.

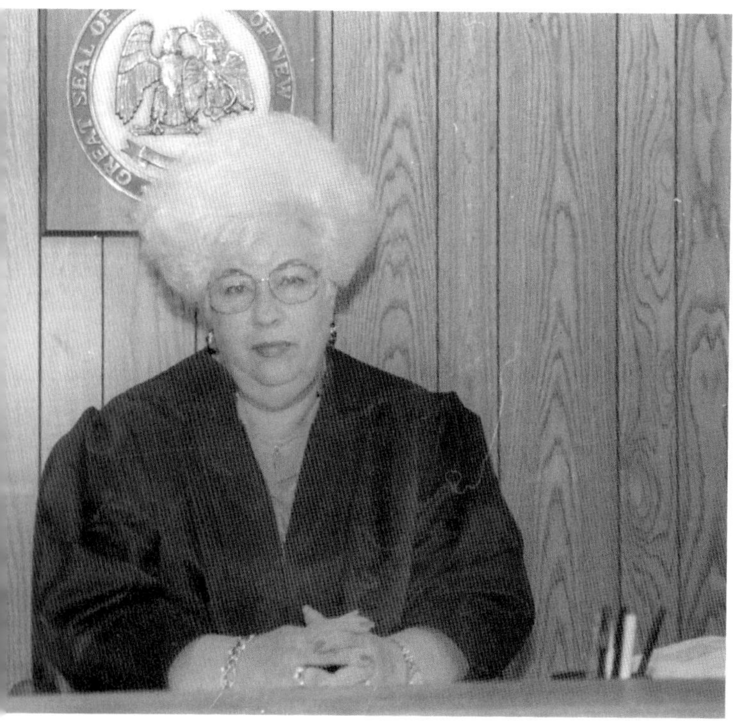

Nancy Beard

After 11 years on the bench from 1983 to 1994, Judge Nancy Beard decided to retire. Beard was known for her fair administration of justice as well as her quick wit and humor, in and out of the courtroom. Beard can trace her Carlsbad heritage back to an 1898 founding family.

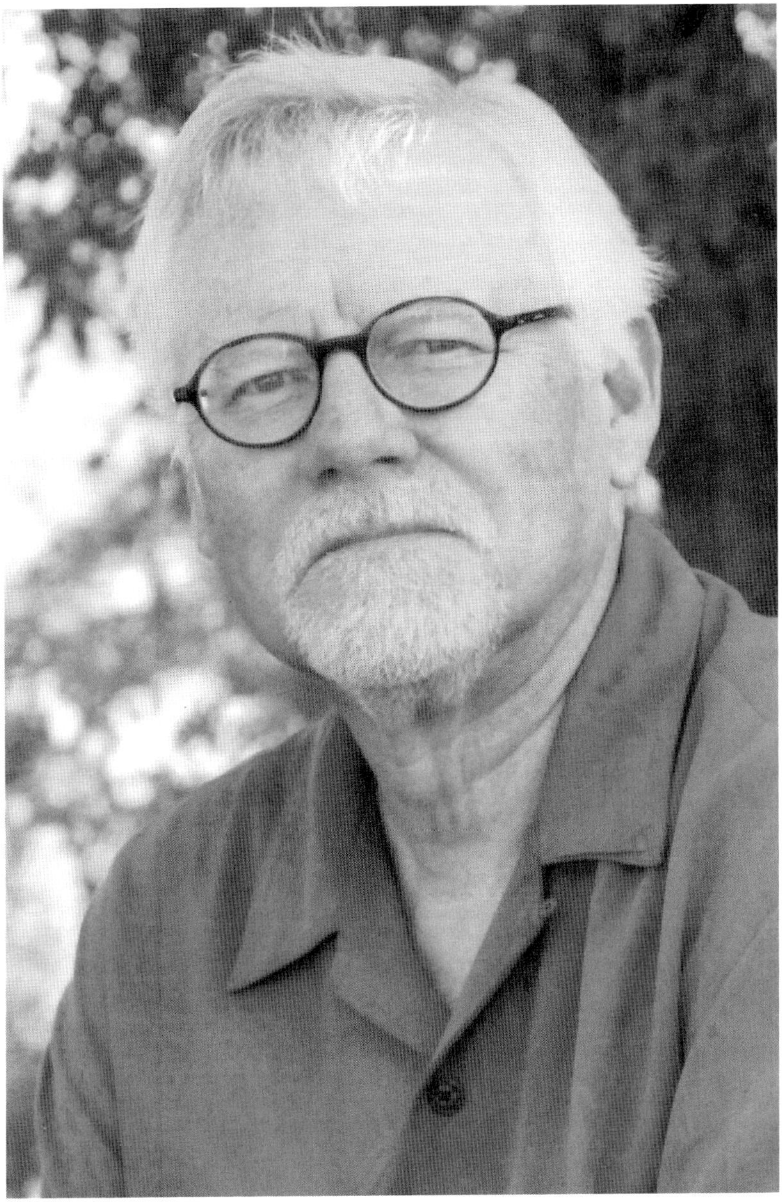

Dwight Pitcaithley

Dwight Townsend Pitcaithley served as chief historian of the National Park Service from 1995 until 2005. A Carlsbad native, he began his 30-year career with the National Park Service at Carlsbad Caverns National Park in 1963. After three years in the US Marine Corps—including six months in Vietnam where he was wounded in 1966—Pitcaithley received a PhD in history from Texas Tech University. As chief historian, he promoted high-quality interpretive programs based on current and evolving historical scholarship. Since 2005, Pitcaithley has taught history at New Mexico State University. He was elected a member of the American Antiquarian Society in 2012, awarded an honorary doctor of laws degree from the University of North Carolina in 2011, and presented the Organization of American Historians Distinguished Service Award in 2005. He married Sabette Stephens in 1968 and has one daughter. (Courtesy of Catherine Pitcaithley.)

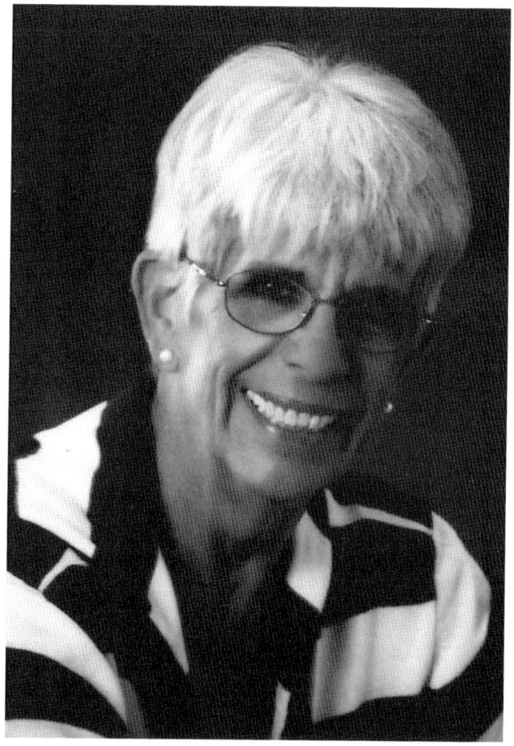

Carolyn Olson

Carolyn Olson came to Carlsbad in 1963 to be a water safety instructor and trainer for the Red Cross. She helped to create an adaptive swimming program for the developmentally disabled. Olson is the local program director and area four coordinator for the Special Olympics New Mexico. Olson serves on multiple boards and received the American Health Care Association National Center for Assisted Living's Hero of the Year award in 2012. (Courtesy of Carolyn Olson.)

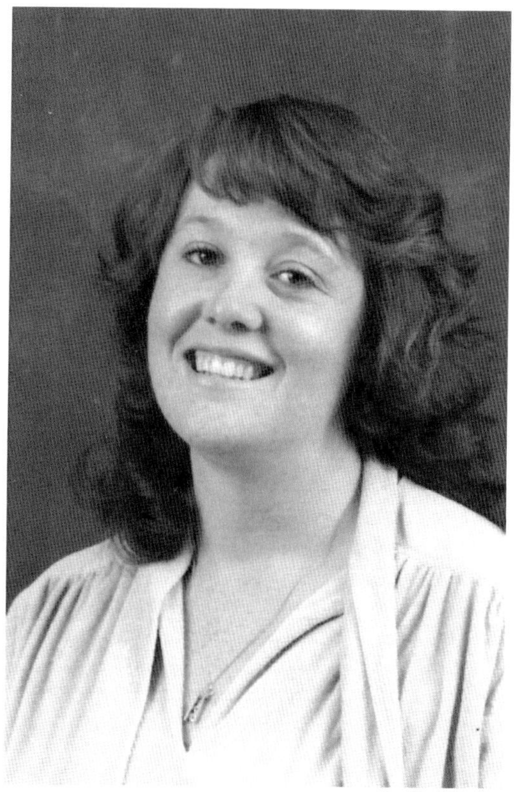

Carye Lou Angell

Carye Lou Angell remembers all the students who attended her middle school science class. Her students will most likely tell you that Ms. Angell's class was the best class they had in school. Known for her hands-on labs, Angell would encourage the class to explore and be curious, all the while learning the main point of the lesson. Angell has an infectious positive attitude and an ever-present beaming smile. (Courtesy of Carye Lou Angell.)

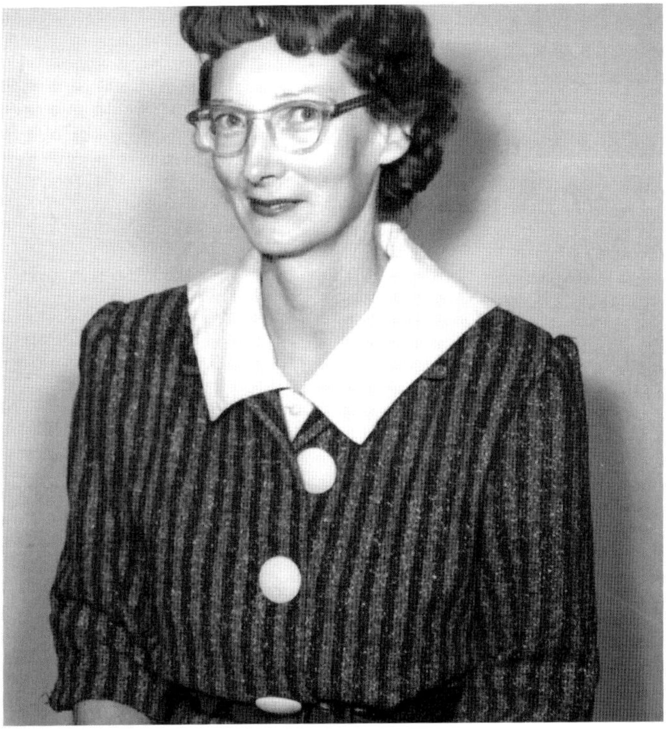

Frances Feezer
As an avid support of the arts, Frances Feezer dedicated much of her life to bringing culture to Carlsbad through her donations of Glenna Goodacre sculptures, which grace the front yard of the Carlsbad Museum and Art Center. In 2003, Gov. Bill Richardson honored Feezer with the Governor's Art Award for her patronage of the Carlsbad Museum and Art Center. This is New Mexico's most prestigious artistic honor.

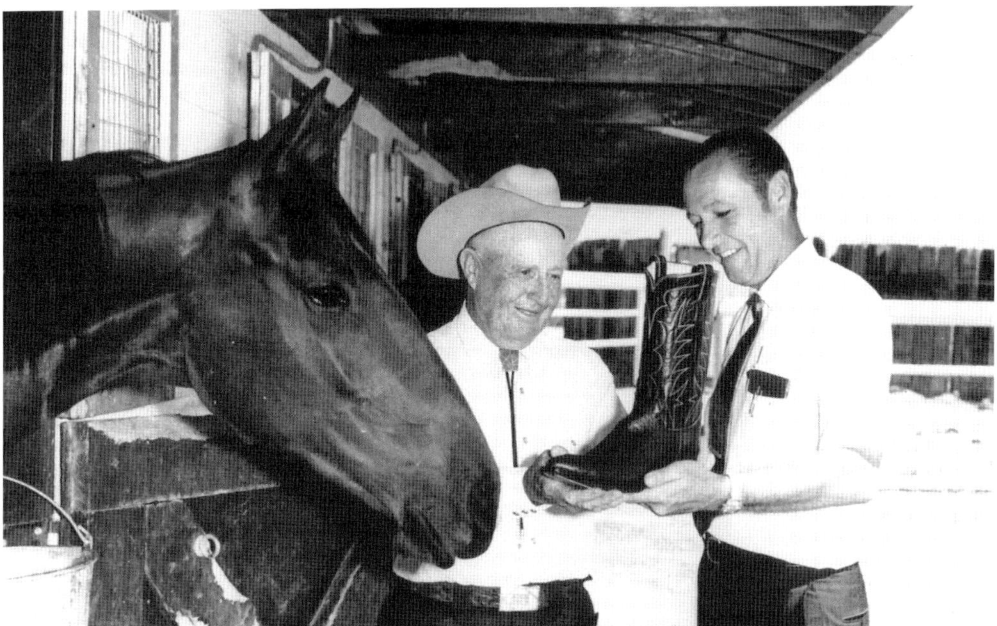

Walter Gerrells
Before his death in 1994, Walter Gerrells had served four terms, for a total of 22 years, as mayor of Carlsbad. Gerrells is touted as a frugal leader, credited with making Carlsbad financially strong. Gerrells was instrumental in bringing the Waste Isolation Pilot Plant and Brantley Dam into existence, creating hundreds of much-needed jobs for residents and turning the town into a city.

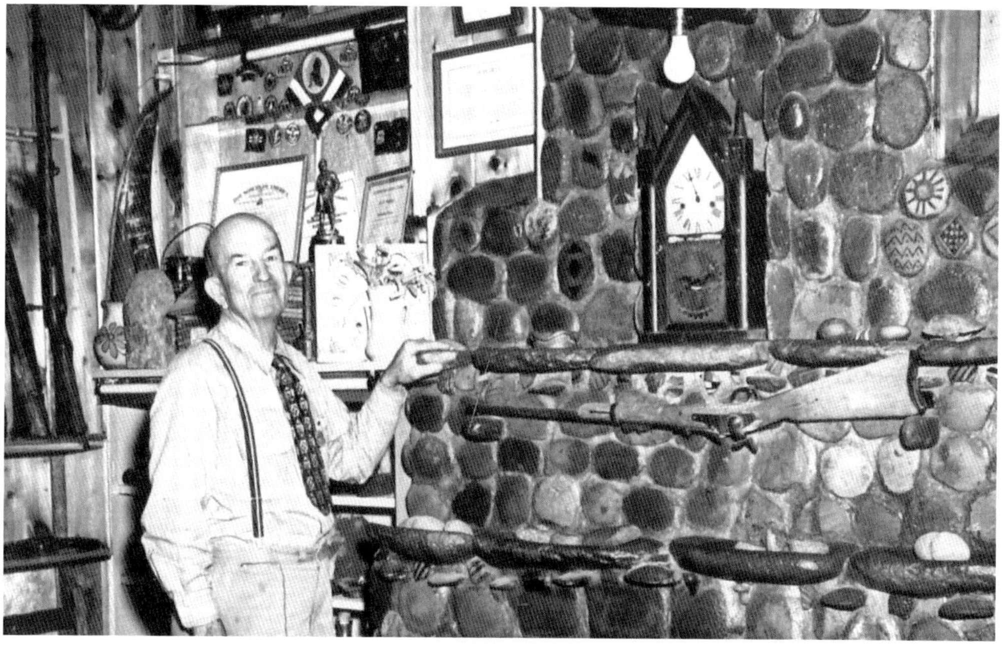

Ira Stockwell

Remembered as Carlsbad's first full-time paid fire chief (serving under 15 different mayors), Ira Stockwell was a well-loved character in town. One of his many talents included gavel making, which had local officials clamoring for the honor of being presented with one of the hand-turned masterpieces. Stockwell worked with schools and brought along his four-legged sidekick, Sparky the Fire Dog, to teach the children the importance of fire prevention. An avid collector of historical items, Stockwell gave tours of his home for civic groups. After Stockwell's death in 1975, his son, Bob, donated much of his collection to the Carlsbad Museum and Art Center for all to enjoy. These items are still on display. Stockwell came to Carlsbad from Kansas with his father on a land excursion and his family was to open the first service station in Carlsbad.

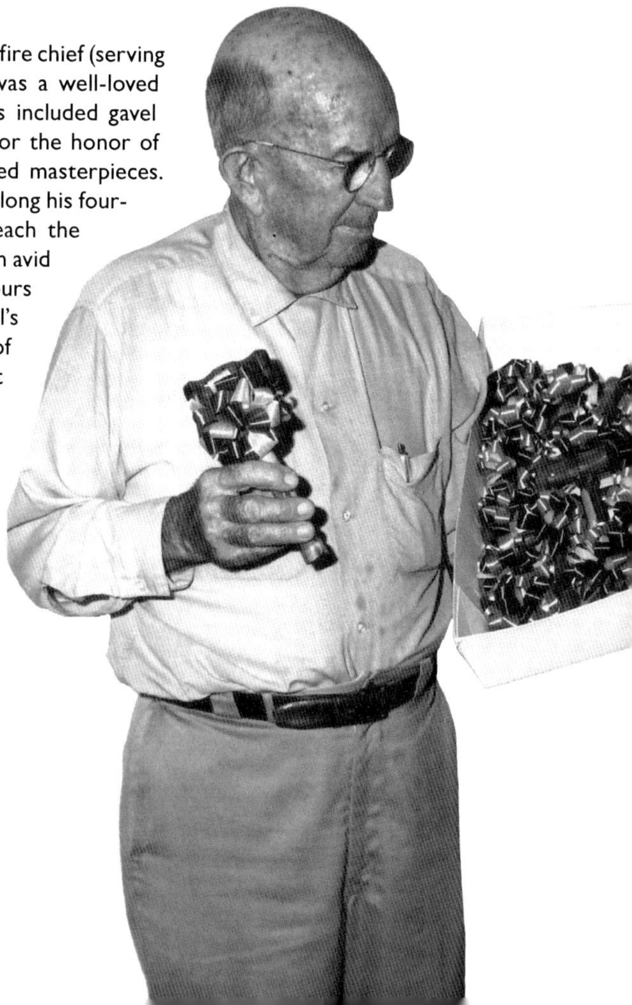

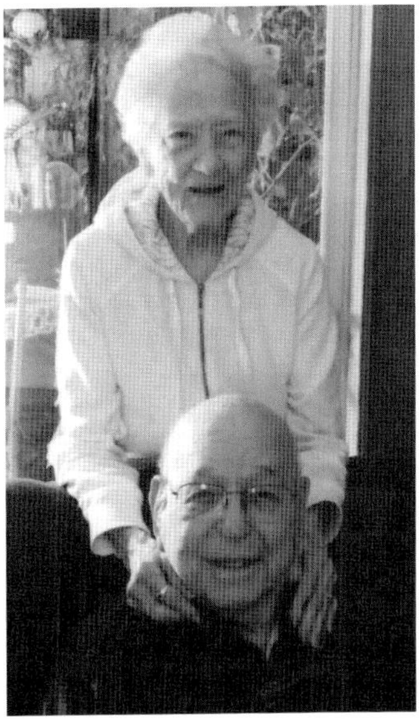

Harvey Hicks

While working in the lab at International Minerals and Chemical Corporation (IMCC), a local potash mine, Harvey Hicks developed a great love for local history and began amassing knowledge of the local native tribes who roamed the area. His weekends were spent combing the countryside for camps. It is probably safe to say that Hicks knew where every settlement was located around Carlsbad. (Courtesy of Valerie Cranston.)

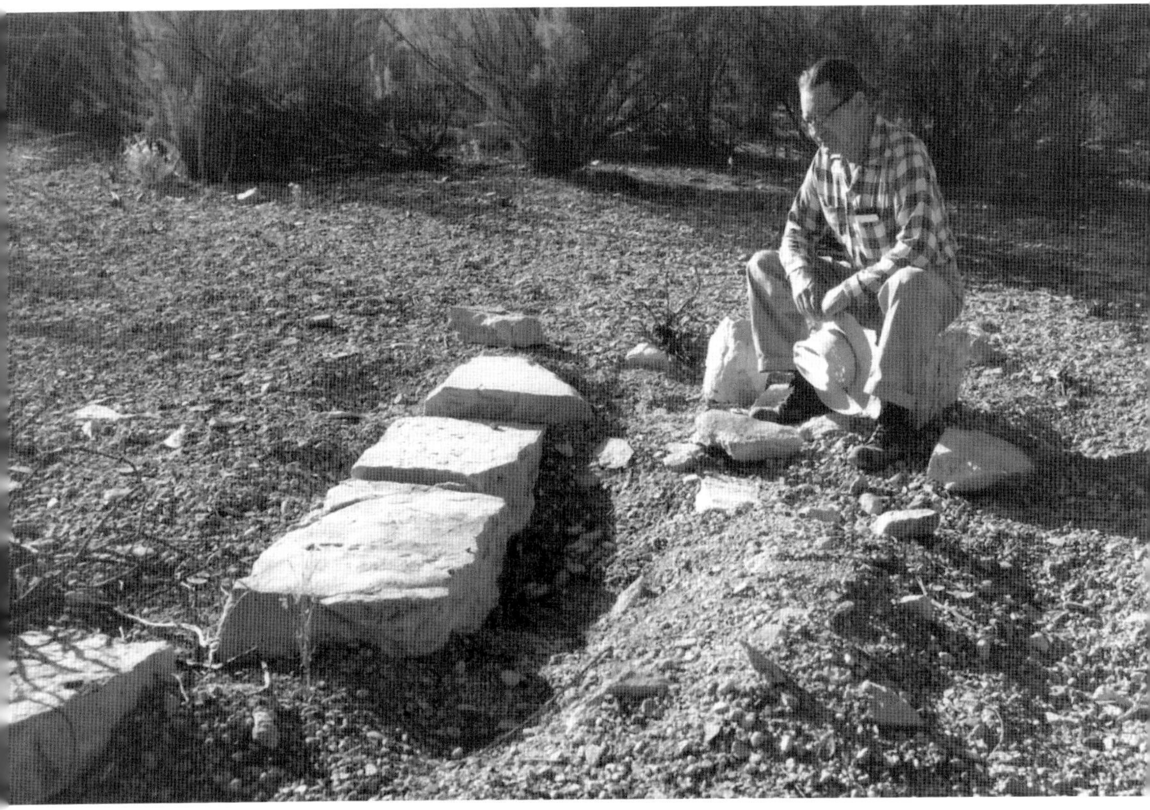

Lee Myers

As the author of *Pearl of the Pecos* and more than 100 articles and booklets, Lee Myers introduced the world to the history of the Pecos Valley. Born in Chanute, Kansas, Myers came to Carlsbad to work as a machinist at a local potash mine. Myers is responsible for collecting oral histories of old-timers. Without his work, this history would have been lost.

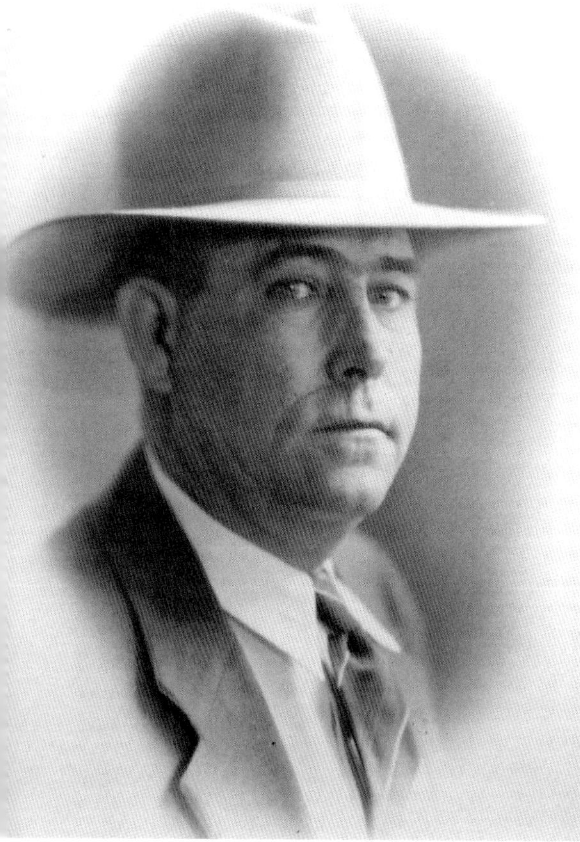

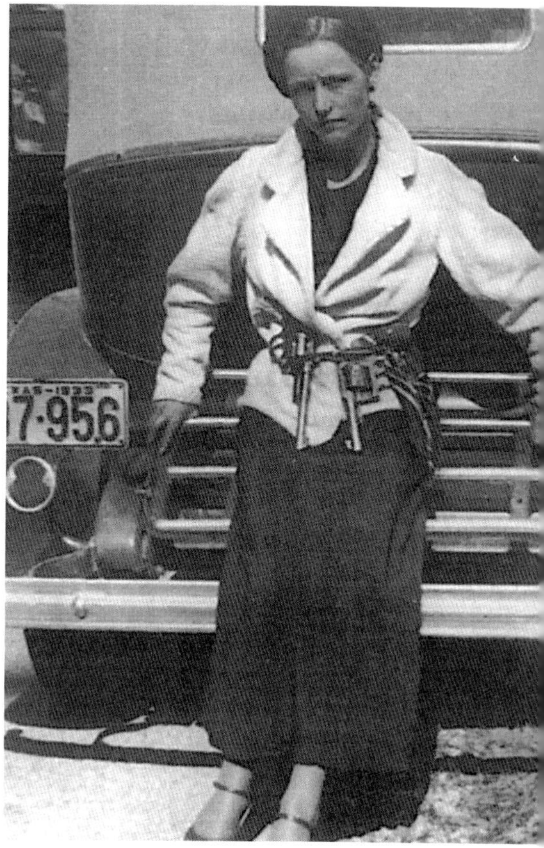

Joe Johns

In 1932, Eddy County deputy sheriff Joe Johns survived a kidnapping by the infamous duo Bonnie and Clyde. Bonnie Parker's aunt, Elise M. Stamp, lived in Carlsbad and was visited by her famous niece but not without being noticed by Johns and reported by Stamps. The duo had stopped for a four-day "cooling off." Further investigation from Johns resulted in him being abducted by the pair, taken to San Antonio, and eventually released. Contrary to rumors, Johns survived to tell the tale.

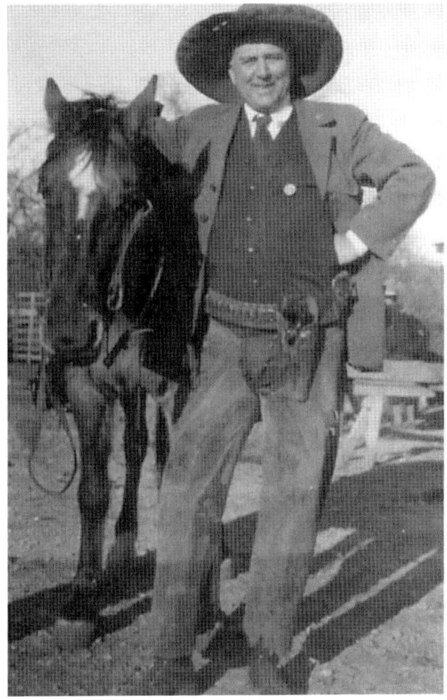

Tom Boles

Tom Boles was the first official superintendent at the Carlsbad Cave, which would later become the Carlsbad Caverns National Park. Boles met many celebrities, such as Amelia Earhart, Will Rogers, and Walt Disney, who came to Carlsbad to see the cave for themselves.

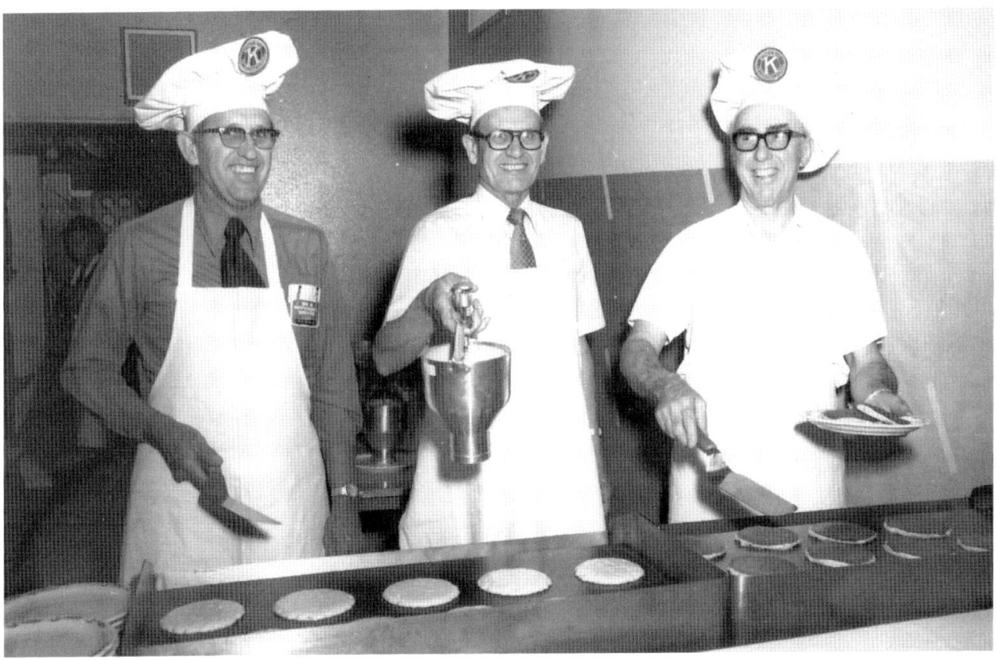

Perry Denton

Like others in this book, Perry Denton could fit into many categories. Known as a Carlsbad mortician, Denton was a pioneer in funeral home services like grief counseling and educational programs on death's processes. Denton also enjoyed photography of wild caves and worked heavily with local civic organizations like the Kiwanis Club, the Carlsbad Chamber of Commerce, and the Odd Fellows Lodge. He was a vital member of the Desert Res-Q Squad.

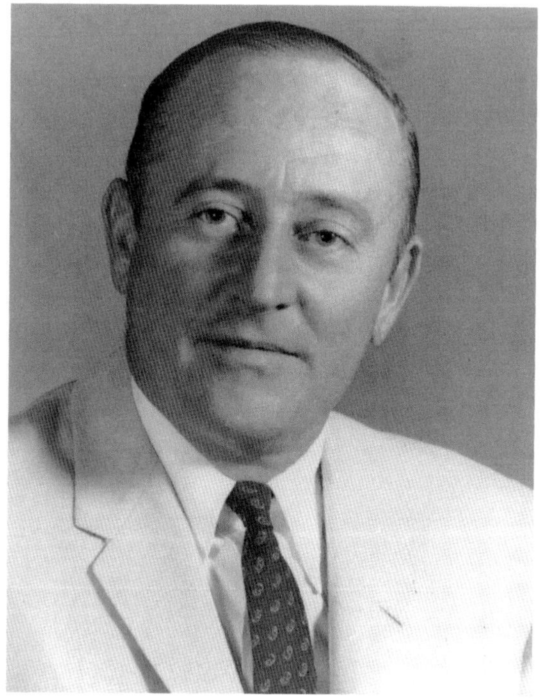

Houston Clark

Carlsbad native Houston Clark became the senior vice president of the Potash Company of America (PCA) after receiving his bachelor of science in chemical engineering at Rice University. Clark also served in the US Navy. He was highly active in Carlsbad as an outspoken city councilor, supporter of the Carlsbad Public Library, and member of the Downtown Lions Club and the New Mexico Mining Association.

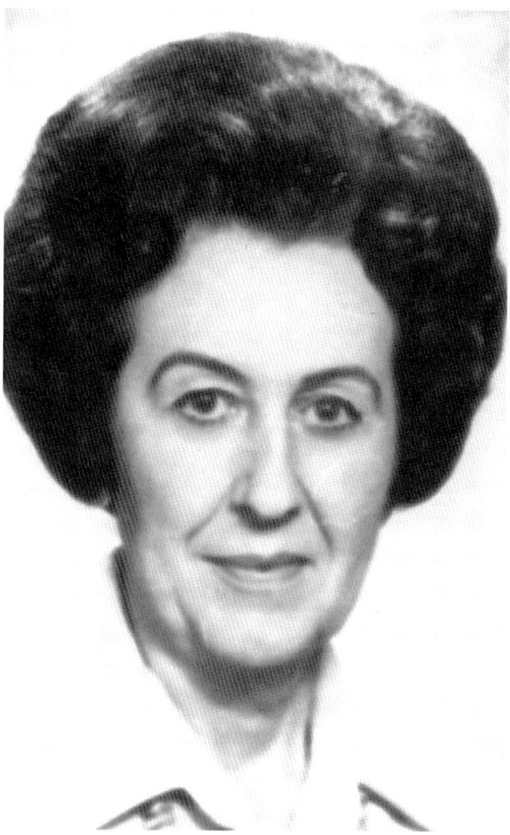

Sarah Jackson

To say Sarah Jackson was active in the community would be a huge understatement. The wife of druggist, Robert Jackson, Sarah was a member of nearly every club and organization in town. A longtime supporter and board member of the Carlsbad Public Library, Sarah served as president for many years and reigned with an iron hand and a smile. She would not stop until her dream was realized.

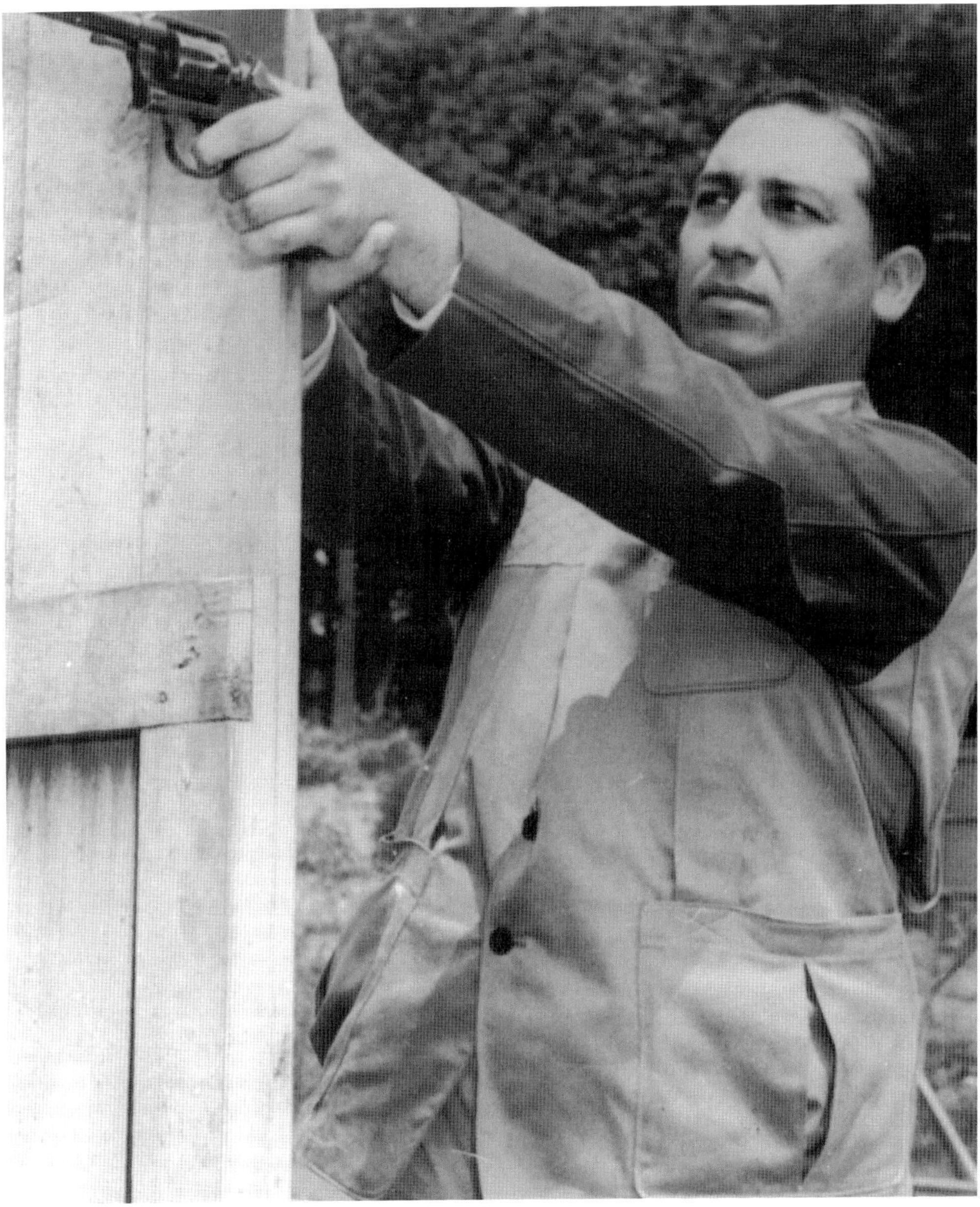

Cruz Zuniga Fernandez

Cruz Fernandez became the first Hispanic American to graduate high school in 1932. Known for his athletic abilities, Fernandez was often dubbed the best player on the team. While attending the University of New Mexico, he participated in the football, basketball, and track programs. He became the first Hispanic American elected Eddy County sheriff, a position he held for 10 years. Fernandez worked for the New Mexico State Penitentiary in Santa Fe, was a staff member of Sen. Dennis Chaves, and was an honorary member of the attorney general's staff. He was working at the State Motor Vehicle Department at the time of his death in 1965. Graduating the FBI Academy with honors in 1949, Fernandez was considered an outstanding law enforcement officer, humanitarian, and political leader in the Hispanic community—one who worked for the underdog.

Dr. Catherine Armstrong

Carlsbad's first pediatrician, Dr. Catherine Armstrong, was a strong advocate for children. Known not to mince words, the doctor laid everything out on the table—the good and bad. Armstrong's methods earned great respect from her colleagues and patients alike. Not one to follow conformity, Armstrong moved to Carlsbad with her son after her husband, who disapproved of her profession, went off to World War II.

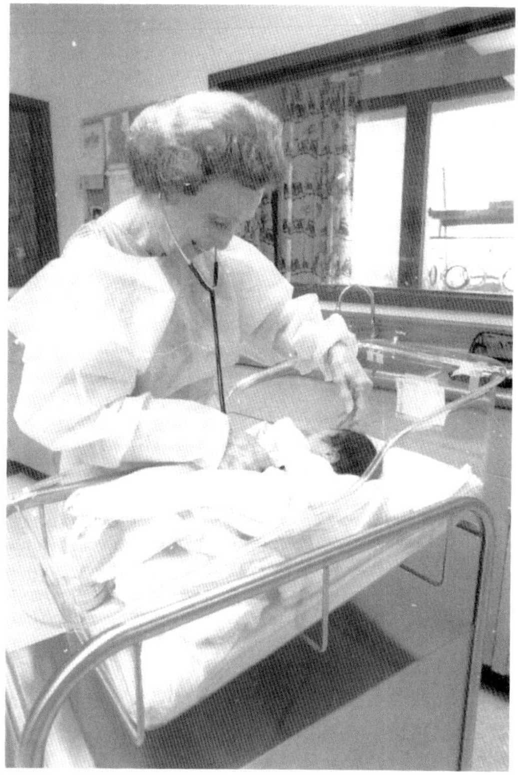

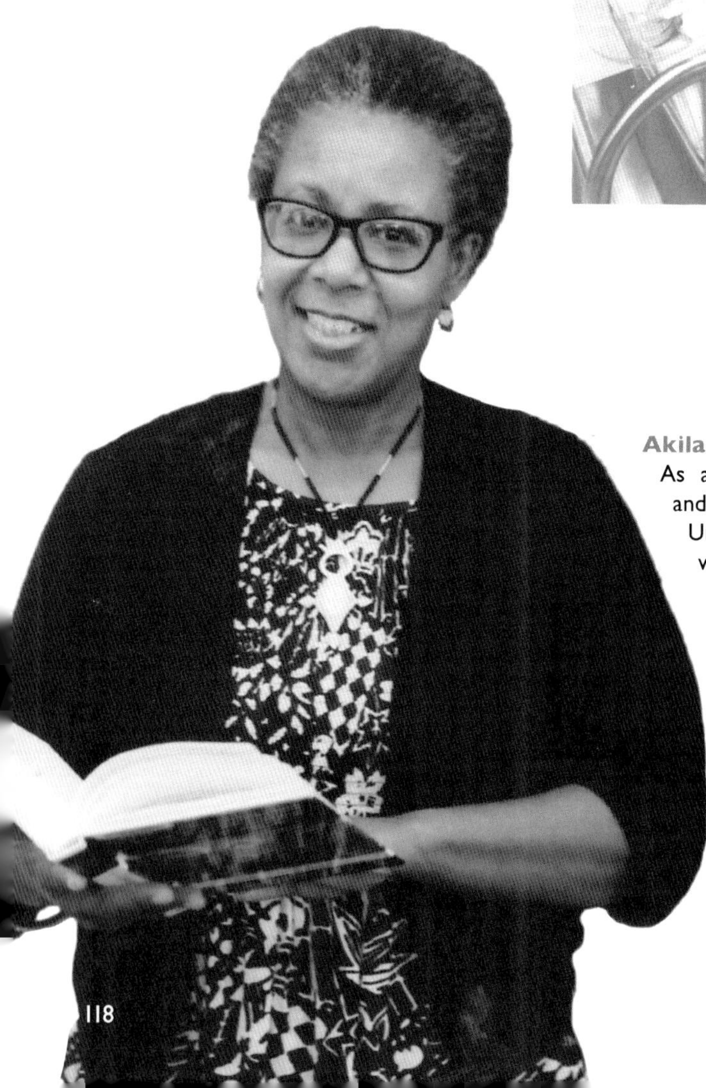

Akilah Shukura Nosakhere

As an author and the library director and professor for New Mexico State University–Carlsbad, Akilah Nosakhere, works hard to bring awareness of the African American community to Carlsbad. Nosakhere highlights African American culture, especially in libraries, through special conferences, and via her own books. (Author's collection.)

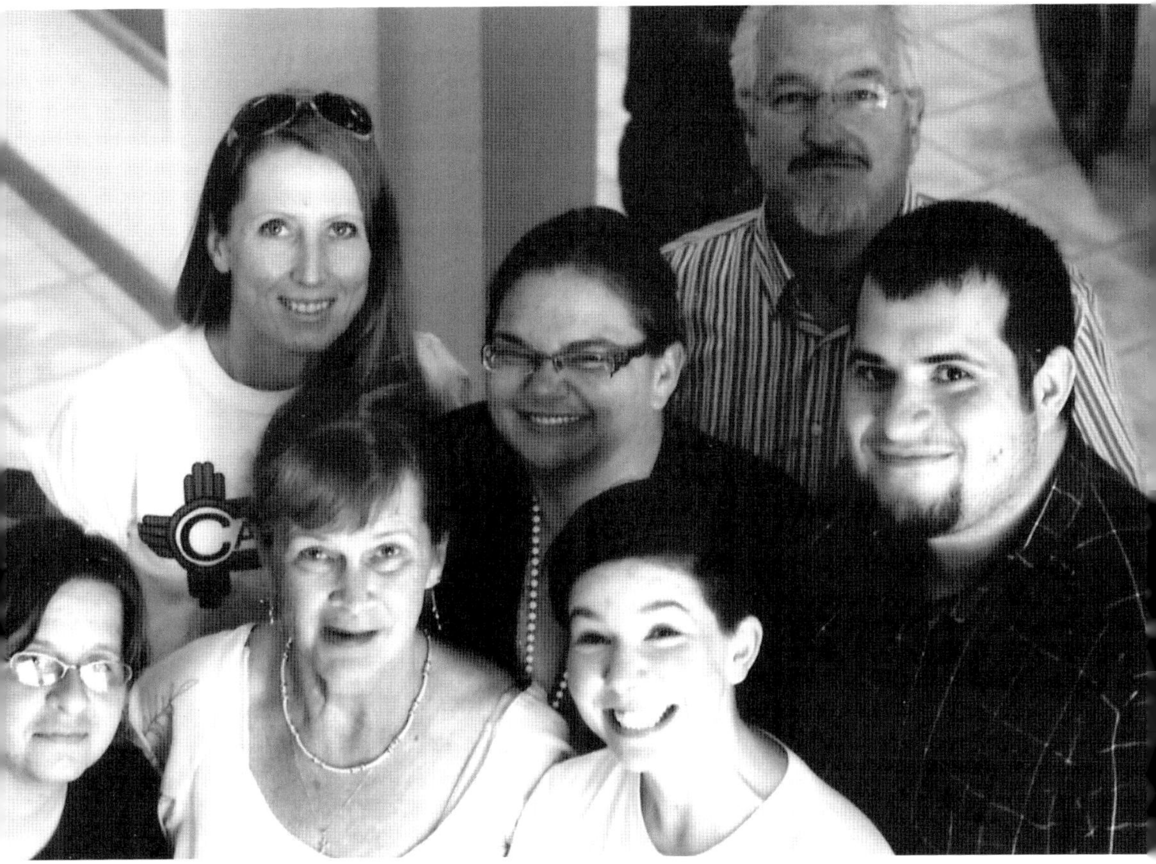

Carlsbad Museum and Art Center

Built in 1931, the Carlsbad Museum and Art Center is the oldest municipal museum in the state of New Mexico. With six permanent exhibits, ranging from a collection of Native American ceramics to a gallery featuring the paintings of the Taos Ten, the museum is a feast for the senses and a highly qualified staff adds to the ambiance. Shown in the image are, left to right: Crystal Mahaffy, Zuzanna Cartwright, Michele Robertson, Dave Morgan, Edward Vanscotter, Tiger Lily, and Cassie Parks. One of the most exciting features of the museum includes the in-progress diorama of early Carlsbad, c. 1905, titled *Little Old Carlsbad*. Once finished, this exhibit, built by Willi Jung and Phil Porter, will follow the history of Carlsbad from the Carlsbad Caverns to the potash industry, with animation and interactive qualities. (Author's collection.)

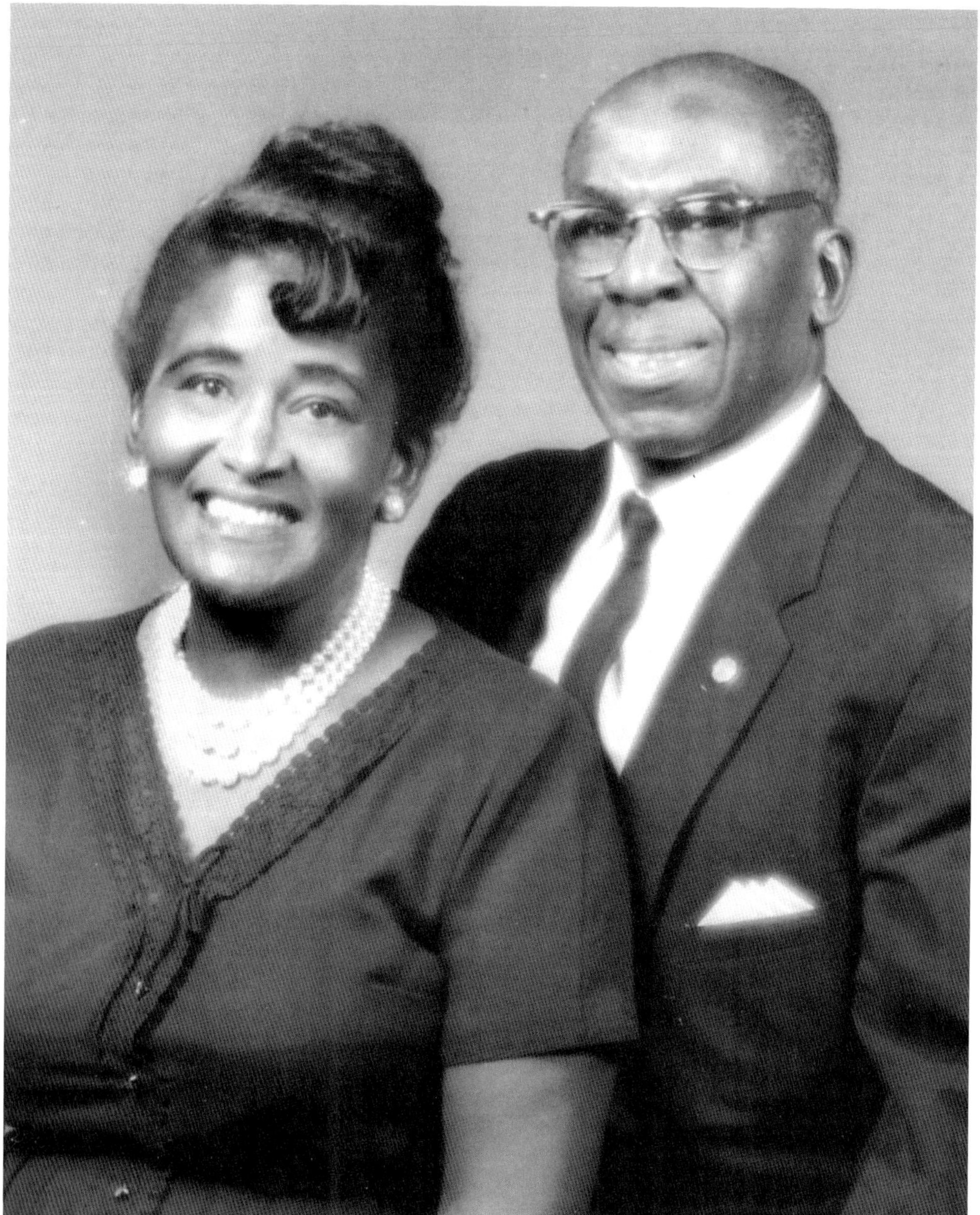

Dr. Emmitt Smith

Described as the "Voice for Racial Harmony" by *Carlsbad Current-Argus* columnist Martha Mauritson, Dr. Emmitt Smith came to Carlsbad in 1949 to teach science and math at the local all-black school. Smith became the first African American principal at the all-black school as well as the larger all-white school. Smith was given credit for integrating local schools, hotels, and restaurants. Smith has a school named for him in Carlsbad, which honors his work with the local school system. His daughter, Bernita Smith-Payne, carries on her father's tradition as an English teacher for Carlsbad Municipal Schools. Before his death in 2003, Smith encouraged children to stay in school, be kind to one another, and strive for excellence and racial harmony.

Roxanne "Rocky" Lara

As a Carlsbad native, Roxanne Lara is familiar with the needs of her community. After graduating with a bachelor's degree from New Mexico State University and a Juris Doctor from Texas Tech, Lara returned home to practice family law at her own firm. Following her father, a Carlsbad School Board member, into public service, Lara served as an Eddy County commissioner chairwoman. Family is extremely important to Lara, as her sister and mother work with her in the law firm. Lara "strongly advocates for and establishes programs to raise the levels of women in leadership to achieve pay equality and reinforce the importance of the woman's vote." Lara is most known in Carlsbad for her work representing abused and neglected children and cases involving private citizens and businesses. She serves on many boards, the Nuclear Task Force, and the Long Range Planning Committee. (Courtesy of Roxanne Lara.)

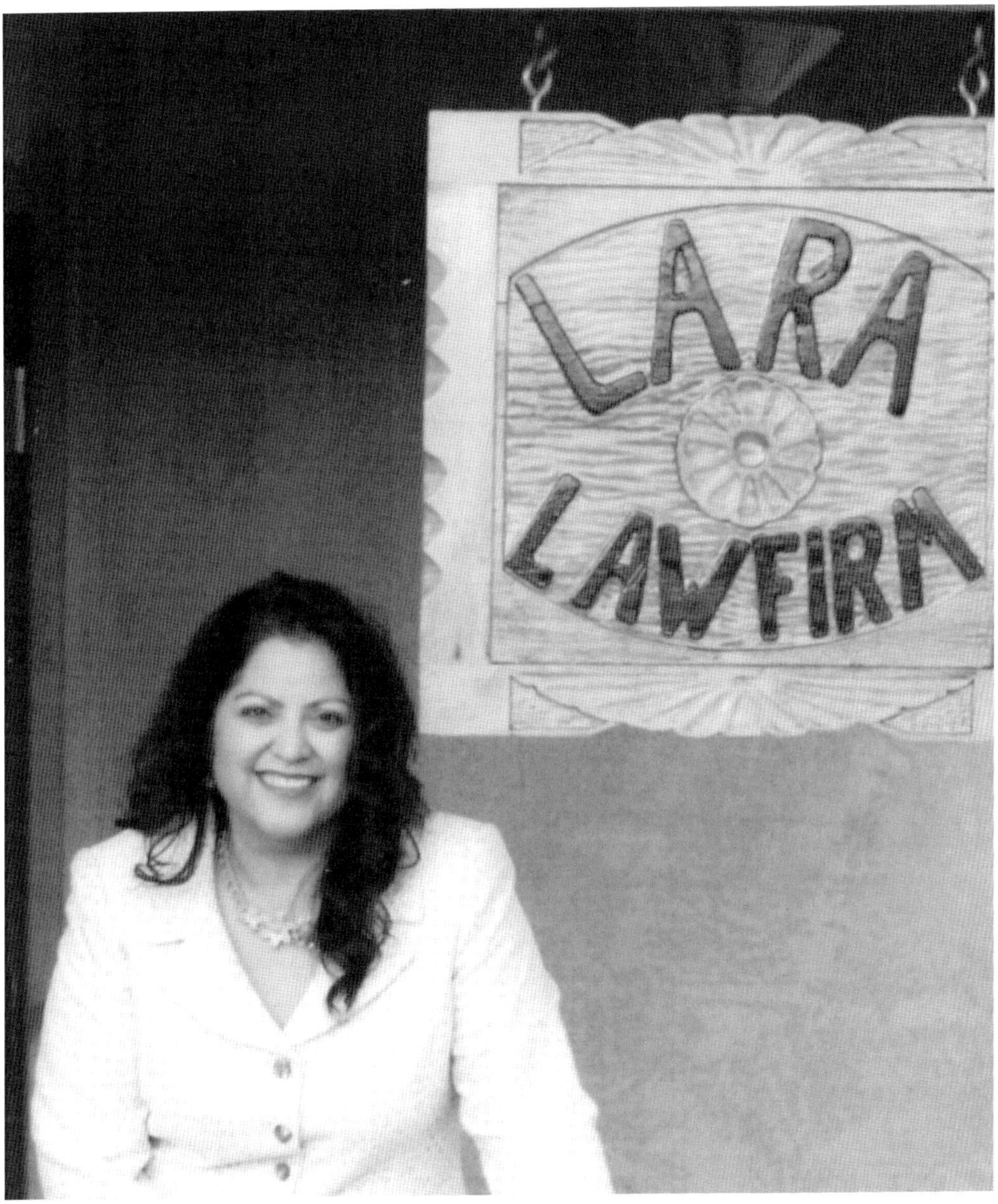

Floyd B. "Skipper" Rigdon

The headstone of Floyd Rigdon states, *Cowboys called him a newspaper man, newspaper men called him a cowboy.* As the publisher for the *Current Argus* for 49 years, Rigdon supported horse racing and rodeos. Rigdon's quarter horse, Beaver, went missing at the New Mexico State Fair in 1943, which shut down all ports of entry, only to find him eating oats in a back tack room.

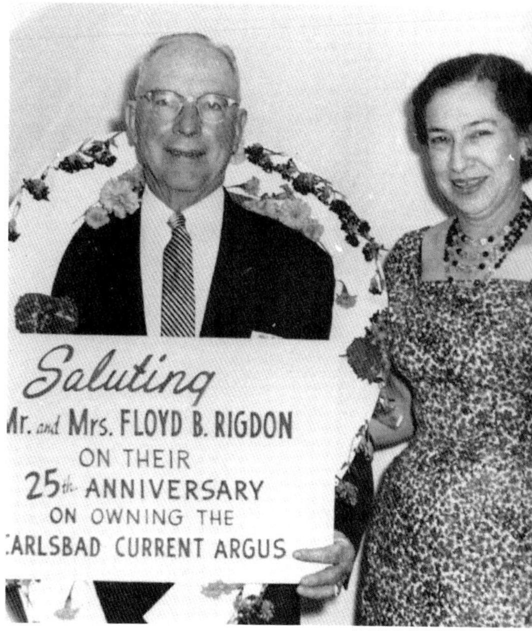

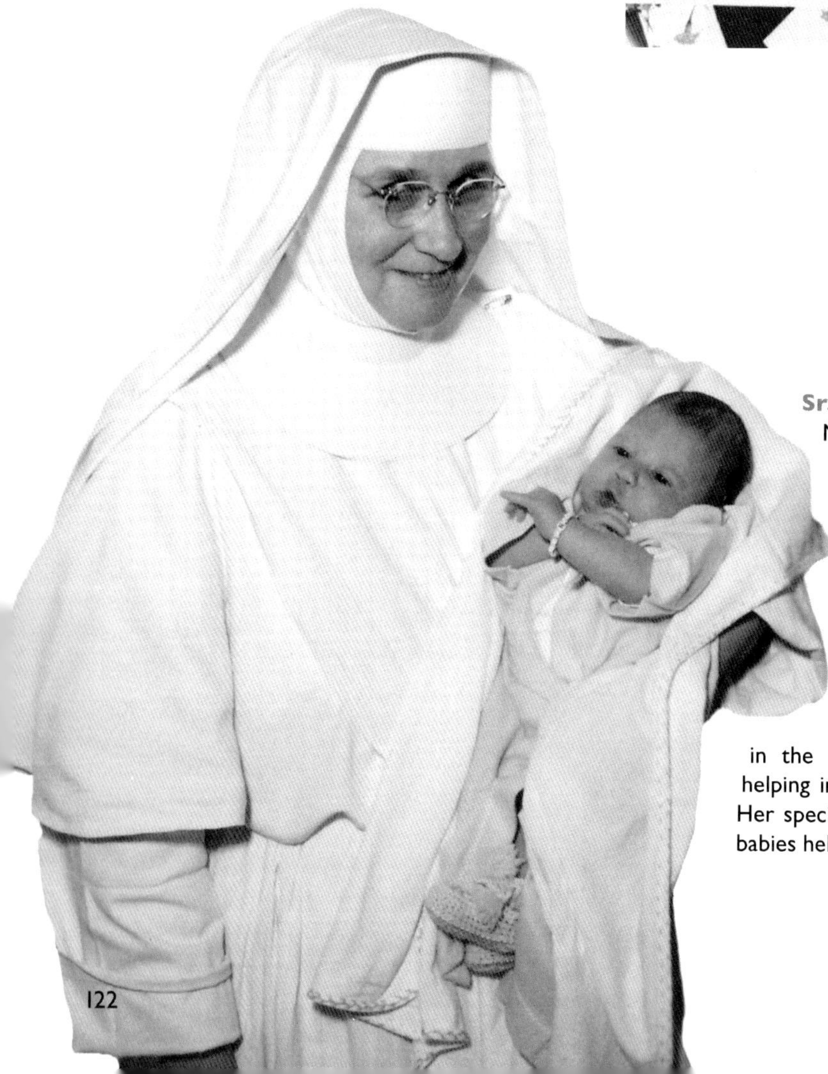

Sr. Mary Benedict

Many Carlsbad residents can thank Sister Benedict for their lives, the author included. Sister Benedict, a member of the Adorers of the Blood of Christ order, was a staple at the Saint Francis Hospital. During her stay, Sister Benedict could be found in the nursery of the hospital helping infants and new mothers. Her special formula for intolerant babies helped them thrive.

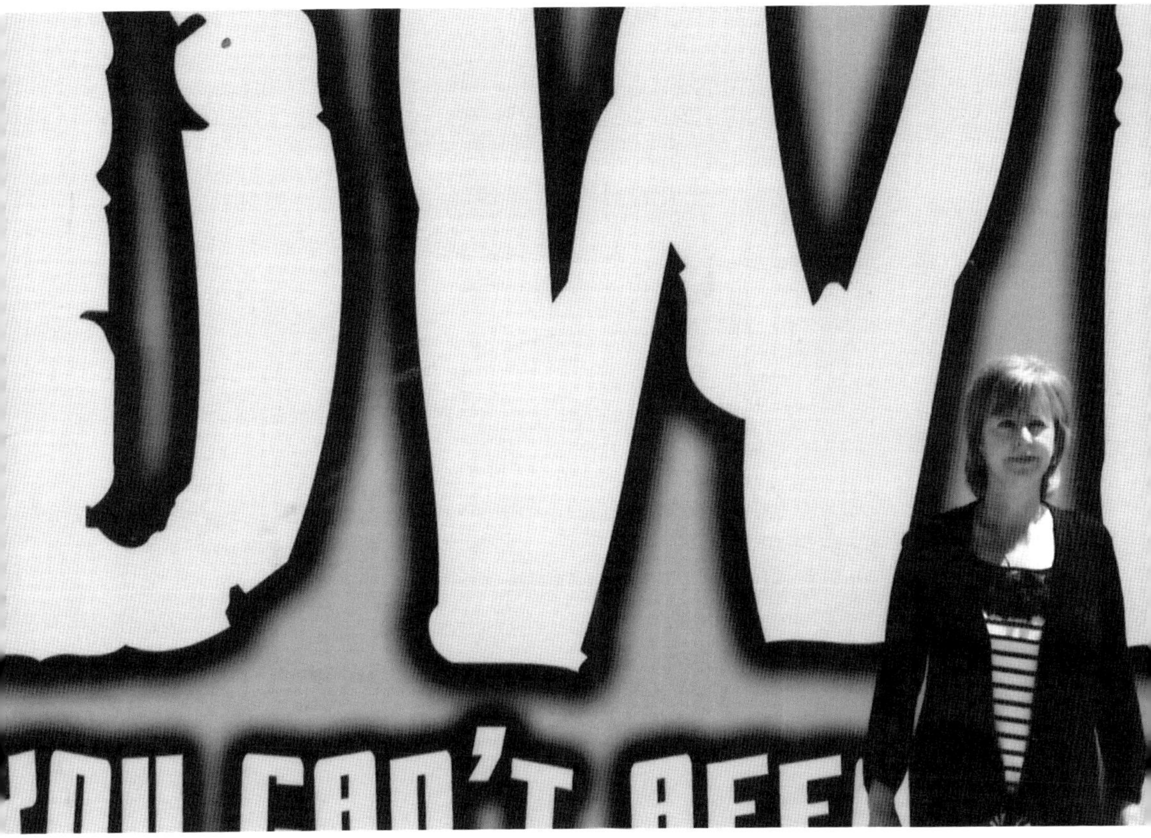

Cindy Holley Sharif

In the early morning hours of November 18, 1978, 19-year-old college student Cindy Holley Sharif's life would change forever. Sharif was the only one severely injured in a near-fatal vehicle accident involving alcohol and an underage driver. Her world as she knew it stopped. Sharif's mother, Janell Whitlock, was told by the emergency room physician that her daughter would never be able to walk and would most likely be a vegetable, but no one anticipated Sharif's great strength, including Sharif. After a week in a coma, she moved her hand and gave the indication she wanted to write something; she was given a paper and pen and wrote, "Ok, don't worry." Greatly relieved, Whitlock knew her youngest daughter was going to be alright, although she would have a long road ahead. A few short months later, with the encouragement of her stepfather, Louis Whitlock, Sharif also began to walk. By raw determination and the grace of God, not only was she able to survive, but miraculously, the only injury to follow her today from this awful journey has been blindness in one eye. Sharif turned tragedy into activism and began her work as the Eddy County DWI program director in 1998. Sharif and her team have worked tirelessly as a labor of love to save the lives of Eddy County residents from DWI fatalities, which occur every 31 minutes. As a Carlsbad native, Sharif is well known in the community but feels highly privileged to "get to do this work." Sharif and her team are striving for a world without impaired drivers who use their vehicles as a loaded weapon. She wants to be best known as a survivor who tried to leave the world a better place.

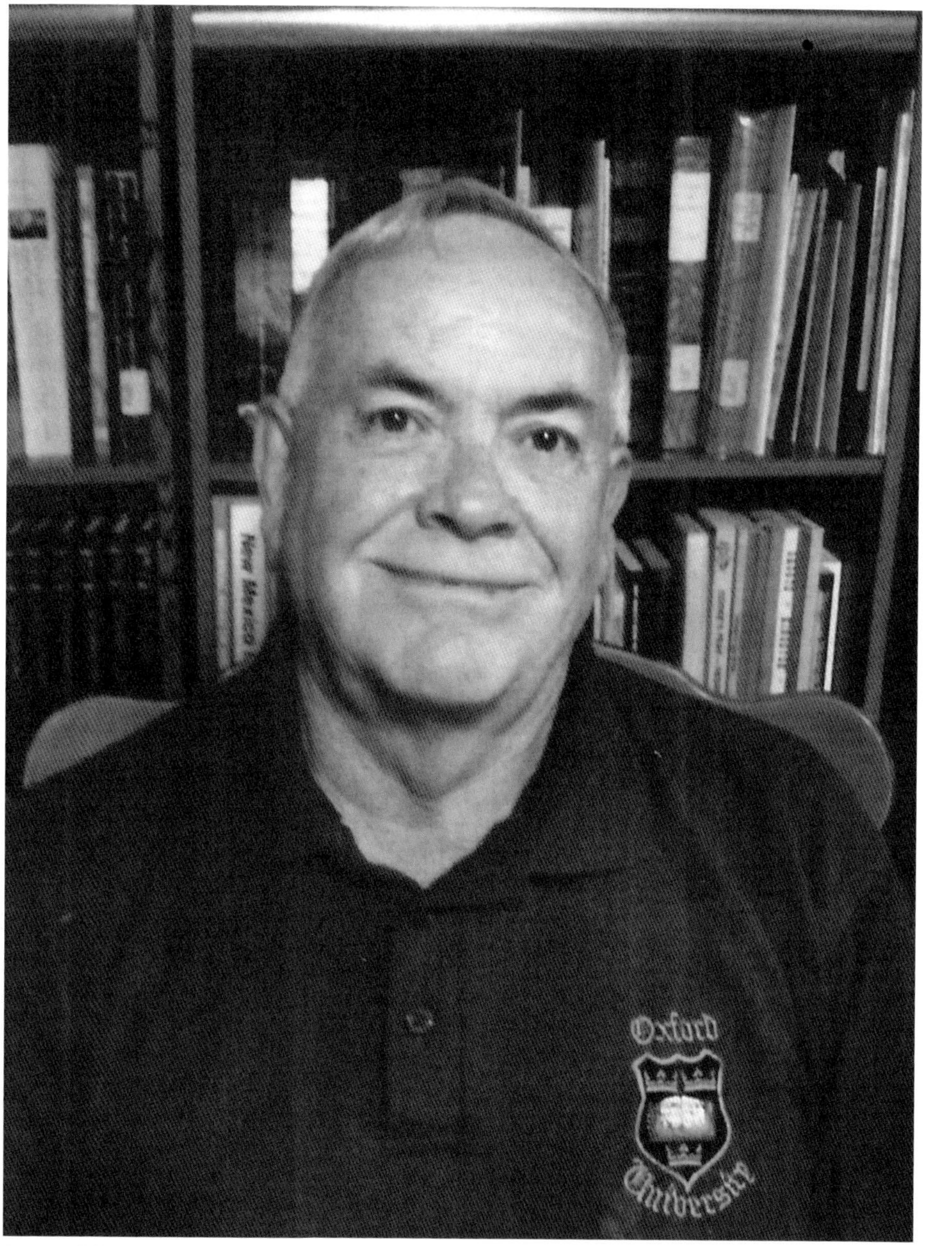

Dr. Doug Dinwiddie

Affectionately known as "Dr. D" to his history students, Doug Dinwiddie feels he is "truly blessed to have been able to work with so many wonderful students" during his 22- year teaching career at New Mexico State University–Carlsbad. Dinwiddie believes in the hands-on approach to history and included site visitations to his curriculum. After receiving his master of arts in history in 1975 from Western New Mexico University in Silver City, Dinwiddie has taught dozens of history courses to what he approximates as 4,000 to 5,000 students. Dinwiddie designed the associate and certificate programs in heritage preservation interpretation and has served as lead advisor for the honor society for about 20 years. He states, "I hope to remain active in the field of history that has been so good to me." Good news for New Mexico! (Courtesy of Dr. Doug Dinwiddie.)

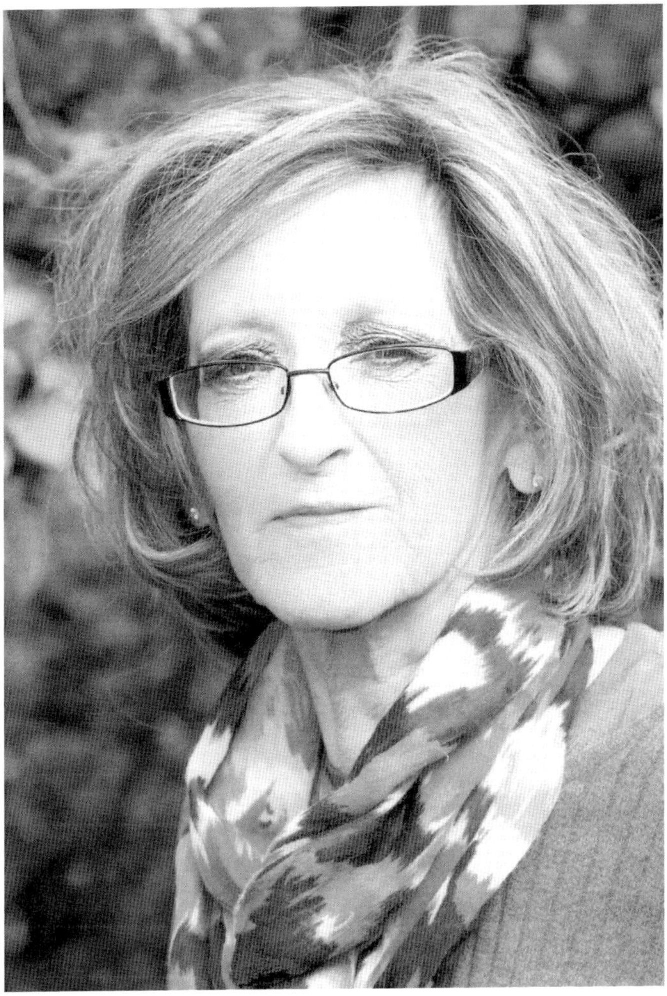

Mary Hess Walterscheid

There is not a busier person in Carlsbad than Mary Walterscheid, who has owned the Garden Mart, Inc.—a full service florist and landscape company—for over 25 years with her husband, Mark. Walterscheid's newest addition is the Hagerman House, a historic home once belonging to James J. Hagerman that is now a place for community gatherings. Walterscheid is a great role model and a shining example of what a good businessperson looks like. She currently serves as the president of the St. Edward's Catholic School Board of Directors, a position that is near and dear to her heart. Walterscheid's other passion is her 20-year membership in the Carlsbad Rotary Club, where she has served as president and is currently the secretary; here, she was instrumental in finalizing the lighting of the historic Flume over the Pecos River. In addition, Walterscheid is a board member of the New Mexico State Florist Association, vice chair of the Mayor's Committee for Long Range Planning–Quality of Life, committee member and ambassador for the Carlsbad Chamber of Commerce, past board member of the Carlsbad Foundation, secretary of the Class Act Board, and past president of the New Mexico–West Texas Teleflora Board. Walterscheid is a mother of four children and "Meme" to 10 grandchildren, ranging from age two months to 15 years. She is a constant fixture at her grandchildren's schools, where she organizes events and volunteers her time. Walterscheid is currently in treatment for cancer and is conducting the fight for her life with grace and dignity; cancer has met its match with Mary Walterscheid. (Courtesy of Mary Walterscheid.)

INDEX

Anaya, Ray, 33
Anderson, Josephine Cox, 7
Andrews, Shane, 28
Angell, Carye Lou, 35
Angell, Steve, 26
Armstrong, Catherine, 38
Balgemann, William, 22
Balzano, Dale, 21
Barnett, Lanny, 16
Beard, Nancy, 35
Bearup, Anson, 6, 7
Beason, Pat, 13
Beaver, Charlie, 18, 19
Bell, Peggi Johnson, 9
Benedict, Mary, 39
Blocker, Dan, 14, 15, 27
Boles, Tom, 37
Bond, Paul, 30, 31
Bowyer, Ralph, 29
Brown, Rosemary, 18
Brubaker, Kay, 13
Bujac, Etienne de Pelissier, 23–25
Burnett, Bill, 17
Buzzell, Laura Cribb, 8
Cabot, Bruce, 14, 15
Campbell, Merwin, 23
Campbell, Stacy Dean, 15
Carlsbad Army Airfield, 27
Carlsbad Caverns National Park, 3, 7, 10–13, 20, 21, 37
Carlsbad Museum and Art Center, 38
Cartwright, Zuzanna, 38
Cavern City Four, 17
Chapman, Martha, 33
Clark, Carla, 13
Clark, Houston, 37
Company B, 25
Cranston, Valerie, 13
Crawford, Abel J., 19
Cunningham, Jason, 26
Cutter, John E., 17
Davis, Ray V., 10, 21
Davis, Ricardo G., 26
Denton, Perry, 37
Dinwiddie, Doug, 39, 40
Dixon, Kenneth L., 11
Dow, Les, 6
Drake, Jack, 9
Eddy County Courthouse, 32
Eddy, Charles B., 1–6
Enchanted Glass Factory, 20
Epstein, Joe, 26, 33, 34
Etcheverry, Sam, 28
Feezer, Frances, 36
Fernandez, Cruz, 37
Fiesta Drive-In, 21
Forrest, Bob, 19
Frederick, George, 17
Freeman, Alfred A., 6
Freeman, Charles, 10
Friesen, Cyndi Ann, 18
Gaffney, F. Drew, 1, 23
Garrett, Patrick, 4, 6, 16
Gerrells, Collin, 19
Gerrells, Walter, 36
Giddens, Frank, 27
Gossett, Adair, 20
Gracia, Andres, 26
Graef, Calvin, 25
Grandi, Billy, 15
Gray, Edward McQueen, 11
Greene, Charles, 4, 7
Gregory, Larry, 16
Gregory, Margie, 16
Grimes, Ron, 16
Hagerman, James J., 4, 5
Harkey, Dee, 6
Harrell, Dick, 15, 27
Haynes, Marilyn, 25
Helm, Ennis, 10, 11
Hepler, Elmer, 28
Hernandez, John, 13
Hicks, Harvey, 36
Howard, Jed, 22, 34
Howell, Velma, 14
Huggins, David, 16
Hughes, Shirley, 17
Hunt, Clyde, 1, 13, 18
Hutchins, Mark, 16
Jackson, Mark, 29
Jackson, Sarah, 37
James, Charles, 25
Johanningmeier, Robert, 12, 13
Johns, Joe, 36, 37
Johnson, Kelley, 30
Jones, Barbara, 8
Joyce, John R., 18
Jung, Willi, 38
Kemp, Dave, 6
Kerr, Cesarine Graves Lewis, 22
Kincaid, Noel, 24
Kindel, Frank, 1, 22
Kirkpatrick, Ed, 12
Knox, Grace, 12
La Caverna Hotel, 21
Lara, Roxanne, 38, 39
Lark, Kim, 33
Leyva, Porky, 29
Light, Robert, 34
Lily, Tiger, 38
Livingston, Carl, 7
Lorentzen, Dorothy Smith, 10, 14
Lucas, James Rees, 15
Mahaffy, Crystal, 38
Martin, Lucille, 12
Mattson, Gerri, 13
Maxwell, Calvin W., 26
McAdoo, Bill, 34
McLenathen, Charles H., 5
Mead, Roderick F., 1, 9, 18
Means, Lewis, 12
Melton, Helen, 32
Merchant, Claiborne W., 5, 6
Meyers, Barbara, 34
Meyers, Norman, 34
Miss New Mexico, 17
Molgaard, Brad, 11
Moore, Carolyn Adams, 17
Moore, Sandi, 18
Morgan, Dave, 38
Mudgett, Bryan, 25
Muncrief, Deedle, 16
Muncrief, Ronnie, 16
Myers, Lee, 36
Niblett, Gary, 11
Nosakhere, Akilah, 38
Nymeyer, B.A., 5

INDEX

Nymeyer, Robert, 1, 10, 13
Ogden, Alisa, 34
O'Hearn, Jim, 17
Ohnemus, Matt, 7
Olson, Carolyn, 35
Oso, Maggie, 10
Pageant of Progress, 16
Palma, Israel, 13
Panagopoulos, Pete, 1, 19
Parker, Bonnie, 36
Parks, Cassie, 38
Perini, Dave, 30
Pitcaithley, Al, 17
Pitcaithley, Dwight, 35
Pitcaithley, Lynne, 15–17
Pompa, Frank, 1, 7
Porter, Phil, 38
Prather-Stroud, Wren, 9, 18
Pratt, Wallace, 23
Rigdon, Skipper, 39
Roberts, John, 16
Robertson, Michele, 38
Robertson, Nora, 12
Rosenberg, Michael, 23
Ross, Cody, 1, 28, 29
Ross, Kenny, 29
Rumpel, Helen, 14
Ryan, Flora, 8
Sadler, Barry, 17
Sepich, Kathryn, 32
Sharif, Cindy, 39
Sherer, Dave, 30
Simpson, Max Coleman, 26
Small, Leon, 17
Smith, Camille, 14
Smith, Emmitt, 38
Smith, Joe Stanley, 25
Spruill, Don, 16
Stell, Joe, 35
Stockwell, Ira, 36
Stuck in the 60s Band, 16
Tansill, Robert, 2, 4, 5
Thayer, Walter, 7
Thompson, Becky, 29
Thornberry, Harold, 17
Thunderbird Indian Dancers, 18
Tracy, Francis G., 4, 5
Trail of the Painted Ponies, 13
Vanscotter, Edward, 38
Walterscheid, Mary, 40
Watson, Ben, 24
Welch, Tuffy, 28
Wertheimer, Linda, 23
Westfall, Frank, 11, 26
White, Charlie, 20
White, Jack Jr., 20
White, Jim, 3, 21
Whitlock, Janell, 31, 32
Whitlock, Louis, 31, 32
Wiseman, Jimmy, 16
Wong, Ping, 19
Wooten, John, 30
Yanez, Lucy, 20

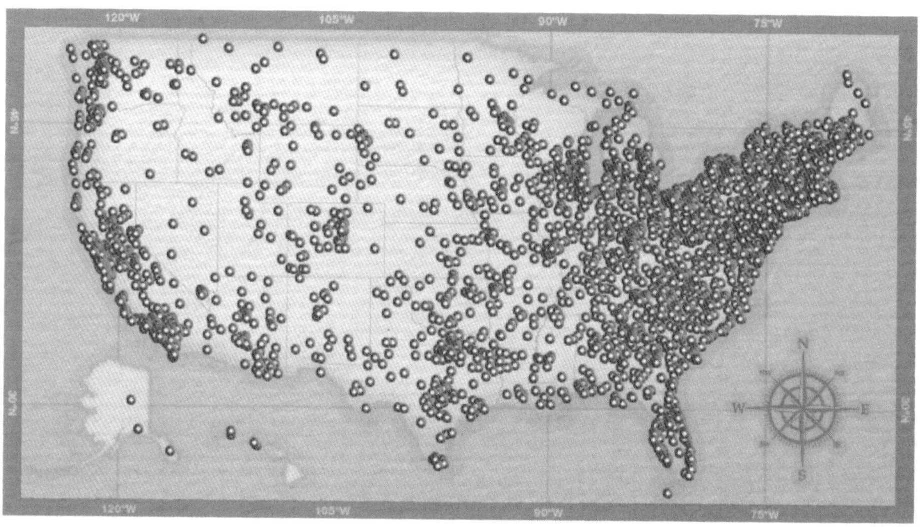

Consistent with our mission to preserve history on a local level, this book was printed in South Carolina on American-made paper and manufactured entirely in the United States. Products carrying the accredited Forest Stewardship Council (FSC) label are printed on 100 percent FSC-certified paper.